THE MYTH AND PRAYERS
OF THE GREAT STAR CHANT
AND
THE MYTH OF THE COYOTE CHANT

Order from:
Five Star Publications
P.O. Box 3142
Scottsdale, AZ 85271-3142
(602) 941-0770 or 800 545-STAR, ext. 43
Fax (602) 941-0069

THE MYTH AND PRAYERS
OF THE GREAT STAR CHANT
AND
THE MYTH OF THE COYOTE CHANT

Recorded by Mary C. Wheelwright
Edited with Commentaries by David P. McAllester
Foreword by Rain Parrish

With twenty-two color plates after sandpaintings
recorded by Franc J. Newcomb and others
Illustrated by Jason Chee

92-485

New Edition
NAVAJO COMMUNITY COLLEGE PRESS
Tsaile, Arizona
1988

The original edition of this publication was published by the Museum of Navajo
Ceremonial Art, Santa Fe, New Mexico, in 1956. This new edition is published
in arrangement with the Wheelwright Museum of the American Indian,
Santa Fe, New Mexico.

*Publication of the New Edition was made possible, in part, by the estate of Laura Gilpin,
in memory of Elizabeth Warham Forster.*

Published by
NAVAJO COMMUNITY COLLEGE PRESS
Tsaile, Arizona

International Standard Book Number 0-912586-58-3 Clothbound
International Standard Book Number 0-912586-61-3 Paper
Library of Congress Number 85-161304

TABLE OF CONTENTS

FOREWORD

There is this strange and persistent fact that is only after a journey to a distant region, a new land, that the inner voice can make itself understood. And to this strange and persistent fact is added another; that he who reveals to us the meaning of inward pilgrimage must himself be a stranger.

HEINRICH ZIMMER

From their earliest period, Navajo philosophy and religion have been admired for their aesthetic qualities. A profound appreciation of Navajo world-view requires an awareness of its significance in the Navajo religion. To the Navajo, beauty is a quality not a form, a content not an arrangement. The art forms, whether "fabrics and jewels," or "soft and hard" goods or mythology express a philosophy in which harmony, order and beauty are paramount and summarized in the words and practices of Navajo ceremonial chantways.

The body of Navajo mythology is intricate and complicated, possessing an extraordinary vitality and wholeness. It provides us with a rare glimpse into the Navajo world of religion and literature which are both distinctive expressions of the poetic narrative. The learned practitioners use the oral tradition and their keen sense of memory to evoke the best elements of an ancient story-telling tradition. They are told with complex symbolism and delicate ritual. Each myth has a plot structure, a pantheon of central characters from the natural and supernatural worlds and an explanation for understanding Navajo social and ethical values. They display a remarkable sense of allegory and poetry. Ultimately, what the myths enable us to experience is the creative integration of Navajo thought and the magnificent powers of the supernatural heros and heroines.

It is to the wisdom and contribution made by Mary Cabot Wheelright and the eminent Navajo Medicine Man Hasteen Klah (Hastiin Tł'aai) that we owe a profound sense of gratitude. The bond and prevision between these two extraordinary human beings grew out of their efforts to share and exchange cultural world-views. She was an adventurer and it was this spirit and curiosity which prompted her to learn the meaning of Navajo religion. Likewise, Hasteen Klah responded with respect and, after taking preliminary caution, shared his ceremonial knowledge. Klah felt that Navajo religion would disappear.

From 1925 until her death in 1958, Mary Cabot Wheelright pursued her work in exploring and collecting the spiritual inner visions of the Navajo people. Her approach to Navajo culture was with a remarkable sense of integrity. With the assistance and support of Hasteen Klah, Wheelright recorded eighteen different ceremonial chantways and worked with forty different practitioners. While some of the versions may differ, they offer a comprehensive explanation of the origins of each myth and symbolism and the meaning of each ritual.

FOREWORD

The Wheelwright Manuscript collection stands as a monumental index to some of the most essential aspects of Navajo thought. They are materials collected with a particular cultural sensibility and we draw from it an understanding of Navajo religion that is rarely shared and attained. Many of the myths, poetic narratives, songs and prayers are supplemented by bilingual transcriptions compiled by Navajo intellectuals as well as scholars of Navajo religion and linguistics. Some of those outstanding individuals who contributed their knowledge were Father Berard Haile, Dr. Harry Hoijer, Dr. Leland Wyman and Dr. David McAllester. The practitioner who contributed his mythology and attendant ceremonial ritual of the *Great Star Chant* was Hastiin Ayóó'áníłnézí of the Táchii'nii clan from Sawmill, Arizona. The sandpainting drawings for the chant were collected by Franc Newcomb, Mary Cabot Wheelwright, Laura Adams Armer, Louisa Wetherill and Maud Oakes in collaboration with sixteen different practitioners and sandpainters.

For the Navajo, the interrelationships of stories, chant and ritual express ideas that are experiential. They involve notions about natural laws which enable us to understand ourselves. The myths and ceremonial rituals are offered for various occasions: the curing of a person who has experienced an imbalance, the blessing of a new dwelling and other times when wishes for protection, happiness and long life are appropriate. At the beginning of the ceremony the practitioners introduce the surroundings of the dwellings, and the practitioner's and patient's relationship to the natural and supernatural worlds. The origins of the Navajo are traced and we are then returned to the present world. The story of the myth is related with all its appropriate rituals. The key to the restoration of harmony and well-being is in carefully acquiring the knowledge of ritual actions and their powers. By participating in this process, by actualizing the myth, we are composing a profound sense of unity with spirit and substance. It is at this moment when the words of the Blessingway songs acknowledge the deep kinship we have with the earth:

> Earth's feet have become my feet by means of these I shall live on.
> Earth's body has become my body by means of this I shall live on.

RAIN PARRISH
Curator
Wheelwright Museum of the American Indian
Santa Fe, New Mexico

THE
GREAT STAR CHANT

THE MYTH OF
THE GREAT STAR CHANT

The myth is given here as told to Mary C. Wheelwright by Ayóó'aníłnézí of the Táchii'nii clan. Ayóó'áníłnézí lived, in 1933, near the sawmill of Fort Defiance. The story comes from a medicine man, Hastiin Bahozhoni, formerly called Diné Tł'óól. Hastiin Bahozhoni lived in Canyon de Chelly until his death in 1907. Ralph Roan-Horse was the interpreter.

The myth of the Great Star Chant includes the stories of the Wind Chant and the Evil-Chasing Chant, two other healing ceremonies which also had their origin in mythical events in the lives of the son of Tł'iishtsoh (Great Snake) and his family. The main characters in the story are:

> Great Star, also referred to as Black Star
> Messenger Wind, also called the Spirit Wind—Nííłch' i Biyázhí
> Messenger Fly—Dǫ'tsoh
> Talking God—Haashch'ééłti'í
> Older Brother
> Younger Brother, also referred to as the medicine man

The relationships in the family in the myth are shown below:

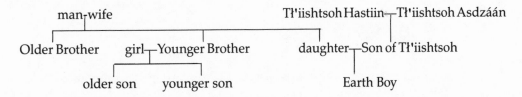

MYTH OF THE WIND CHANT

The Marriage of the Son of Tł'iishtsoh

A poor family is taught the useful arts by a stranger.
He marries the daughter, reveals that he is the son of Tł'iishtsoh.
He continues teaching the family: a baby is born.
The family journeys to visit Tł'iishtsoh and show him the baby.

The Baby is Lost and Recovered

They lose the baby and camp by a lake.
They play games to the east of their camp,
They play games to the south of their camp,
They play games to the west of their camp,
They play games to the north of their camp
  and discover that the baby has disappeared.
They search three days for the baby.
A messenger tells them how to make suitable offerings.
Talking God, after offerings, helps them.
They search under the lake and see Tł'iishtsoh.
Black Wind, after offerings, helps them.
Tł'iishtsoh is drawn through ceremonial hoops.
Tł'iishtsoh is transformed into the baby, now a young man.

The Origin of the Wind Chant Ritual

The Winds show the ritual to the family.
Description of the Wind Chant ceremony.

The Story of Older Brother and Younger Brother

Older Brother disregards warnings, eats intestines, becomes ill.
They learn how to invoke supernatural help.

MYTH OF THE EVIL-CHASING CHANT

Older Brother disregards warnings, eats a snake, becomes ill,
They learn the Great Snake ceremony.
Older Brother disregards warnings, kills a woodrat, becomes ill,
They learn Gila Monster Medicine and Shaking-hand.
Older brother disregards warnings, shoots whirlwind, becomes ill,
They learn Cyclone Medicine.

MYTH OF THE GREAT STAR CHANT

The Story of Younger Brother's Visit to the Sky

He is tricked by Coyote and transported to the sky.
He disregards warnings and returns to the Hole-through-the-sky,
Fight with the Rock Wren, Origin of Rock Wren Medicine.
He disregards warnings and goes to the White House of the Eagles.
He raids the Bees with the Eagle People,
Origin of Bee Medicine.
Origin of the use of eagle down in the Water Chant.
He disregards warnings and goes to the Blue House of the Hawks.
He raids the Wasps with the Hawk People,
Origin of Wasp Medicine.
Origin of the use of hawk down in the Hail Chant.
He disregards warnings and goes to the Yellow House of the Hawks.
He raids the Rock Wren with the Hawk People,
Origin of Rock Medicine.
Origin of the use of Hawk down in the Male Shooting Chant.
He disregards warnings and goes to the Black House of the Eagles.
He raids the Left-handed Wind with the Eagle People,
He gives eagle down to the higher powers and to Great Star.
Great Star teaches the ceremony to Younger Brother.
Ceremonial usages (note: dreams showing Great Star sickness; taboos learned
    from the Great Star Myth), Younger Brother's healing apprenticeship.

Younger Brother's Return to Earth

He rescues his family from Coyote.
He gives the Great Star Chant over his family,

The Preparation: purification, rites of sacred hoops and woltáád (untying of
    knots) preparation of medicine.
Great Star comes to assist.
First Day: plaques, the Black Star sandpainting.
Second Day: plaques, the Blue Star sandpainting.
Third Day: plaques, the Yellow Star sandpainting.
Fourth Day: plaques, the White Star sandpainting.
Younger Brother's family assists in ritual.

The Sacred Company Journey for Power

They go to the east to Coyote and learn Coyote songs.
They go to the east to Darkness Hooghan,
Younger Brother's older son learns the chant here.
They go to the south to Blue Hooghan,
Younger Brother's younger son learns the chant here.
They go to the west to Yellow Sunset Hooghan,
Younger Brother's wife learns her ceremony.
They go to the north to White-Ray-of-Life Hooghan,
Younger Brother's older son learns his ceremony.

The Sacred Company Continues to Journey for Power

They go east to the Great Sea,
They learn songs and prayers from Water Monster.
They go south to the End of Rivers,
They learn songs and prayers from Water Horse.
They go west to Holy Water,
They learn songs and prayers from water monsters.

Part of the Water Chant Story

Story of the White Butterfly and the origin of the
    water monsters. They learn songs from Hummingbird.

Part of the Hail Chant Story

They go to the ice home of White Thunder,
With Bat's help they vanquish White Thunder,
They learn songs and prayers from White Thunder.

The Sacred Company Continues to Journey for Power

They go east to Black Belt Mountain (Sisnaajiní),
They discuss ceremonies with Black Wind and Black Thunder.
They go south to Mount Taylor (Tsoodził),
They discuss ceremonies with Blue Wind and Blue Thunder.
They go west to Sparkling Mountain (Dook'o'oosłííd—San Francisco Peaks).
They discuss ceremonies with Yellow Wind and Yellow Thunder.
They go north to Dibé Nitsaa Mountain (La Plata Mountains).
With Rock Wren's help they again fight and vanquish White Thunder.
They learn further songs and prayers for White Thunder.

The Sacred Company Continues to Journey for Power

They go to Tséhołhot'ááya,
They learn the Black Wind ceremonies.
They go to Coiled Mountain,
They learn the Blue Wind ceremonies.
They go to Naadahas'éí,
They learn the Yellow Wind ceremonies.
They go to the Mountain of Light,
They learn the White Wind ceremonies.

The Sacred Company Continues to Journey for Power

They go to the hooghan of Salt Woman.
They fight with the Red Ant people,
They learn the Red Ant Medicine.
They go to Shooting Water,
They fight the water monster.
They learn songs and sandpaintings, the great prayer

of invocation and liberation, and details of the sand-
    paintings.
They go south to Hairy Mountain,
They fight the bears,
They learn prayers and rituals from the bears.

The Final Ceremony Given Over Older Brother

The powers and sacred knowledge of Older Brother, Younger
    Brother and their relatives.
Gopher is offended, origin of scarcity of food.
Water God is offended, origin of the scarcity of water.
Salt Woman is offended, origin of the scarcity of salt.
Older Brother and Younger Brother leave the people of the earth.

MYTH OF THE WIND CHANT

The Marriage of the Son of Tł'iishtsoh

In the northeastern part of the Dibé Nitsaa Mountains, at Tsé'ááto, lived a family of the Táchii'nii clan: the father, mother, daughter and two sons. The father belonged to the Tsi'najinii clan. They were so poor they had to use their own hair to make traps to catch birds for their food. They set the traps near water and roasted the birds on spits before the fire. To keep themselves warm at night they moistened their bodies and rolled themselves in feathers. The women wore nothing but kilts made of woven yucca fiber, and the men wore only Gee strings.

They moved from Tsé'ááto because of lack of food, and journeyed for two days without finding any. Then they came to the San Juan River, and from there traveled two days more to the Ch'ooshgai Mountains. There they found food and spent the next four days eating and resting. One day a strange man met them and asked them who they were and whence they came. They answered, "From Tsé'ááto," and then the stranger left, saying that he lived nearby.

On the following day he came again and told them of a place where they could get many plant seeds to eat. Then he returned, this time bringing a leg of deer as a present, but again left without making himself known. On the fourth day he came again bringing half a deer. The father of the family said that, as the stranger had been so good to them, they had all agreed that the daughter should become his wife. The stranger said that he would be glad to take her and he made himself a brush hooghan near where the family was living. Then he said he would have to go and tell his father and mother of his proposed marriage, and that he would come back again that evening. When he returned, he said that his father and mother approved of his marriage. The girl's father said to him that it was the custom that when a family offers a girl to be wife to a man, the man should give presents to the girl's family, and in return that the parents of the girl should be willing to help the couple if they were in trouble or need. The stranger told them who he was: "I am the son of Tł'iishtosh (Great Snake) of Nahodiisgiizh."[1]

---

[1] A place southwest of Crown Point, where smoke comes out between the rocks.

Tł'iishtsoh had told his son to give a present to the girl's family. The young man, who had the power to draw the deer to him, brought in a yearling and killed it. He told the family to come out and cut it up and take the meat; this was his gift to them, but he himself did not touch it. The next day he killed two deer, one for himself and his wife, which they ate, and one for the girl's family. The third day he killed three large deer, one for himself and wife, and two for his wife's family. Then on the fourth day, he killed four big deer, kept one for himself and wife and gave three to her family. He used the rays of the sun to draw the deer to him and killed them with a club near a certain tree, then cut the meat with flint knives and the bones with a double hatchet of stone.[2] The deer were butchered on a pile of brush.

The family knew nothing about how to prepare the buckskins, and the son of Tł'iishtsoh showed them how to do it. He began by pulling out one of the poles under the body of the deer and trimming it until it was smooth; then he laid it against a tree and threw the skin over it. He took one of the sharp bones of the leg and a sharp-edged rib and showed his father-in-law how to use these to clean the hair off the skin; then he told the family to take the brains out of the deer and rub them into the skin until it was soft. The son of Tł'iishtsoh brought in a deer every day after this, and his father-in-law kept on cleaning and preparing skins in the same spot day after day, so that there grew up a great pile of hair where he worked. This gave the name, Biyahdiigai, to this place.

Then the son of Tł'iishtsoh taught his wife's family how to make buckskin clothing. He took two skins for the back and front of a dress, with the head-end of the skins upward, and sewed them together along the sides, using an awl made of bone. The custom which forbids a son-in-law ever to look at his wife's mother began at this time. That is why he built his hooghan some distance away from that of his wife's family. He now made a dress for his mother-in-law and clothing for the older brother of his wife. For the latter he made breeches, sewed up at the sides with a fringe, and a shirt with a short fringe under the sleeves and down the sides. Then he also made suits for his wife's younger brother and his father-in-law. He showed them how to tan the deer pelts with the hair on, and they sewed two or three pelts together to use as blankets to wrap themselves in at night.

They had always roasted everything on sticks before the fire, and the son of Tł'iishtsoh said to them one day, "Why don't you boil any of your food?" So they began to think about this, but they did not know where to get a pot to boil in. Far off to the east they saw smoke which came from Kin dootł'izh and the two brothers of the girl decided to go on a journey to that place where the Ancient Ones lived.[3] When the two brothers arrived there, the people wanted to know where they got their buckskin clothing. They longed to get some for themselves and asked if the brothers could bring clothing to trade for their pottery. So the brothers left Kin dootł'izh and went back to the family. They told them what they had seen and heard, and that the people there needed deer meat and buckskins, so the two brothers took meat and

---

[2]This method of drawing the deer to a certain place and killing it with a club is used so as to kill without shedding blood.

[3]This was Aztec Pueblo.

buckskins and went back to Kin dootł'izh. They traded their meat for pottery, cups, dippers and bowls, and they exchanged buckskins for turquoise, white shell and jade and stone beads. They also brought back to the family bows and arrows and quivers. This trade, which took place in the fall, brought a great change of living to the family: They were warmer and better fed than ever before, and so they spent the winter there.

The Baby is Lost and Recovered

In the spring the time came when the wife of the son of Tł'iishtsoh was to have a child, and in the month called Seedplanting (June) the baby was born and it was a boy. The son of Tł'iishtsoh said he wanted his father and mother to see their grandson and that they must now take the baby and go visit his family. Since he had been married he had hunted constantly and had brought in a great many deer, so there was much meat and many buckskins ready for travel supplies. The family also had pounded dried meat mixed with wild rose berries which keeps for many years without spoiling.

So the entire family, including the two brothers, the son of Tł'iishtsoh and the baby, all set out to visit the family of Tł'iishtsoh. The son of Tł'iishtsoh told his wife's people that he would go ahead and they were to follow him. The two brothers led the family; both were carrying bows and arrows and they sometimes shot at things as they went along. They traveled in this way for twelve days, following the trail of their brother-in-law.

On the morning of the thirteenth day, they came to a lake with many bulrushes growing in it. It was all covered with rushes except for a circle of clear water about three feet wide around the edge, and there were many trails leading to the water from all directions. The family camped at the north of the lake, but when they looked for the tracks of the son of Tł'iishtsoh they could not find them anymore. This happened in the Month-of-ripening (August). The next morning, after they had breakfasted, they felt happy and decided to play games and have a good time. They put the baby down on the ground a few feet from the lake. Then they began picking up handfuls of sand and piled it in a heap about seven or eight inches high and in the top they made a hole and each of them spat into it until the hole was filled. Then they scratched away the sand at the bottom of the pile, saying, "Cheedi, Cheedi!" ("Scratch, scratch!") until they came to the damp core in the middle of the pile. Whichever direction the core should fall would show the direction in which they should travel to find the son of Tł'iishtsoh. It fell toward the mother of the girl.

Then they played a hide-and-seek game. The old woman put her hands over her ears and closed her eyes and her husband stood by her and shouted in her ears, while the two sons and the daughter went to hide. When the mother looked up she could not see them and she went hunting for them. She found one boy and told him to hold on to the back of her dress. After that, as she found the others, she said, "Hold on to those who are found." So she led them all back to the old man, her husband, and he said, "Give me one of the little ones." She said, "No." The old man offered various plants in exchange for a child but she said she did not want plants. She asked him to give her a smoke and he did this by picking up sticks and rolling them in a bulrush leaf to make her a cigarette. She took a puff and said, "That is nothing but

11

dirt!" and she threw it at him. He rushed after her, playfully trying to touch one of the children holding on to her, while she tried to prevent it as well as she could. But as she grew tired the old man managed to touch one of the children. The one who was touched fell out of the line, and the old man touched the others one by one until he had caught all of them. He said they were all his now, then they had a good laugh about it. They played these games east of where they were camped.

After they had finished playing, they all went to see how the baby was. When they came to where they had left him, they found that he had been moved closer to the water. They took up the baby and went to their camp to spend the night.

The next day they again hunted in vain for the tracks of Tł'iishtsoh's son. So they played the same games again to the south of their camp and left the baby near the lake. When they played the sand game, the core of the pile fell toward the old woman again, and when they went back to the baby he had been moved still closer to the lake. They took him up and went back to their camp to sleep. On the third day, after hunting in vain for any track to lead them on their way, they dug a hole about three feet deep and placed the baby in it to keep him safe. Then they went on to play games again, to the west of their camp. When they played the sand game, they said the old woman must dig too fast, and that was the reason why the core always fell toward her. This time instead of scratching below the pile of sand they blew it away, but the core still fell toward the old woman. This time, when they looked for the baby, they found he had been moved still closer to the lake, and they took him up and went to their camp and slept. The fourth day of their stay in this place they looked for the track of the son of Tł'iishtsoh as they had done everyday, but again found no trace of him. They went off to play their games to the north of their camp and this time, to keep the baby safe, they hid him in a hole again and also covered his legs with sand.

As before, when the pile of sand was blown away, the core fell toward the old woman. But when they looked for the baby they could not find him at all, nor was there any track to show where he had gone. They thought he might be in the water and hunted for him among the bulrushes, for the water was only as deep as their knees. They held each other's hands and went on hunting all day long. Next day they searched again among the bulrushes, digging with their hands. They also dug up the place where the baby had been left, but all day long they found nothing. When they came back at night, they consulted as to what they should do.

On the third day of the search they still had no success and went on digging late into the night. Suddenly, they heard someone call from the darkness to the east, saying, "What are you doing?" and they answered, "Who are you? You may know something about the way to find our baby."

They called to him to join them but they had to call four times before he would come in. When he entered, they saw it was Dǫ'tsoh, the messenger.[4] He sat down with them and said that the baby was in the same spot where they had left him, but that he had been taken down into the earth. He said, "You are to blame, it was all your fault. Remember that when the son

---

[4] "Big Fly," the white-headed fly, called messenger because he acts as advisor and interpreter between gods and men.

of Tł'iishtsoh was married he gave presents to his wife's family, and he said that the wife's people must do the same. But you have not done this." The family asked what they must do now. Dǫ'tsoh told them that they should have brought an offering to Tł'iishtsoh, called nitł'iz, made of powdered turquoise and white shell, jet and abalone. Dǫ'tsoh told the family that the only way of finding the baby was to bring this offering of nitł'iz at once to Tł'iishtsoh's place and also to put a shell full of it into the lake. He said, "You must not sleep tonight," and then he left them.[5] After he had gone, they wished they had asked him many more things, for they still wanted to know more.

Dǫ'tsoh then went and told all that had happened to Haashch'ééłti'í (Talking God). After their sleepless night, the people heard the voice of Talking God, calling from the east, at the first light of dawn. Then he called again, and then again, and then he appeared. They told him the whole story and asked him where the baby was, saying that they believed he knew how to help them. But Talking God said nothing, shook his head, and went about as if looking for something. They said to themselves, "We must give him something for his help." They offered him two buckskins and a white shell and now he nodded his head.

Then Talking God ran toward the lake from the east and gave his call. In the same way, he ran from the south, then from the west, and then from the north.[6] As he gave his call from the north, they saw the water in the lake rise in the center and open like a door. When the door in the lake opened, Talking God, followed by Older Brother and the mother of the baby, went in single file to the opening and found twelve steps leading down in the lake. The old man, the old woman and Younger Brother stayed on the bank.

Under the lake, Haashch'ééłti'í (Talking God) led Older Brother and his sister from the bottom of the step through fields of flowers. As they went, they saw Tł'iishtsoh above them to the north with his tongue sticking out, ready to strike, but they did not see the baby. Then they searched toward the east, and then came back to the place where they started at the bottom of the steps. Then they searched to the south, and in that direction there were beautiful birds of all kinds, called ayásh, including a very lovely one called chooshghalii (tanager). Then they searched toward the west, and then toward the north, and after they had gone, thus, in each direction, they went back to where they had started at the bottom of the steps from the upper world. Talking God was searching with them, but they did not find the baby.

Suddenly they heard Níłch' i Biyázhí (the Messenger Wind) speaking to them from above saying "Tł'iishtsoh is the one who took the baby away. The offering that he needs is a buckskin with a pierced turquoise tied between the ears." So they asked Older Brother to go up to the earth above and bring a buckskin with a turquoise tied to it, and place it before Tł'iishtsoh. These things he did. And then as they looked toward the east, they saw a man appear dressed in black flint. No one saw where he came from. This man, who was the Black Wind, set up in

---

[5]If the patient goes to sleep on the night of a ceremony being given over him, the sickness will go on, and when he comes out in the morning to draw the dawn into him, it will do him no good.

[6]Adooldiz is the term for these movements or dance that he made.

the east a black ceremonial tsibąąs[7] which had a head on it with a blue top, a white face, and a yellow stripe on the chin. Next he picked up the buckskin offering and laid it over Tł'iishtoh, the Great Snake, with the head of the buckskin at Tł'iishtsoh's head. Then he picked up Tł'iishtsoh in the buckskin and threw him through the tsibąąs. When he did this, the skin of Tł'iishtsoh cracked open at the head and the people saw hair sticking out. (The nitł'iz offering which the family had put into the lake was for the Wind People who lived there, and the four Winds had taken the offering and divided it. When Talking God and Older Brother and the mother came down into the lake, the Winds had already prepared the tsibąąs in readiness for this ceremony.)

Now the Blue Wind appeared in the south and put up the blue tsibąąs. This had a white face, yellow stripe on the chin, and top. The Blue Wind picked up Tł'iishtsoh in the buckskin and threw him through this tsibąąs, and this time the Great Snake's skin split to his shoulders. Then, to the west, appeared the Yellow Wind and set up the yellow tsibąąs. This tsibąąs had a white face, yellow chin, and black top. He picked up Tł'iishtsoh in the buckskin and threw him through this tsibąąs, and this time the Great Snake's skin split so the people could see that he was human to the waist. At the north appeared the White Wind and set up the white tsibąąs. This tsibąąs also had a white face, yellow chin, and black top. The White Wind threw Tł'iishtsoh through this tsibąąs and the snake skin split so that he was human to his ankles. Next appeared the All-colored or Rainbow Wind and set up in the center, overhead, the tsibąąs made of many plants of all colors. He picked up Tł'iishtsoh in the buckskin and threw him through this tsibąąs. The skin peeled off entirely and they saw, to their surprise, a grown person who had been their baby four days before.

The Origin of the Wind Chant Ritual

Then the Black Wind came and stood facing east with Talking God behind him. He called the rescued youth to stand behind with the Yellow Wind on his right, the White Wind on his left, and the Blue Wind and All-colored Wind behind him. Behind the latter stood Older Brother and then the mother. They all moved toward the east, south, west and north, and as they circled round, the Winds instructed them. They were told that they were all to be nourished by the flowers used as medicine. This medicine was to be rubbed on the body, made into infusions and used as an emetic. They were told that the birds, too, were to be used for

---

[7]Tsibąąs are ceremonial hoops made of various kinds of branches and variously decorated. They are large enough for a person to pass through and the passage is a symbolic transformation rite. Such concepts as star symbolism, concentration of sacred power in an enclosed space and purification are also associated with ceremonial hoops.

The "head" described here is the upper end of one of the hoop withes. The branch has been cut through at an angle and a face painted on the resulting oval wood surface.

medicine. Pollen should be powdered over them when the feathers were to be used as incense and pollen should be put in moccasins with the feathers to give power. The winds also showed them mountain tobacco to be used as medicine, for incense and for smoking. The mountain tobacco of the east and west has blue flowers and that of the north and south has white flowers. All this they were taught by the four Winds, for this part of the story had to do entirely with the Wind Chant Ceremony.[8]

The Wind Chant Ceremony

This is what is done in the Wind Chant Ceremony (Nítch'ijí). In the hooghan they make the sandpainting on buckskin called "Jóhonaa'éí Iikááh," and the prayer called "The forcing words of prayer for the patient" is said:

> Talking God came for me and went through
>   the first black tsibąąs for me;
> Talking God came for me and went through
>   the blue tsibąąs for me;
> Talking God came for me and went through
>   the yellow tsibąąs for me;
> Talking God came for me and went through
>   the many-colored tsibąąs for me.

The patient and priest and the patient's family go through these different colored tsibąąs in this order. Then they all turn around and go back through the various tsibąąs and into the hooghan. The patient then sits on the sandpainting and white corn pollen is put on his feet. The black tsibąąs is placed nearest the hooghan and they begin passing through the tsibąąs going eastward in the order given in the prayer.

On the second day, the ceremony is held at the south, but there is no sandpainting on buckskin in the hooghan. On the third day, the ceremony is held to the west, and on the fourth day it is held to the north. Each day, new tsibąąs are made. At the end of the ceremony the sandpainting on buckskin is given to the medicine man.

The size or number of sticks that go into the tsibąąs is not fixed, but the top of each stick must be faced toward the hooghan when the tsibąąs are set up and all must be tied together with the growth of the wood. On each side of each tsibąąs, near the ground, two plants are

---

[8]In the ceremony, when they say "Walking-with-the-Wind," (Nítch'ihołdiiskai) it refers to this part of the story. There are five songs sung for the trip the travelers took towards the east, five for the south, five for the trip to the west, and five for the trip to the north. In the story the tsibąąs were set one in each direction, but the people were told that in the future they should be set in a row.

tied. Three of the four used at the south are made of pinyon, one is made of rose. For the west, three are made of cedar and one of rose, and for the north, three of hard oak and one of rose are used.[9]

The Story of Older Brother and Younger Brother

Earlier in the story it was told that when the son of Tł'iishtsoh was killing the deer for his own family and for the family of his wife, he and his wife never ate with the rest of the family. It was also told that they never ate the intestines, or heart, or lungs of the deer. Before the family returned to the upper world from under the lake, the Winds told them that these parts of the animals should never be eaten. They were also told that they must never lie down in places where water had run, as in arroyos, nor lie down to sleep with their heads close to any tree, particularly one that had been struck by lightning. They were told that if they disobeyed these prohibitions they would disappear, as the baby had disappeared, and be brought to this place under the lake.

Then led by Haashch'ééłti'í (Talking God), the boy who had been rescued, Older Brother and the boy's mother, in that order, all went up to the shore of the lake where the rest of the family were living. The old people asked where the baby was. (Talking God had vanished as soon as they reached the upper air and the Messenger Wind had told them that he came from Tséniichii'. He said that hereafter the lake was to be called Awéé'náá'ołí, Baby-floating-in-a-circle). Older Brother and the baby's mother said, "This is he who was the baby, who is with us." So the others greeted the youth and they all went on their way back to their home because they felt that this was not a good place to stay in.

Their meat was nearly gone because there was no game near this lake. The two brothers traveled ahead of the family with their bows and arrows trying to get food. They tracked deer and other animals but could not find them; they even tried to get rabbits or rats and squirrels, but with no success. While his two uncles hunted, the youth stayed with the others.

One day in their travels they came to some people who were living in the same way this family had lived before the son of Tł'iishtsoh had taught them how to make buckskins and clothing and had shown them a better way of life. These people were an old man, a women, a son and two daughters. The two hunters told them how they had been trying to get food, and that they could not find any. The people asked the travelers where they got such nice clothes. The brothers told them about this and the two girls were much fascinated by them and followed them around. One of the girls said that she would like to have clothes like theirs and the brothers said they would try and get some clothing for them. Younger Brother decided to marry the younger of the two girls, and he took her for his wife.

The two brothers then went back to their own family and Younger Brother told them that he had married. He said that he wanted his wife to have a buckskin dress and asked his sister

---

[9]When the ceremony is one of songs only with no prayers, it is given like the one witnessed by M. C. Wheelwright at Newcomb in 1932 where the row of tsibąąs began with the black one toward the east.

to make one. When it was made he took it to his wife. All the rest of her family wanted clothing also and the two brothers brought clothing to this poor family until they had provided for them all. These people were living west of the lake where the baby had been lost and the brothers and their family, after stopping there, went on westward on their travels.

Older Brother Eats Intestines

One evening they saw a very fresh track of deer and Older Brother insisted that the family camp there while he went east after the deer. The family made camp and he followed the tracks and came up to the deer, which was lying down, shot it and killed it. He left it there, went back to his family and brought them to camp near the dead deer. They butchered it and built a big fire and when this had burned to coals the meat was all cut up ready to cook. Older Brother and his sister and her son, who all had been warned by the Messenger Wind not to eat either the head, intestines, liver, or heart of any animal, forgot all about this. Older Brother put on the coals the forbidden parts of the intestines called ach'íí'náhiniiste'e'é and cooked them. As they cooked, they curled up and moved. Even when they moved, the people did not remember that they had been forbidden to eat this, for it looked so good; they took it off the fire, laid it on some green brush and all began to eat it. After they had been eating for some time, there were only two inches left of the intestines. When Older Brother picked this up and put it in his mouth, it jumped down his throat before being chewed, and that piece of intestine turned into a snake inside of him. During the night he suffered very much: his stomach swelled to a very large size. The others tried to keep it from swelling, even tying it down, but it kept growing and they did not know what to do, or who could help them.

Suddenly Dǫ'tsoh, the messenger fly, appeared. He said that there was a snake inside Older Brother, sent as punishment since they had disobeyed what the Messenger Wind had said and had eaten what they should not. Dǫ'tsoh told them that there were four Hastói (Elders) who lived on a high rock mountain who might help them, and that Younger Brother was the one who should go there to ask them for help. So he went, and when he reached there he found a hooghan. As he entered, one of the Hastói was lying by the door, to the east. Younger Brother laid down a buckskin as an offering and begged for help, or for some ceremony to help his brother. But the Hastói said he could not help because he had no knowledge about the sick man. Younger Brother asked another Hastói at the south of the hoohgan and got the same answer. Then he asked one to the west and one to the north, but each said he could not help. Suddenly Younger Brother realized that these were all the Winds that had met the travelers below the lake, only these Winds were older. As they could not help, Younger Brother took his buckskin offering and went back to his family. When he got back, the family said, "Next time take two buckskins and try again." So he went a second time, but the same thing happened and he could get no help. So he went a third time, taking three buckskins, and a fourth time taking four, but with no success, and he returned discouraged to his family.

Dǫ'tsoh came again after this and said, "Don't take valuable things like buckskins. Cut out a diamond-shaped piece of the center of each buckskin, cutting with the grain and remembering in each case in which direction the head of the skin was and at this end paint the Sun and at the other end paint the Moon. Fold it together and set it, making a pouch for tobacco, with the Sun on one side and the Moon on the other. Now take a piece of lók'aatsoh (reed) and cut off a short section for a k'eet'áán offering.[10] In the hollow reed put mountain tobacco and hazééłda'a (squirrel) plant.[11] For this offering the squirrel plant should also be chewed up and blown all over the k'eet'áán. Some mountain tobacco should be put in the pouch." The k'eet'áán is called biyeel and is half white and half blue, for the Sun and Moon. (This is where the blowing on of the squirrel plant decoction on the body of the patient ceremony began.)

Dǫ'tsoh said, "This k'eet'áán and the pouch are what the Winds want." He told Younger Brother that when he came to the hooghan of the Winds with this offering, he was to enter and pass, sunwise, to the Wind at the west side. Here he was to hold out the offering over the Wind's right foot, then pass it up over his head, down to his left foot and leave it there. Then he was to offer the pouch in the same way, leaving it at the Wind's left foot also. He said to Younger Brother, "Don't tell the Winds that I told you to do this," and then he disappeared.

So Younger Brother went again to the house of the Winds and offered the k'eet'áán and pouch to the West Wind, as Dǫ'tsoh had told him to do, saying to him, "I offer this, asking for your help." The Wind did not move at first, but finally he picked up the k'eet'áán and smelled of it, and then picked up the pouch. He seemed angry and, looking up, said, "You are the one who planned this, Nihookǫ́ǫ'haniihii (He-who-knows-everything)!" Younger Brother looked up and saw Dǫ'tsoh overhead and realized that it was to Dǫ'tsoh that the Wind was speaking. Dǫ'tsoh said, "I have been here all the time. I don't roam."

Then the Wind passed around the offering to the other Winds who all looked at it carefully and smelled of it. Younger Brother grew impatient and tried to hurry them, but they went slowly, and finally the West Wind took out a pipe, shook the mountain tobacco out of the k'eet'áán into it and smoked it slowly. Then he passed the pipe around until the Winds had smoked up all the tobacco. Then the Wind said to Younger Brother, "Go out and bring in my medicine pouch." Younger Brother went out to do as he was told and at once Dǫ'tsoh appeared before him and said, "Don't bring the medicine pouch in but let the Wind bring it in, and don't ever lose sight of the Wind when he goes with you to your family. No matter what he does, you must follow him. If he tells you to wait for him, or go behind a tree, or out of sight, don't do it, but always watch him. If you lose sight of him, even once, it will be much harder for him to cure the patient and he may die." Then Dǫ'tsoh went back to his place over the hooghan and Younger Brother came back and told the Wind that he could not find the medicine pouch. The Wind sent him out for it three times more and then went out himself, brought it in, handed it to Younger Brother, and said, "You carry it for me." Younger Brother brought it out of the hooghan and waited outside; the West Wind took the lead and Younger Brother followed him on the way to his family.

---

[10]A k'eet'áán is a section of hollow reed about the size of a cigarette which is filled with sacred materials and used as an offering.

[11]This is a medicine plant which has a strong odor, a round leaf and a pod containing black seeds.

Before they had gone far the Wind told Younger Brother to go ahead and that he would come after. The boy refused and the Wind asked him why he did this. Younger Brother did not answer but still refused to go ahead and kept the Wind in sight constantly; the Wind tried this strategem four times but Younger Brother persisted in refusing to obey him.

They reached the home of the patient and the Wind gave him the pouch to hold. It had a hole in the center and was only a fingerlength long. Then the Wind began to spread out his medicine and as he did this the pouch grew larger and larger. The Wind took out powdered herbs, zaa'nił, and stirred them in water. He took some of the decoction and blew it over the patient's stomach, then made him drink some of it and rubbed some on his body and the swelling went down and he was cured. This happened on the fourth day after Older Brother had swallowed the intestine which turned into a snake. The Wind warned the patient again not to eat intestines of deer, not to lie with his head next to a tree, and not to kill woodrats or burn cactus.

The family had thought that this was the Black Wind who had come. They had not recognized him because he was not dressed in his blue flint armor. After telling the family who he was, he left them.

Now that Older Brother was well, the family stayed in this place, and Younger Brother wanted to bring his wife to live with his own family. He went to his wife's people and asked them to join his family. They said that they could not come at that time, but that he should take his wife with him back to his family; he did this and joined his own people again. The rest of her family said they would come later.

They were now living near Tsé'édééh, to the south of where they had been and they moved a little way off from the place where Older Brother had been sick. It was now autumn and there were many ripe seeds growing nearby which they could eat. They saw many tracks of deer, but the hunters, when they followed the tracks, could find no game.

MYTH OF THE
EVIL-CHASING CHANT

Older Brother Eats a Snake

In their hunting, they came to a place called Chį́įshtah Násk'id, a semicircular mesa which has a plant (chį́įstah) growing on it. This was south of where the family was living. There the brothers came across a creature like a snake under a bush, and they noticed that there were marks like deer tracks on its back. They had not noticed, when they were under the lake, what Tł'iistsoh, the Great Snake, had looked like. When they saw this awkward beast under the bush, they thought it might be useful to them as food. Older Brother wanted to kill the creature, but Younger Brother said that he did not think they should. They went away and left it, but Older Brother still wanted to kill it. Three times they came back to the strange beast and went away again, undecided. When they came back to it for the fourth time, Older Brother decided to kill it. He cut its head off and its tail, took the intestines out, put the body on a flat rock and built a fire near it. By this time it was evening. For protection from the wind, they made a little brush corral. Then they began to cook the beast, which was very fat, by turning it from side to side near the fire. When it was cooked, they took it off the fire and laid it on some plants they had picked. Younger Brother said, "We should not eat this food," but Older Brother insisted that he would eat it, and did so. Younger Brother left his food untouched and went to sleep on the north side of the fire, while Older Brother slept to the south of the beast's remains.

Sometime in the night, Younger Brother got up and rebuilt the fire. He saw the remains of the reptile nearby, and his brother asleep. Later on, he got up for the second time and found things the same as before. When he woke for the third time, everything was quiet. At the first ray of light, he rebuilt the fire again, as it was cold. There was not light enough to see much, but he heard a noise like the rattle of a snake and, as the early morning light came, he looked over to where the remains of the reptile were. He could see nothing there, and, when he looked for his brother, all he could see was a beast like the one that they had killed, shooting out its tongue at him. Younger Brother was frightened. He called out, "I told you not to eat that," and he ran away, leaving everything. As he reached his home, the sun rose. He told the family what had happened to his brother: that he had eaten forbidden food, and what he had seen in the dawn.

They all began thinking what could be done to restore Older Brother to himself again and they decided to send Younger Brother again to Tsé'édééh to the Wind People to beg them for help. So Younger Brother went to the Winds, but they answered as they had on his first visit. They said they knew nothing about it and could not help, and Younger Brother returned to his family.

Then the family sent the Messenger Wind to Wind Rock, the home of Haashch'éélti'í (Talking God), to see if he would be willing to help. When the Messenger Wind brought Talking God back to the family, he led them to the place where Older Brother had been turned into a snake. All they could find of Older Brother were four footprints leading to the entrance of the corral. His clothing and his bows and arrows were there, but there was no trace of him. They all were searching, except the old man and his wife and the wife of Younger Brother, who stayed in the camp. Talking God ran off to the east, then to the south, west and north, looking for tracks, while the rest hunted around the bushes and the rocks everywhere, but found nothing.

All this time, the youth whose father was the son of Tł'iishtsoh, knew everything that had happened or would happen in the future, because he had been given this wisdom by Nítch'i Biyázhí (the Messenger Wind) speaking in his ear. But he never had told anyone that he possessed this knowledge. After the family had been hunting for four days, the youth told them that he knew there was a mountain in the shape of a coiled snake, called Dził Náneests'ee'é, to the south. There lived Tł'iishtsoh, the Great Snake, in his den, and there he had taken Older Brother who had been turned into a snake.

Talking God said to the people, "You stay here and I will go and bring back my grandson," and he left and went to the den of Tł'iishtsoh. When he got there, he went inside and said, "I come after my grandson." All he could see in the den were Tł'iishtsoh Hastiin and Tł'iishtsoh Asdzáán[12], and they answered him roughly, "No creature that walks the earth should enter here. You must go." So he went out and returned to the family. The next day Talking God and the youth who had knowledge set out together for Tł'iishtsoh's home, but when they got there they were ordered out in the same way and returned to the family. On the third day Younger Brother went with them, but Tł'iishtsoh told them that Older Brother was not there, and sent them all away. On the fourth day Talking God, the youth, Younger Brother and the mother of the youth all went to Tł'iishtsoh and begged him to give them back Older Brother. Tł'iishtsoh only grew angry and sent them home again.

All the Winds knew what was happening to the family and Dǫ'tsoh, the messenger fly, now appeared at the camp where the old man and woman and the wife of Younger Brother were waiting. He told them that the youth's name should be Ni'bitádidíín Yeeneeyánii Ashkii (Nourished-by-the-growth-of-the-Earth-Boy, or Earth Boy). When Dǫ'tsoh had told them this ceremonial name he left, and the wife of Younger Brother left the old people and joined her husband and the others. She told them about this name which Dǫ'tsoh had given the youth, and also that the youth knew everything that went on, and therefore he was the only one who

---

[12]Great Snake Man and Great Snake Woman.

21

could find his uncle, Older Brother. Then she went back to the old people. Younger Brother now spoke to his nephew by his real name, Ni'bitádidíín Yeeneeyánii Ashkii, and said, "My nephew, you know where my brother is and where and how I can find him. You are the only one that can bring him back—will you help us?" Earth Boy said, "Yes, I will do what you ask," for he had been called by his real name which had great power.

They were camped now between the home of Tł'iishtsoh and a place called Wooded Hill. Earth Boy said, "Over there, at Wooded Hill, live five Hastói (Elders), four Fire Gods and One Water God. Those are the only people that can bring Older Brother back to himself." So Talking God left to visit Wooded Hill and found Dǫ'tsoh there when he arrived. He said the Hastói had been looking for Older Brother and were planning to come and help. Then Talking God spoke to them all. He told them of the troubles the family had been having and that they begged for help to bring Older Brother back to himself. Haashch'ééshjiní, the Fire God and the Water God agreed to help, and they followed Talking God back to the family. Then Talking God, Fire God, Water God, Earth Boy, his mother and Younger Brother, all six of them, set out for the home of Tł'iishtsoh. Fire God, armed with his fire-stick, led the way.

When they came near the home of Tł'iishtsoh, Fire God told them to wait and that he and Water God would go on alone. He carried his fire-stick as his only weapon and Tóneinilí (the Water God) carried his water pot. As soon as Tł'iishtsoh saw them coming into his house, he ordered them out, even while they were begging to him to help their grandson. Tł'iishtsoh said that there was no grandson of theirs in his home. Four times they asked for help and four times Tł'iishtsoh refused, and he continued to order them to leave. Then Fire God grew angry and said, "Do you mean that my grandson is not here?" Tł'iishtsoh said "Yes" and told them to go. Fire God repeated his question four times and four times Tł'iishtsoh gave the same answer.

Then Fire God took out his fire-stick and put it down, steadying it with his foot. He spun the stick and at the first spin smoke arose, but Tł'iishtsoh paid no attention. At the second spin, smoke filled the den and still Tł'iishtsoh did not seem to mind. The third time the stick was spun, fire came and spread everywhere, but Tł'iishtsoh still paid no attention. At the fourth spinning of the stick, it exploded, and Tł'iishtsoh called for mercy, saying, "Surely you can have your grandson." Then Water God began sprinkling water from his pot and put out the fire.[13]

Tł'iishtsoh had rolled Older Brother up in a dark cloud and put him up in the rafters of his house. He told Fire God and Water God that in exchange for Older Brother they must repair his home which had been burned, and they must also give him a shell, cut into a diamond shape. (Tł'iishtsoh now wears this on his head.) Also, they had to be willing to learn his ceremonial song and his prayer and his tsibąąs ceremony.

The first thing that he showed them was how to make a black mountain[14] outside the

---

[13]From the beginning of the story to the time Older Brother ate the snake, all the story belongs to the Wind Chant. After this happening, the story belongs to the Evil-Chasing Chant.

[14]This is a symbolic ridge a foot long and six inches high made of earth or sand of the appropriate color.

22

hooghan toward the east, at some distance. Beyond that, toward the east, he made a blue mountain, then a yellow mountain, and then a white mountain. Next to the hooghan between it and the black mountain, he set up a tsibąąs (ceremonial hoop) of rose branches. Next to this he placed a white tsibąąs, next a yellow one, then a blue one, and then a black one. All these tsibąąs were set up between the black mountain and the hooghan. Now he took the black cloud out of his hooghan, unrolled it, and out came Older Brother in the form of a snake. Tł'iishtsoh warned them that no one should stand on the north side of the path of mountains and tsibąąs while this ceremony was going on.

Tł'iishtsoh then picked up Older Brother, still in the form of a snake, and passed along the south side of the row of tsibąąs and mountains. When he reached the east end of the path, before the white mountain, he stood on two white bear tracks which were made there and prayed to chase the dangerous powers away. Then he stepped over the white mountain. After this he stood on yellow bear tracks, sang a song, prayed, and stepped over the yellow mountain. So he stepped over the mountains and came to the tsibąąs of rose. All this time he was carrying Older Brother in the form of a snake. Then Tł'iishtsoh threw Older Brother through the rose tsibąąs and when he landed on the ground he became a human being again. Tł'iishtsoh followed through the tsibąąs, picked Older Brother up, and carried him back to the hooghan through all the other tsibąąs. He said to the people, "This is what I want you to learn to do to protect yourselves against dangerous powers. That is why I have been showing you this ceremony which is for chasing dangerous powers away."

(When the baby was changed into a snake it was only because the family had not given presents to the son of Tł'iishtsoh; therefore that first ceremony was of the Wind Chant form. But in the case of Older Brother, he had killed Tł'iishtsoh, which was forbidden, and then had eaten of the dead forbidden thing, hence the Evil-Chasing Chant form of ceremony was necessary.) Then Tł'iishtsoh gave them more warnings. They must not eat intestines, heart or liver of deer, nor kill or eat woodrats or rabbits. Nor might they eat anything that had died naturally or had been killed by another animal, or by accident. Also, they must not watch anything suffering or dying.

Older Brother had been a snake for four days, and as a result was now numb and deaf. Tł'iishtsoh told the people to take him back to the place where he ate the snake at Coiled Mountain, and there they would find plants of all kinds, some bitter and some sweet, also many berries. He said they must get a piece of bark or wood from a tree that had been struck by lightning, and pound the wood and herbs up and mix it with water and give this to Older Brother to drink. "He must drink as much as he can, and what is left he must rub all over his body." Fire God and Water God, with Older Brother and the others journeyed back to the place where Older Brother had eaten the snake (Chįįshtah Násk'id). They gathered the herbs and bark and prepared them as Tł'iishtsoh had directed. Older Brother drank the infusion and vomited. Out came the pieces of snake that he had eaten, and he was cleansed and was as well as he had been before. After this, Fire God and Water God left and went to their home. The others rejoined the rest of the family at their camp. Now Younger Brother had learned the Wind Chant and the Evil-Chasing Chant and could cure many evils, but Older Brother had only learned the Wind Chant.

Older Brother Kills a Woodrat

They broke camp and moved again, so as to forget the trouble that had happened in this place (as is the custom now), and traveled westward. The two brothers went off hunting, and one day they came to a place of many woodrats' nests. Here Older Brother killed a woodrat. Younger Brother said, ''Don't you remember you were told not to kill these?'' Older Brother answered, ''Yes, but the woodrat is not for me, it is for my mother. I am not going to eat it.'' He gave it to the old woman and then the brothers went off hunting again, this time toward the north. Older Brother was hunting further off, while Younger Brother was nearer to the camp. As they walked along, Older Brother called to the other and said ''Stop shooting rocks at me!'' for something had hit him on the ankle. Younger Brother came running to him and found him sitting down. ''I didn't shoot at you,'' he said, and, looking at the ankle, he saw a red spot near the bone. Older Brother told Younger Brother to follow the rest of the family and leave him, so Younger Brother did this, and the family camped after a time. Meanwhile, Older Brother was trying to follow them, but his ankle hurt him so that he could hardly move. Finally Younger Brother and his nephew, Earth Boy, came back to help him, and carried him to the camp. By now his whole leg, up to the knee, was swollen, and he was suffering greatly. The rest of the family, meanwhile, had eaten the woodrat, as they had nothing else to eat. Earth Boy knew what was happening and the cause of it, because the Wind had spoken to him, but he kept quiet and said nothing.

The family talked over this trouble and wondered who could help them, and then Earth Boy told them that the cause was the killing of the woodrat. The accident came from the Yellow Wind to punish Older Brother. The Yellow Wind had hit him on the ankle with a cactus. The reason cactus was used was because woodrats eat it. The family was still thinking what help they could get for Older Brother's suffering, and they remembered that Tł'iishtsoh had helped them the last time. They decided to go to him, but Earth Boy said, ''No, you must go to the home of Yellow Wind. He is the one who did the harm and he alone can help.'' So they prepared nitł'iz, an offering of jewels, and Younger Brother went off with it to the home of the Yellow Wind. He gave him the offering in a small shell basket, saying, ''I bring you this as an offering, and want you to come and cure my brother.''

The Yellow Wind looked at the offering and was satisfied. He asked Younger Brother to bring him his medicine pouch. Younger Brother went out to do this and found that this time the medicine pouch was quite large. He brought it to the Yellow Wind who said, ''Take this with you and I will come tomorrow.'' Younger Brother begged him to come at once as his brother was suffering, but the Yellow Wind said again, ''I will come tomorrow, he will still be alive then.'' (The medicine man always does this now, sending the pouch first, and always says, ''I will come tomorrow.'') When Younger Brother reached his family, Older Brother said to him, ''Why didn't you bring the Yellow Wind?'' Younger Brother said, ''I begged him to come, but he said he would come tomorrow.'' Older Brother scolded him for not bringing the Yellow Wind at once.

On the following day the Yellow Wind came, as he said, and, opening his medicine pouch, he brought out some herbs and stirred them in water. This is known as zaa'nił. He gave

24

it to Older Brother to drink and made another decoction and rubbed it on his hurt leg. At once the swelling went down and ceased to ache and Older Brother felt all right for a while. Just as the Yellow Wind was leaving, Older Brother had a convulsion, twisting his body about. The Yellow Wind said, "There is nothing much the matter with him, but he must be covered." He laid Older Brother down with his head to the north and spread a buckskin over him. Then he drew four zigzag lines on the ground to the east of the patient, four to the south, four to the west, and four to the north, and then crossed each group with a straight line.[15] After making each cross he rubbed out that group with his feet and in this way passed around the patient, praying as he went. After this, beginning at the north, he made four straight lines at the patient's head and rubbed them out, then at the west, the south and the east, rubbing out each in turn. After this he took the buckskin off the patient and he was well again.

Older Brother had this convulsion because the medicine contained substance which came from Gila Monster and also pollen that had been shaken onto Gila Monster, and so had strong power. So today, in the ceremony, they offer a prayer to the black Gila Monster who comes from the top of Naadahas'éí, south of the meteor crater near Flagstaff. The prayer says, "Come down and help me find the sickness of the patient."

Yellow Wind lived at Naadahas'éí with a black Gila Monster as guard to the east, a blue Gila Monster to the south, a yellow Gila Monster to the west, and a white Gila Monster to the north. The Shaking-hand came from this convulsion of Older Brother's and he began now to be able to read thoughts and to have second sight.[16] Before Yellow Wind left, he repeated the prohibitions given to the people. He added that they must not lie in the path of the wind in places through which it sweeps, and then he left them. Older Brother was the ancestor of those who never do what they are told, and always do what they are told not to do.

Older Brother Shoots the Whirlwind

For a time everything went well. The wife of Younger Brother said she wished her father and mother could join the family. The family agreed to this and they traveled back to the region near Tsé'édééh where her people had been living. However, when they reached there, the girl's people had gone. Earth Boy, who was a member of the Snake Clan, could always draw game to him and kill deer whenever they were needed. He went hunting and killed many deer, and his uncles brought in the meat so the family lived well there through the winter. During the next summer, they moved further away toward the home of Tł'iishtsoh. The wife of

---

[15]This is a rite to restore the patient when hysterical. Similar zigzag and straight lines stop the approach of the cyclone (page 55). See page 40 on jidiitłah rite.

[16]Shaking-hand is a form of divining which may be used in diagnosing sickness. It consists of a shaking movement of the hand and forearm which is interpreted in somewhat the same way as is the movement of a divining rod. A person who has this gift may need the help of a medicine man in interpreting; such a person may also have the ability to read thoughts. Star gazing is another form of divining in which the practitioner actually sees visions; a person who has Shaking-hand is merely acted upon by external phenomena.

Younger Brother had a boy baby born there, but her family had not been found yet. Every day the two brothers went hunting but they were not successful; it was their nephew, Earth Boy, who killed the game and Older Brother and Younger Brother took turns going out to bring in the kill.

One day Older Brother was walking alone and saw a little Whirlwind coming towards him. He tried to dodge it but it hit him; he turned to avoid it but still it pursued him. He tried to dodge it four times and then he grew angry and shot at it with his bow and arrow. As he did this, he noticed that the Whirlwind was turning anti-sunwise. When he shot his arrow into it, the Whirlwind stopped and where it had been there was a person lying on earth. This was the son of Left-Turning Wind who lived at Ni'hodiits'a' (Road-of-the-Left-Handed-Wind) to the south. At the same place lived Níyoltsoh (the Cyclone). Older Brother knew it was very dangerous to have shot the little Whirlwind. He was frightened and ran home and was very much excited when he told what he had done. Meanwhile Earth Boy knew all about this as the Wind had told him, but he said nothing.

Older Brother asked what he should do and Earth Boy said, "Nothing can help you now. None of the Winds can help you; neither the Black, the Blue, the Yellow, nor the White Wind, and neither Fire God, nor Water God, nor Talking God, nor Tł'iishtsoh. The Cyclone is the one power that nothing can face." Just then they heard the roar of the Cyclone and saw a whirlwind of black clouds and lightning coming toward them. Earth Boy said to his uncle, "No one can help you now but yourself."

Then Older Brother asked the rest of the family to help him build a hooghan, and they gathered everything that has prickles, such as cactus and yucca, and they covered the hooghan with these. Next, Older Brother built a fire of hard oak inside the hooghan. Picking up a coal, he burned a crescent on his breast, with the opening to the left. Then he did the same on his back with the opening to the right; this is called "shield-of-fire." Then, walking out of the hooghan, he stuck an arrow in the ground pointing east, another pointing south, one to the west, and one to the north. Facing the Cyclone, he went to meet it as it came closer and closer. When it drew near, he took out a flint and made a zigzag mark on the earth across the path of the Cyclone. Next to the zigzag he made a straight line, then another zigzag line, then another straight line. He went back into the hooghan and everyone watched to see what would happen. The Cyclone came as far as the marks and could not pass them, though sometimes it nearly succeeded in breaking through.[17]

Then Older Brother went out of the hooghan and found that the Cyclone had stopped, and when he came to where it had been, he met a man coming toward him. When they met, Older Brother realized that this was the Left-Turning Wind. The Wind spoke and said, "I was not so big after all. You have more power than I have. Now if you will restore my son whom

---

[17]This is also an Evil-Chasing Chant episode. Beginning with the shooting of the Whirlwind, there is a ceremony called akéé'dahoodzoh (meaning "drawing out by arrows from the body"). In the ceremony, the priest who treats the patient rubs ashes all over him and presses an arrow to the patient's body.

you have killed, I will teach you three ceremonial songs. I promise that I will go away and never bother you or any of your people again as long as people exist."

Older Brother agreed to restore the son of the Wind. He went to the body, pulled out the arrow and put pollen of flowers and powdered birds' feathers on his own feet and hands. Then he moved the body of the Whirlwind from the east, south, west and north with his hands and rubbed his whole body. He pressed his feet to the feet of the Whirlwind, and he came to life. Then Older Brother spoke to the Left-Turning Wind and said, "Take him now and make him well." So the Wind and his son left and Older Brother went back to the hooghan covered with cactus and named it Blessed Hooghan because even the Cyclone could not touch it. The family stayed there the rest of the summer, and when winter came they went back to Tsé'édééh, whence they had come. Here there were plenty of deer which Earth Boy could always kill.

During the next summer, Younger Brother's wife had a second boy. He saw that there were too many living together in the family and said, "I will move away with my wife and two boys. You must all help to build a new hooghan a little way off." The rest of the family decided to move again and said that where they settled the next time they would build a hooghan for Younger Brother and his family. But Younger Brother decided to move first and the rest did not move after all, but stayed at Tsé'édééh. Younger Brother told his nephew, Earth Boy, that he would have to supply both families with food. Whenever he killed something, he was to bring meat to Younger Brother's family as well as to the outfit of his own parents. The nephew agreed to do this.[18]

---

[18]This is where the Great Star Chant branches off from the Wind Chant.

MYTH OF THE GREAT STAR CHANT

The Story of Younger Brother's Visit to the Sky

Younger Brother had been thinking of all the things that had happened to his older brother. He said to his wife that there should be a ceremony over Older Brother, and then he went back to his family and explained what he thought should be done. But he did not know what ceremony should be given, or how to do it, so he spoke to his nephew about it. Earth Boy said, "There were several little ceremonies given over Older Brother by the Winds, Tł'iishtsoh and the others, and now we must combine these in one ceremony." After talking this over, Younger Brother went back to his home. The day after this, he decided to go to the medicine man at Tsé'édééh. He said, "This ceremony should be given here at my home. After I have seen the medicine man, we will build a ceremonial hooghan for it."

So he left the next day and went to Tsé'édééh to the home of the Black Wind. He begged him to come and give the first big ceremony over his brother but the Black Wind said, "No, I think the medicine man at Coiled Rock is the one who should give the first ceremony. Let me get him, and I will be his assistant."

When Younger Brother came back to his home, his wife told him that while he was away, a man had come whom she did not know. Younger Brother asked his wife if he knew the man and she said, "No, you don't know him."

Then Younger Brother went to the rest of the family and told them what the Black Wind had said and where he was advised to go for a medicine man to give the ceremony. The next day he went to Coiled Rock and came to the house of Tł'iishtsoh and begged him to give the ceremony over his brother. Tł'iishtsoh said, "No, I cannot do that, but go to Naadahas'éí Bílátah. You will find the Yellow Wind there and he is the one to give the ceremony."

When Younger Brother got back to his home, his wife told him that the stranger had again visited here. Younger Brother asked the rest of the family who this could be, but no one knew anything about him. The stranger had asked Younger Brother's wife where her people were, and she had said that her husband was away finding someone to hold a big ceremony over Older Brother.

Younger Brother went back to the rest of the family and told them that Tł'iishtsoh had advised him to get the Yellow Wind to hold the ceremony. The next day, Younger Brother went to the home of the Yellow Wind and asked him to come give the ceremony over his brother.

Yellow Wind answered, "No, I cannot, but over yonder, at Yáhóógai, you will find the White Wind. He will perform the ceremony over your brother and I will help him."

Back at home, Younger Brother's wife told him the same story of a visit of a stranger. He said, "Why didn't you question him more about where he came from, and who he is?" All that she had learned was that the stranger lived nearby. Younger Brother told his family what the Yellow Wind had said, advising to visit the White Wind, and asked whether they thought that these Winds that he had seen would be good helpers in the ceremony. Everyone thought these Winds would make very good helpers.

Next day, when Younger Brother was ready to leave to visit the White Wind, the stranger appeared. Younger Brother asked him who he was. He answered, "I came to see the ceremony that I heard was going to be given for your older brother." Younger Brother told the stranger he was nearly ready to start after the medicine man, and the stranger said that he wanted to go with him for a short distance. He said that he knew where there were some young eagles on a rock ledge which he wanted to get. He needed a man, he said, like Younger Brother to climb the rock, which he could not do, to chase the young eagles down from the nest. "The medicine men need eagles for the ceremony, and these eagles are not very far from the home of the White Wind. If you will help me get the eagles, I will go afterwards and get the medicine man, for I know him very well."

Younger Brother, by this time, had recognized the stranger as Ma'ii (Coyote). He agreed to go with him and they set out. Finally they came to Tsé'édééh (south of Zuni) where they saw a pointed rock with a ledge where there was a nest of crows. Coyote had been there earlier and had painted the crows with white earth so that they looked like young eagles. (This kind of white earth, dleeshłigaii, is now used to whiten the bodies of the dancers in the ceremony.) When Younger Brother and Coyote came to the rock, Coyote pointed to the nest and said, "You see how pretty those young eagles are. When they spread their wings you can see their heads and breasts are white, and their tails are striped with white." Younger Brother started to climb the rock and Coyote laughed, saying "How pretty your eagles are going to be!"

Younger Brother climbed up to the nest and as he did so Coyote blew at the rock and it grew so tall and steep that Younger Brother could not get down again. Then Coyote went back to Younger Brother's wife and told her that her husband had gone forever, he did not know where, and that Younger Brother had told him to take his place with his family.

Meanwhile, Younger Brother, who had got to the top of the rock, found that it had grown up to a circular opening in the sky. The rock grew up into this opening and Younger Brother tried to step off the rock onto this new country where he found himself. He tried to the east, to the south, to the west and to the north, but every time the sky moved back when he stretched out his foot. Then he remembered that he had with him some nitł'iz[19] and, taking out the black nitł'iz he offered it to the sky to the east. Then he tried again to step off the rock and succeeded in doing so. The rock sank back to earth leaving Younger Brother in the country of the sky.

---

[19]An offering in the form of powdered white shell, turquoise, abalone shell and jet, the four sacred jewels.

He started walking east and there he found a long white house. Then he saw to the south a blue house, to the west a yellow one and to the north a black one. He noticed people walking back and forth who looked at him strangely. He felt that he wanted to get away from them: they kept crowding around him in an unfriendly way and, when he spoke, they did not understand him. He found an opening in the crowd towards the northeast and walked away from these people for quite a long distance. Here he came upon another black house and saw that to the south there was a blue house, to the west a yellow one, and to the north a white one. These houses were set in an outer circle around the first houses that he had seen.

At this black house the people were very friendly: he found that they understood his speech and they gathered around him asking questions as to how he got up to this place. They said he should not be up there because he belonged to the earth and that no Earth People should come up so high in the sky. He told them that he wanted very much to find a way down to the earth again. They were talking outside the house, for they had not entered it yet, and one of these friendly people told him that he had better stay in this black house. He said that there were many bad people around and that Younger Brother must not go off alone.

Then they took him inside that black house and explained to him that it was the home of Sǫ'tsoh, the Great Star (also called the Great Black Star in the story), and that the people here were all his friends. He looked around and called them Diné (The People[20]), and then he noticed that in the middle of the house there was a star for their fire. They told him that he should stay there that night, and they prepared some food made of seeds for him, called ch'il bináá'łees'áán. It was just like what he had below on the earth and he ate it with the Star People. They told him that they would help him to reach the earth again. He learned that the white house, the one he had first come to in the sky, was the home of the Eagle People; the blue house at the south was the home of the Chicken Hawk, the Grey Hawk, the Grey Barred Hawk, and two other smaller hawks: there were four kinds of Hawk People living in the blue house. In the yellow house lived all the Yellow-Winged or Yellow-Tailed Hawks. In the black house at the north lived the Black Eagle, also the White-Headed Eagle, the Buzzard and the White Eagle: all the big Eagle People lived in this house.

Then they said, "You are now in the house of the Black Star People. To the south, in the blue house, live the Blue Star People, the house at the west is the house of the Yellow Star People, and at the north is the home of the White Star People." They told him that as soon as he arrived in the sky everyone knew that he was there and that he belonged to the earth, for the Wind had told them. The Black Star People dressed in black flint, the Blue Star People in blue flint, the Yellow Star People in yellow flint, the White Star People in white flint and the Many-Pointed Star People, who lived overhead, were dressed in flint of all colors.

He Goes to the Hole Through the Sky

The Black Star People also said to Younger Brother, "Don't go near the place where you came up from the earth. Stay with us and you will be safe, and, when we think you are ready to go

---

[20]"Diné" is the Navajos' name for themselves.

back to the earth, then you can go to the opening." Younger Brother wondered why they told him not to go near the opening to the earth. He hid himself the next day from Sǫ'tsoh, the Great Black Star, the chief of the Black Star People, and then went back to the hole through the sky. He felt very lonely while he was looking down.

Suddenly Tsénoolch'óshii (Rock Wren) appeared and put a great rock on top of Younger Brother and then went away again. Younger Brother found that he could not move and could not get out from under the rock. Sǫ'tsoh waited for him to come back but he did not come. Then Sǫ'tsoh began searching for him in the houses of the Eagles, and in the other Star houses, and all around the sky, but could find no trace of him. Then the Wind came and told the Star People what had happened to Younger Brother: that he was hidden under a great rock. The Star People went to the opening to the earth and found the rock and tried to lift it off, but it was too heavy. They called the Thunder to help them and he tried to move the rock with his fire which is the lightning. He laid this crosswise and tried to move the rock with it, or to break it, but did not succeed. So, knowing who had placed the rock there, they looked for Tsénoolch'óshii and surrounded him, keeping him prisoner, until he agreed to move the rock off Younger Brother.

He said he would release him on condition that Younger Brother learn from him three songs to be used in the ceremonies of the Earth People, particularly of the Evil-Chasing Chant. He also made the condition that his rocks should be used in ceremonies. They all agreed that these songs and ceremonial objects belonging to the Wren should be taken back to the Earth People, and then he said that he would let Younger Brother stay among the Sky People and would not trouble him again. Younger Brother went back to the home of Sǫ'tsoh, and the Star People warned him again that it was dangerous to go to the opening down to the earth or to the houses of the Eagles or the Hawks.

He Goes to the White House of the Eagles

He slept at the home of Sǫ'tsoh and next morning began wandering about and wondered why he was not to visit the Eagle People. Finally, he went to the house of the Eagles, and as he neared it he saw people going in and followed them. He found it was like a great kiva[21] inside, and he found that it was full of Eagle and Hawk People. They knew that he was a stranger, so he sat very quietly and found they were talking about going on a raid. They said, "We must all join together and start tomorrow morning." Younger Brother wondered where they were going. They all crowded around him and said, "We are going to raid near where Sǫ'tsoh lives." He said he would like to join them, but they said, "No, Earth People cannot go with us."

The meeting had lasted a long time and it was now night. Younger Brother came out of the Eagles' home, and all this time the Star People were searching for him. He went straight back to the home of the Black Star People and they said to him, "We were looking for you, where have you been?" He answered, "I was with the Eagle People."

---

[21] A sacred underground chamber, in the Pueblos, where preparations, initiations and secret rituals take place.

Down on the earth, his nephew, Earth Boy, had known long ago that Younger Brother was to go up above the sky, and he had given his uncle the power to hear the Spirit Wind, Níłch'i Biyázhí, though Younger Brother did not know that he had this power. It was the Spirit Wind which had suggested going to the opening in the sky and to the Eagles' houses, even though the Stars had counselled him not to. But he did not understand yet why he was impelled to do these things. Sǫ'tsoh warned him of the danger as a way of testing him, because he meant to teach Younger Brother his wisdom.

Younger Brother spent that night with the Black Star People. The next day, they told him not to go wandering off towards the white house of the Eagles because there was danger there, but he did go, in spite of their warning. He saw people running by and realized that they were Eagle People on their way to the raid, and he asked if he could join them and they forbade it. But he followed them, whereupon they tried to make him turn back, and this happened four times. Then they said to him, "We are very light and swift and move quickly. Even with this advantage, many of us are killed, but you would not live a moment on this raid." So Younger Brother said, "I will go and watch you from a distance."

So he followed until they came to a place where there were many big and small yuccas. He went on to the top of a hill to watch and saw the Eagle People preparing to fight. They were sharpening their claws, getting bows and arrows ready and practicing shooting, but he could see no houses or people and wondered who was to be raided. Finally, the Eagles gathered together and rushed to a place where there was a great round clump of yuccas on a little hill. Younger Brother saw them swoop down to this place, and then he saw a great swarm of bees which came out and attacked the birds, scattering them in all directions. The bees managed to bring down a good many Eagles by getting into their wing feathers. At last the birds gave up the attack and flew back, still followed, and many of them being killed, by the bees. Soon Younger Brother saw the bees coming back to their home.

Now he picked a bunch of ch'ildiilyésii (one of the four sacred herbs) and walked towards the home of the bees. When he got there he found a big hole going down among the yuccas. He began to pull up the yuccas around the hole and as he did so he heard the bees buzzing below. He put some ch'ildiilyésii into his mouth and chewed it up into little pieces and blew it at the bees as they came out of the hole. As it hit them, they fell to the ground. He kept digging down into their hole until he got down about three feet and most of the bees, by this time, were killed. Still he dug deeper and found at the bottom of the hole a bigger space and two huge bumblebees there. He took up the smaller one and pulled out its sting and let it go. As he did so, he said, "Now you must be pleasant and not harm people any more." Then he took up the bigger one and pulled out its sting also. He split a leaf of yucca and took from it a fine fiber with which he tied up the big bumblebee. Then he put the bee in his belt. Carrying the bumblebee with him, he went to one of the eagles that had been killed and pulled from the eagle five little pieces of down. Then he blew some of the ch'ildiilyésii on the bird and it came to life and flew away. He went to all the other Eagles that had been killed and brought them to life again in the same way. In doing this he collected quite a handful of down; this is called "feathers-of-the-living" (hinááh bits'os).

Younger Brother started to go back to the house of Sǫ'tsoh, the Great Star, and as he went he was met by twelve people (Tohí Dine'é) all dressed in white and carrying white flutes. They said to him, "You have some lovely feathers in your hand, what are you going to do with them? We should like to have some of them." He replied, "They are feathers of the Eagles," and he divided the feathers among these twelve people. They said they came from the Blue Star House and were the Water People, and explained that they went up to the sky by means of "wood kicking" (tsiilkaalii). Younger Brother watched them go off toward the east and saw them no more.

He was still carrying the big bee and some of the down that was left. He went up to the house of the White Eagle People at the east and stopped outside the door, listening to the talk inside. He heard them say that the raid was unsuccessful. They told how many had been killed and someone asked, "Where is the Earth Person (Nihookáá' Diné)?" Someone else said, "The bees killed him for he couldn't get away quickly." Then Younger Brother went into the house of the Eagles and, as he did so, he took out the big bee and unrolled the yucca fiber so that he held the bee on the end of a string. The Eagle People were much surprised to see him and asked him how he got away. But when he let the big bee fly about the house on the end of the string they were all frightened and tried to get out of the door.

Younger Brother laughed and said, "Come, there is no harm here. I have conquered your enemies the bees." At first the Eagle People were afraid of him, but, finally, he persuaded them to come near and he told them how he had killed the bees with ch'ildiilyésii. Then he said, "You thought that many of your people had been killed, but they are all alive and well."

Then he left the Eagles' house and walked over the opening down to the earth. He dropped the bee through the hole in the sky, saying, "You go below and be useful to the Earth People and be good." That is where the bumblebees come from and why they are used in the ceremonies. An incense is made of the wax of the bees and called yátaał niłch'i.

When night fell, Younger Brother went back to the home of Sǫ'tsoh and he was asked where he had been. The Star People said that they had been searching for him again and that it was dangerous for him to go away like that. He told them what had happened and how he had conquered the bees and cured the Eagles that had been killed. He also told them of meeting the Tohí Dine'é (Water People) and giving them presents of living feathers, and of sending the bee down to the earth. He showed Sǫ'tsoh some of the living feathers that he had and asked him if he needed anything like this. Sǫ'tsoh was much pleased and took the down. He inhaled the smell of it and said, "Yes, this is what I needed for my ceremonies." Then Younger Brother realized for the first time that Sǫ'tsoh was a medicine man.

He Goes to the Blue House of the Hawk People

Younger Brother spent the night there. Next morning they told him not to wander about, but he hid from them and then went to the opening down to the earth. After that he decided he would go to the blue house of the Hawk People. When he got there and went in he found many Hawk People there who were also planning to go raiding, and he listened and heard them say that they were going next day. Then he went back to the house of the Sǫ'tsoh and stayed there over night. Next morning he saw the Hawk People going towards the south. He tried to follow them but was forbidden because they said it was dangerous for him. He asked to go four times and, being refused still, followed after the raiding party. They came to a place where many yuccas and other plants grew and he went up on a hill to the south to watch what happened. The Spirit Wind told him that the wasps were to be raided that day. All Younger Brother could see was that the Hawks were swooping up and down and that many were falling to the earth, for the wasps got into their feathers and hurt them until the Hawks retreated. Younger Brother watched the wasps coming back. When the last had disappeared into their home, he broke off some more of the ch'ildiilyésii and went to the home of the wasps. He found it was a hole under tsá'ásdzi', "the slim yucca," and he pulled this up and dug down into the home of the wasps. As they came up he blew the chewed-up ch'ildiilyésii on them until they were mostly killed. As with the bees he found two big wasps, one of which he let go having taken out the sting. The other he bound up in yucca fiber, having taken out his sting also, and he carried him to the Hawks who had been killed, and healed them by blowing ch'ildiiyésii on them. From the first Hawk he took seven pieces of down and from the others that he cured he took three or four or five pieces of down. All the Hawks were healed and flew away.

As he was going back he was met by twelve people whose faces were painted yellow across the chin, blue across the mouth, black across the eyes, and white across their foreheads. Each had a feather on his head. They were the Níló Dine'é (Hail People). They traveled on a cyclone and on the lightning. Younger Brother asked them if they needed any of the hawk down and they all said, "That is what we need." He gave seven pieces of down to the first of them, and five, four, three, two and one to each of the rest, and they went south and disappeared. All the Hail People's bodies were spotted with white.

Younger Brother went on to the blue house of the Hawks and as before listened to the talking. Then he entered and took the wasp from under his clothes and let it fly, holding it by the yucca string. When the people heard the buzzing of the wasp they dashed for the door, trampling on each other. Then he picked up the wasp and, laughing, called the Hawk People in and told them that it was harmless. They all came back when he told them there would be no more trouble with the wasps, and they thanked him for removing the danger from them. He told them also that the Hawks that they thought were dead were well again. Then he went to the opening down to the earth and dropped the wasp through it. He told it to be good and useful to the Earth People in the ceremonies to be used for incense made of the honey known as ayahdadi'nił and also as ayeel, an aperient made of the wasp itself. Then Younger Brother went back to the house of Sǫ'tsoh and told him everything that had happened. He showed him the hawk down and gave him what remained. Then he spent the night there.

He Goes to the Yellow House of the Hawk People

Next morning they warned him against going west to the yellow house of the Hawks. They told him that it would be all right for him to stay among the Star People, or to go to the white or blue house of the Eagle and Hawk People, because they were friendly to him for what he had done for them. But he decided that he must go to the yellow house in spite of what

Sǫ'tsoh, the Great Star, had said. When he got there he found that they also were planning to go raiding the next day, and as before he asked if he could go and was refused. He stayed with the Yellow House People until it was dark, then went back to Sǫ'tsoh's home. He spent the night there and next morning near the yellow house he saw the people running to the west. He asked to go with them four times, and was refused. After that they forgot him, and he went on to a hill at the south to watch what happened. There was a ridge of thin layers of rocks known as Tsét'ą́hii and the Spirit Wind spoke in his ear, saying, "That is what they are planning to fight: it is the home of Tsénoolch'óshii (the Rock Wren)." The Hawks swooped down over the home of the Wren and the Wind hit the thin rocks, breaking them and making them fly up and hit the hawks. It killed many of them. The Wren threw many rocks also and many of the Hawks were killed until they retreated. When they had gone, all the thin rocks went back to the ridge where they belonged. The Wren had promised after he had released Younger Brother from the great rock at the opening down to the earth that he would never harm him again. When Younger Brother went toward the home of the Wren on the ridge he found him jumping about, full of joy. Younger Brother walked up to him and said, "Why are you killing people? You promised not to harm anyone any more." The Wren said, "It is because the Hawk People make raids on me that I kill them. I am only protecting myself. You go and tell them not to raid me anymore, and there will be no more trouble." So Younger Brother left the Wren and picked up one of the thin stones, carrying it with him. When he came to the first Hawk whose bones were badly broken by the stones, he brought to him some herbs called azeenitł'iní ("hardening medicine"). He chewed this up and made it sticky and used this on the broken wing and leg of the Hawk. Then he took from him nine pieces of down, and went on and cured the other hurt Hawks. He left the badly wounded ones to rest while the ones who were slightly hurt went off to their homes. From each he took some of the down.

While he was tying up the down that he had collected, he was met by twelve more people whose faces were painted like those of the Hail People, and who had one feather in their hair. Their bodies were painted white and spotted with white and black. They were people of the Naa'at'oobika'jí (Male Shooting Chant). Younger Brother asked if they would like some of the down and they said, "Yes." He gave the first of them nine pieces of down and the others five, four, three, two and one apiece. After receiving the down they went off and disappeared to the west. Then Younger Brother went to the yellow house of the Hawks carrying the rock, listened outside as before, and heard them telling of how many had been hurt and wondering whether he was alive. Finally he came in with the rock in his hand. It had blood on it, for when he went over to the home of the Wren after the fight he saw that many of the rocks had blood on them. When he brought the rock into the yellow house he said, "Where shall I lay this?" The Hawks were all terrified and rushed out, but he called them back and told them that the rock was harmless. He said that there would be no more trouble if they did not attack Tsénoolch'óshii, and then he said, "Come and pick up this rock and put it away." At first they were afraid but finally one picked it up and put it aside. Younger Brother left and went back to Sǫ'tsoh, and he told him of the raid and the whole story of what had happened to him and spent the night there.

He Goes to the Black House of the Eagles

Next morning the Black Star People warned him not to go to the black house of the Eagles at the north, that there were people there who gave sickness such as leprosy, syphilis and tuberculosis. He was warned to beware of them and to stay among the Star People and the Eagles that he knew. But again the Spirit Wind told him not to be afraid to go to the black house, though Younger Brother still did not know why he should be impelled to go. So he started out and went into the Black House and found many people talking about a raid for the next day, and as before he asked if he could join. They said, "No." He went back to the Black Star People at night but did not tell where he had been. The next day he went back to the black house and saw the people running off to the north, and as before, he asked if he could join them and they refused four times. He followed nevertheless and came to a place of sand dunes where a few prickly plants grew called tł'oh dahnaayizii (tumble weed, or "the plant that rolls"), and he could see nothing there except the dunes and these plants. The Spirit Wind in his ear said, "Those plants are what they will fight, but what moves them is the Left-Handed Wind. When it is attacked it whirls these plants up against the turning of the earth and against the Eagle People." Now the Eagle People were ready to attack and the Left-Handed Wind whirled the plants against them. They began to retreat, and many fell with the rolling plants stuck to them. Younger Brother afterwards went to where these plants were growing and picked up one and brought it to the first Eagle that was hurt. He found that the rolling plants were sticking to the Eagle's body. He pulled them off, and then used "hardening medicine," which he chewed up until it was sticky. He put it into the wounds made by the plant and so closed the wounds. Then he took from this Eagle twelve pieces of down. Afterwards he went to the others that were hurt and took nine, eight, seven, six, five, four, three, two and one from each Eagle after healing it. While he was tying up the feathers there appeared, again, twelve people to meet him. One was Doonikéí (the name of a Pueblo Clan), and two were Blue Racer Snakes, and nine were Atsá Dine'é (Eagle People). These people as well as the three other groups of people that he had met were all Eagle People. However, they had higher and different powers from the ones who lived in the big houses which he had been visiting. He gave the first of these Eagle People twelve pieces of down and then to the next nine, eight, seven, six, five, four, three, two, one apiece, and they disappeared to the north. He went back to the black house of the Eagles and as he came heard them talking about the fight, and that he probably had been killed. Then he walked in with "the-plant-that-rolls" in his hand and threw it into the fire. As it caught fire it rose in a flame and circled over the Eagle People. They all rushed for the door and he was left alone. "The-plant-that-rolls" dropped to the floor in ashes, and he called the Eagle People back and told them that the plant was not harmful any more. He told them to make friends with all those that they had been fighting with, and that all their troubles had come from their raids; that those they had been fighting were only defending themselves. Then he left and went back to Sǫ'tsoh and told him everything that had happened, and of meeting the Eagle People. He offered Sǫ'tsoh all the down that he had left, and this time Sǫ'tsoh said to him, "I was very anxious to get these feathers, my son, and I thank you." He had known all the time what Younger Brother was doing and what was going to happen, for Níłch'i Biyázhí, the Spirit Wind, had told him.

The Great Star Teaches Younger Brother

Then Sǫ'tsoh, the Great Black Star, began to teach Younger Brother many things about his medicine. He said, "When you went on the first raid with the Eagle People of the white house, you remember that you pulled up yucca roots when you were fighting the bees. Those roots you must use when you wash the patient of his impurities. You must use the shredded leaf of the yucca in tying the tsibąąs (ceremonial hoops) and you must use the prickly end of the yucca for untying the wooltáád[22] that you will use in the ceremony. You must also use this yucca fiber when you have the Spruce Tree Rite over the patient. In the Wooltáád Rite you must use for the sacred bundle five leaves of the yucca with ch'ildiilyésii, tóyikááł, tsé'azhiih, and tł'oh nástasii in each bundle. These four holy plants are to be in each bundle between five leaves of yucca. On the first night of the ceremony you should use five of these bundles in the treatment of the patient. On the second night of the ceremony you must use seven bundles with seven leaves of this slim yucca, and on the third night nine of the bundles with the yucca called ye'ii bitsá'ásdzi, and four holy plants. On the fourth night you must use twelve bundles with the horned yucca called tsá'ásdzi niteelí niteelí and the holy plants."

Sǫ'tsoh also said, "You must use ch'ildiilyésii for decorating the wand in the Anaa'jí ceremony.[23] Also, you must use it for the ant'eesh or blackening of the body in the Anaa'jí ceremony. This blackening frightens away evil powers. In the other ceremonies when blackening is done, the paint used in blackening the body is made of the ashes when ch'ildiilyésii is burned."

Sǫ'tsoh said to him, "The medicine of the people that you met in the sky, the Water Chant People, the Hail Chant People, the people of the Male Shooting Chant, and the Eagle Chant People will be used, combined as one medicine, for one incense and one kétłoh infusion.[24] If the patient has a sickness that comes through any of these people, you must use this incense and kétłoh to check the sickness until the main ceremony can be performed." He also told him that for the Great Star Chant, also the Eagle Chant and Hail Chant, a gourd rattle must be used. He said that a buffalo hide rattle should be used in the Male Shooting Chant, and that no rattle should be used in the Yo'iijí or Bead Chant. Sǫ'tsoh told him that the bees and wasps, also their wax and honey and the "life feathers" should be used in combination in the sicknesses which come from these four people. Sǫ'tsoh said to him that the flat rock that he carried away from the home of Tsénoolch'oshii (the Wren) should be used for a dish on which

---

[22]The wooltáád rite is basically an untying of knots on the theory that pain and evil influences are tied within the patient's body. A hoop or bundle of feathers or of herbs is held to the afflicted part, and the string tied in slip knots is pulled loose and released.

[23]The Anaa'jí, or war ceremony, is a three-day exorcism of alien ghosts. It is given for returned veterans, young people who have been away at school, and other Navajos who have been exposed to non-Navajos. It was also given to make peace with the spirits of those killed. In the Creation Myth, it was first given on the return of Naayéé' Neezghání and Tóbájíshchíní from killing the monsters that were infesting the Earth after the Emergence from the lower world of first men and gods.

[24]The kétłoh infusion is an unheated lotion said to be especially good for allaying headache and fever. This mixture of herbs, especially mints, and water is drunk by the patient and is also used to bathe or moisten the patient and other participants. It may also be sprinkled about the hooghan and be used to moisten some of the ceremonial equipment.

a plant called ałtahdeedlííd should be burned to make the paint to blacken the body. This plant should be used in place of tł'oh dahnaayizii "which you burned in the Eagle's home." This last plant should be used in the kétłoh infusion in the future, but not burned.

Sǫ'tsoh said to him that he must use the tops of the yucca plants and of other prickly plants, such as pine and pinyon, ground up fine and put in water to make an internal medicine called zaa'nił to be used in the Great Star Chant. Another medicine, ayeel, which was to be taken internally, must be made of the following things: the wax and honey of the bumblebee and of the wasp, the four kinds of yucca, tsá ásdzi'nit'eelí, tsá asdzi'ts'óóz, ye'ii bitsá'ásdzi', tsá'ásdzi' bidee' and the tips of them, also pine, fir, pinyon, cedar, grey fir, grey short pinyon, also the tips of all of these, and the four cactus called "tall cactus," "round cactus," "salty cactus," and the Entranyas cactus, and the tips of all these; also the lichen which grows in circles on the rocks and is black, yellow, blue and white.

Sǫ'tsoh said to him there will be four Dáádiníléí, or Guardians of the Entrance, used in this ceremony, the Wren, the Bat, Dǫ'tsoh the Fly, and the Spirit Wind. From these Guardians, dried substance, such as hair and feathers, will be used, and in the case of the Spirit Wind the dried substance will come from the rock that grew up into the sky.[25]

Sǫ'tsoh said that the hardening medicine which Younger Brother had used to heal the wounded Eagles should be used in the following way: it should be combined with its roots and the roots and sticky juice of the tall cactus. These should be rolled together into a ball with all of the other medicine mentioned rolled inside of it. This is ayeel, which combines everything and is protection against any sickness. It is used in the form of the ceremony called Diyin k'ehgo Hatáál, which means holy form of the Sacred Chant. Sǫ'tsoh told him that when a male patient takes the ayeel and swallows it, the medicine man sends it to the left side of his body. The medicine man does this by a rite called ats'íís, which consists of pressing his feet to the feet of the patient, his knees to the patient's knees, his shoulders to his shoulders, and his back to the patient's back, his head to the patient's head, in each case touching the patient's right side first. Then the medicine man turns the patient's body from side to side, placing one hand on the patient's breast and one on his back, having previously moistened his hands in the kétłoh. The medicine man should treat a female patient in the same way, only the medicine should be sent to the right side of the female patient. The reason that the medicine should be sent to the left side of a male is because a man uses his left arm to hold his bow, but a woman uses her right hand most, therefore the medicine is sent to the right side. After this rite is over no one should slap the patient on the shoulders or back, for if the patient is slapped it misplaces the ayeel and this would cause sickness. The patient should be very careful not to do any of the forbidden things mentioned in the story, for if he does he also disturbs the medicine and this would cause sickness. The male patient when he first goes through this ceremony should be given a name. When he is given this name a small turquoise is tied to the left-hand side of the top of his head, and the life feather should be tied at the left-hand side of his head. The turquoise should be given to the patient to keep, but the feather should go back to the medicine man as it belongs to his medicine bundle.

The dried substance, called ayásh bąąh nanoogáád, is taken from the Bat, Wren, Dǫ'tsoh

[25]Probably this is all in the form of powder.

the Messenger, and the Aniłt'ánii (Corn Beetle), and from the ayásh or group of birds such as the bluebird, the yellowbird (tsídiiłtsoí)and the tanager. These are mixed and tied up into a small bag of buckskin and one feather is put into the mouth of the bag. This is the bag for the male patient. When the patient is a female she should have a small piece of abalone shell tied on the right side of the head when she is given a name, and the life feather should be tied on the left side of the head. She should keep the shell, but the feather belongs to the medicine man. No one who has had this Great Star Chant should ever carry ice or snow, for if he does he would move the ayeel in his body, and that would give him pneumonia. This ayeel remains in the body of the patient during the rest of his or her life.

Sǫ'tsoh told Younger Brother about how to paint the body of the patient. On a male patient a four-pointed black star should be painted on the stomach with a white border around it, and a figure of the black Sǫ'tsoh above,[26] and on his back a blue star with a blue figure above it. On the first day of the ceremony they should paint the lightning, extending from the hands of the black figure of Sǫ'tsoh down the arms of the patient, in black. On the second day the medicine man should put a blue line above the black lightning arrow line on the patient's arms. On the third day a yellow line should be added above the blue, and on the fourth day a white line above the yellow.

On the legs of the patient there should be the same colored lines as on the arms, to be painted in the same order, toward the front of the body, and on the sole of each foot there should be painted a black arrowhead pointing toward the toes.

For the female patient, the figure of Sǫ'tsoh on the front of the body should be painted blue, and the figure on the back should be black, and the two lightning arrows on the front of the body should be blue, while the arrows painted on the arms should be of straight lightning. On the first day they must be painted black, ending in a blue arrowhead in the palm of each hand. On the second, third and fourth days of the ceremony the other lines mentioned before are added to the paintings on the arms and legs. On the legs of the female patient the lightning is straight with blue arrowheads. On the left leg the arrow points up, and on the right leg it points down, while on the soles of both feet there should be blue arrowheads. After the patient's body is all painted, the medicine man, using the tips of two fingers dipped in white earth, should mark the whole body with double white spots. Both the male and female patients' faces should be painted alike, with a stripe of yellow across the chin, stripe of the blue across the mouth, black across the eyes, and with a white forehead. A male patient's forehead should be painted with wavy lines, the forehead of a female in straight lines.

On each of the four days which are the last of the nine-day ceremony, the day should begin by making the sandpainting and then painting the body of the patient, and on the last day the turquoise and feather should be tied on the patient's head, and then he should be given ayeel. The dried substance, ayásh bąąh nanoogáád, should be placed in his moccasins, and then he should put them on and go outdoors and draw the sun into his body. Meanwhile ground corn meal mush must be prepared, which the medicine man must bless by sprinkling with corn pollen in the form of a cross. He then must feed the patient from the four directions, and then everyone may eat this ceremonial food. The one who should paint the body of the

---

[26]See illustration.

patient is the assistant to the medicine man. Before he does the painting he should paint a black arrowhead on the soles of his own feet, and black crooked lightning extending down the inside of his arms, ending in a black arrowhead on the inside of each wrist. The rite of painting the body of the patient is called azdoosjjh. After the assistant has finished painting the patient he should wash himself.

When this ceremony is completed, the medicine man should prepare for the "beating of the basket." This is the ceremony of singing on the last night, when they sing all night. When the dawn comes the patient should go out and draw the dawn into him, and then go home with the feather and turquoise still tied on his head. The paint must be left on four days. At the next sunrise he must come back to the ceremonial hooghan, and the medicine man should remove the feather and put it back in his bundle. After four days have passed, the patient takes a bath and then ties the turquoise to his hair, or headband, or hat.

Sǫ'tsoh told Younger Brother that the making of the ceremonial fire should always begin the ceremony, and that on the first four nights of both the five- and nine-day ceremony they should hold the rite of wooltáád (untying of knots). In the five-day ceremony the body painting must be done completely on the last day. But in the nine-day ceremony one line of the body painting should be done each day beginning on the fifth day of the ceremony, and there is no jidiitłah[27] ceremony on the fourth night. On the first four days, early in the morning when it is a nine-day ceremony, they must make nitł'iz for the náá'iiniih rite, which means delivering offerings to those above. This is used instead of the k'eet'áán rite. The nitł'iz is made of powdered turquoise, jet, and white shell which is put in small bags and left on the hills nearby. The patient can choose to whom the offering should be made: to Coyote, Earth Thunder, the Wind, Darkness, the Ray of Dawn, the Yellow Sunset, and the Blue South. Sǫ'tsoh, and the different Stars, the Sun and Moon and all the others who come into this story can have offerings given to them, even the plants, such as yucca, cactus and pinyon. The offering to Water is to be given at Be'ek'id Náhábąsí (Turning Lake), or to Tónahelįįh[28] and Tónáálį, a place where water falls into a hole, or to Tóniteel the Great Sea, or to Na'ní'áhí which is a Water Bridge. The patient can choose five from among these powers to whom the offering should be given. All of these powers know when this ceremony is being given anywhere, through the Spirit Wind, and they will protect the patient. The patient also protects the powers. The ceremony gives him this power to protect them and to realize it. Through the Spirit Wind a mutual relationship between the patient and the powers is established.

If the medicine man has given the patient the rite of ats'íís, the pressing of his limbs and

---

[27]This ceremony is to prevent fits, or to resuscitate a patient from a seizure such as that which may be caused by too powerful a ritual medicine, or the appearance of whatever brought on the need for the ceremony. A practitioner dressed as a bear, or some other power associated with the seizure, appears suddenly while the patient is protected by a sandpainting. If this causes a convulsion, the patient is covered with a buckskin and treated with prayers while the medicine man surrounds him with four groups of four zigzag lines which he draws on the ground, crosses with a straight line, and then erases. Then he makes four groups of straight lines around the patient and the buckskin is removed. (See pages 25–26.)

[28]A mythical place where two waters, male and female, cross each other. At this place are the whirling logs of the famous sandpainting from the Night Chant. The log of the female stream points west to east and is turning south, the log of the male stream points north to south and is turning west.

body to those of the patient, he is not supposed to use his feet and hands to hit anything, but must use a whip or stick; his hands and feet are sacred.

Sǫ'tsoh told Younger Brother that while he was in the sky Nííłch'i Biyázhí (the Spirit Wind) whispered messages in his ears, but that when he returned to the earth the Spirit Wind would go down inside of him, and then at night would go out to bring back messages to him. When we dream, that is the spirit inside of us speaking, and when we hear sounds in our ears, or feel a prickling in our throats, or a twitching of our nerves, or a popping in our noses, that is the Spirit Wind telling us either to do or not to do something. It is a warning to pay attention. When we sleep, the Spirit Wind comes out and travels among other Spirits and brings back messages to us, and when our ears ring he is telling us what to do, for he has been out traveling and he is trying to give us a message, but our minds get in the way.

DREAMS REVEALING GREAT STAR SICKNESS

The medicine man, Ayóó'áníłnézí, said that for him to dream of deer that are well and strong is fortunate for the patient that he is treating. If he dreams this just before he is summoned to a patient he always knows that the ceremony will be successful. He always had that dream until a Navajo years ago asked him to go hunting and he killed some deer, and since he did that he cannot depend upon this dream. It does not matter what creature you dream about as long as it is healthy, but if it is weak or sick or deformed it is a bad dream. If you dream of success, even of a fight, it means success in whatever you undertake. If you dream of Coyote, or of being on a rock that you cannot get down from, or of going through a small hole in the rock, or that you are flying, or of the waves falling over you, or being in an arroyo with a river rushing on you, or of defending yourself against an enemy, then you have a sickness that will be helped by the Great Star Chant. This is true also if you dream of bees or wasps, or flying rocks, a whirlwind coming, or of thunder, bears, snakes, or of prickly things. If you dream of Sǫ'tsoh, or any Stars which frighten you, four or five times, then you are suffering from the sickness which belongs to Sǫ'tsoh, and the painting of the body is to protect you against this trouble. This takes the place of the symbols that protected Older Brother from the Cyclone when he faced it alone.

Taboos and Causes of Sickness

Sǫ'tsoh told Younger Brother that even if a person is well and has not had the ceremony, the forbidden things spoken of in this story should be remembered and added to the ones mentioned; that one should not burn a tree that has been struck by lightning, or lie on the home of the red ant (Wóóláchíí'), or spit on his home, or defile it, and no one should burn a hawk's nest, or sleep under or on top of a rock or under a lightning-struck tree. If anyone does these things he is bringing trouble on himself, and this is still true, that these things will bring the sickness that comes from Sǫ'tsoh. In order to overcome this, ayeel should be offered.

Sǫ'tsoh told him that small pieces of cut-up deer meat and meat from a doe belong to the medicine bundle of this ceremony. He also said that if a male and female sheep are killed, and all the medicine plants, and the bees, wasp, cactus and prickling things which Younger Brother used in the upper world are boiled together and given to the patient to eat, then he can eat all the forbidden things without being hurt by it.

Sǫ'tsoh told him that sickness also comes if a splinter from a tree has entered the patient's body; even if it is pulled out, the sickness coming from this will return again, if you are to have the tree's sickness and this is true of injury by stones or cactus, for this sickness moves about until it finds a weaker part in your body; and this requires different kinds of ceremonies and offerings. Sometimes ayeel or nitł'iz, or sandpaintings, may be the cure for this sickness. Injuries coming from the shaking of thunder, or snake bite, or being hurt by the wind are hard to cure because there are so many ways of giving offerings, and so many ceremonies such as the Eagle Chant, Hail Chant, Male Shooting Chant, Bead Chant, or the Blessing Chant, all have to do with these sorts of injuries, and the right kinds of offerings must be given in order to cure the patient. All these things were told to Younger Brother by Sǫ' tsoh, the Great Star, and they are true to this day.

Younger Brother's Healing Apprenticeship

After Sǫ' tsoh finished telling Younger Brother all this, in came a young man with a message saying, "There is a very sick man I want you to cure." Sǫ' tsoh told this young man, who was an Eagle, to take the medicine pouch, and that they would come next morning and hold a ceremony. Sǫ' tsoh knew that the sickness came from the bee's sting, and that the sting had renewed itself after being pulled out. When he reached the patient he opened his medicine pouch and began to give the nine-day ceremony, which was held in the way that has been told about in the story. Younger Brother watched and saw for the first time how to give the Great Star Chant. Sǫ' tsoh told him that as many as four patients can be treated at once in the ceremony. Younger Brother noted carefully all the rites, and remembered where the songs came, and how the sandpaintings were made, and learned the prayers, because Sǫ' tsoh told him that he was to give this ceremony on the earth. Then they went back to the home of Sǫ' tsoh, and in order to test Younger Brother's knowledge, after a few days when another summons came to give the ceremony, Younger Brother acted as assistant to Sǫ' tsoh.

During a whole year Younger Brother helped Sǫ' tsoh give ceremonies for the Eagle People of the white house, mostly for injuries by bee stings and things of that kind. When summer came no ceremonies were held, and in the fall they heard of a sickness at the blue house of the Eagles, and the Blue Star medicine man was summoned. Knowing that Younger Brother was a good assistant, Blue Star asked for him. At this ceremony there were two patients, both suffering from a wasp-sting infection, and Younger Brother was taught how to doctor more than one patient at a time. He noticed at the ceremony of Blue Star that songs which Sǫ' tsoh gave were reversed and changed. The sandpaintings and untying of knots rite and the giving of medicine, were different, and Younger Brother remembered it all.

For a year he stayed with the Blue Star and the Blue Eagle People, singing over as many as four patients at once. He learned all that Blue Star showed him, and only occasionally visited Sǫ' tsoh. After the summer had passed he heard of another sick person, among the Yellow Eagles. Yellow Star was summoned to cure him, and he asked Younger Brother to come and be his assistant. So he went and found three patients, the leaders of the Eagle People, and Younger Brother memorized all these ceremonies which were a little different from the other two, staying with Yellow Star People for that year. During this time some of the Yellow Eagle People had caught a sickness from the sticky medicine treatment, called rock sickness, with pain like appendicitis. Yellow Star and Younger Brother treated patients for this, as many as four at a time.

After the summer passed there was sickness at the Black Eagle's house of the four leaders, Black Eagle, White-Headed Eagle, White Eagle, and Buzzard. White Star was called as medicine man and asked Younger Brother to help him. He found these ceremonies different but remembered them all, and was told by the Spirit Wind that this was his last apprenticeship. He asked White Star for a medicine pouch of his own, and this was made for him by all the Stars: they made him a medicine man.

Soon after this, he went back to the house of the White Star, and the rest of the Black Eagles grew sick from the prickles from the bushes which the Cyclone had blown into them. This had infected them and had made sores all over their bodies. Younger Brother took ch'ildiilyésii and rubbed it on their bodies, and made them drink it. He treated them for this sickness during a year, treating as many as four patients at a time. During these ceremonies Younger Brother used the medicine pouch of White Star but not his own.

Now he had finished learning the Great Star Chant of the Black, Blue, Yellow and White Stars, and White Star told him to go back to his father, Sǫ'tsoh, the Great Star. He also told Younger Brother that he should go back to the earth, but that before he went all the different Stars would come to see him and say good-bye. Younger Brother asked them all to come to the home of Sǫ'tsoh, and when they came they discussed how to send Younger Brother back to earth without harm. Sǫ'tsoh asked the others to give some gifts to take with him. He himself gave the youth a bolt of lightning, and a black cloud, and a small star to use for star gazing. Sǫ'tsoh told him again that in the future the Spirit Wind would be inside of him, and that he would speak to him in dreams. Then the other Stars asked Blue Star what he would give. He gave Younger Brother a bolt of sheet lightning, a blue cloud, and ak'ah, or fat, used for ceremonials and known as tł'ahnaashchíín. He also told him that he would be helped in the future by his dreams. Then Yellow Star offered heat lightning, a yellow cloud, and a big star. He, too, spoke about the Wind giving the youth help in dreams, and that he could use the big star for star gazing. The White Star gave him the rainbow, a white cloud, and some fat for his ceremonials, and spoke again about his dreams. Then they gave him the rainbow as a road back to earth.

Younger Brother Returns to Earth

They all went back to their own homes that night. They had told Younger Brother that they were going to send him back to earth at noon the next day, and he spent the night with Sǫ' tsoh. Next day, at noon they all went to the opening down to the earth. As Younger Brother stood there he looked up and saw all the four Great Stars above him, and with them Sǫ'tsoh Deeshzhah, the Many-Pointed Star, who was dressed in all colors. The Great Stars were dressed in their flint clothing. Then Sǫ'tsoh let fall the black cloud, which dropped just below the opening. Blue Star dropped the blue cloud, which fell below the black cloud and stopped. Yellow Star dropped the yellow cloud, which fell below the blue cloud and White Star dropped the white cloud, which went beyond the yellow cloud and stopped. Then all the Stars shook down powder, which made fog to hide Younger Brother from the people of the earth as he descended. Sǫ'tsoh gave him the bolt of lightning, and he carried with him all the clouds and lightnings and the rainbow, the ceremonial fat and his medicine pouch. Younger Brother put the lightning under his feet and it jumped with him from the opening into the black cloud. Then he laid the straight lightning under his feet and it took him to the blue cloud. Laying the heat lightning under his feet he landed on the yellow cloud and then putting the rainbow under his feet he went to the white cloud which was on the earth. So he landed there in a fog and no one could see how he came. Immediately thereafter the fog, rainbow, clouds and lightning all disappeared.

To Younger Brother when he came back to earth everything seemed strange, but he recognized the tall rock which had taken him to the sky, for he returned to the earth close to it. He remembered the direction where his people had been living and so he went there, but found that the place where they had lived was empty and there was no one in the hooghan. He walked round to the west inside the house and suddenly a sound came in his throat. He remembered the Stars had told him that this was one of the signs telling him to be quiet, and that he would get a message. So he did not worry any more, but brought in wood and built a fire, for night had come. As he sat by the fire he heard a noise coming from over the doorway to the east, and he knew the noise came from the pinyon wood poker which had been left there by his family. Soon the poker dropped to the ground and spoke, for it had been given the Spirit which knows all about things. It said, "Four years ago your wife and children were taken away to the south by the Coyote," and he also said, "Always the people of the earth will make use of me, they will never do without me." (That is the reason today that the medicine man begins all ceremonies by making the pokers.) Then Younger Brother took up the poker and put it back over the door. He had brought from the sky food that he had been given in the ceremonies, and when he started living on the earth he used this food. He took out of a small pot about two inches in diameter, a pinch of corn meal, a pinch of powdered horse tail plant and a little of all his sky foods. He mixed this with water and drank it, and this was all he used for food now.

Younger Brother then left this place, going south, journeyed all day long and reached a hooghan. He walked in but found no one there. He had the same experience again, only this time received a warning in a twitching nerve on his body, and then the poker made of pinyon wood spoke to him and told him to go south to another place where his family lived. There again he found no one. He was warned by a ringing in his ear to be quiet, and this time a poker made of oak spoke and told him that his wife and two children, with one child born to the Coyote, had gone west and that they had left three years ago. The next day he went west searching for them and found no one in the hooghan there. Warned by a popping in his nose, he kept quiet and made a fire, and the cedar poker spoke to him, saying that his wife and the Coyote and his two children, and two children of the Coyote had gone north. He spent the night and went on again; and at the fourth hooghan he found help from the poker of hard oak. The poker told him his family had gone from there a year ago toward the east. The next day he left and went far to the east, and at noon he came upon this hooghan and saw smoke coming out of it. He saw two young Coyotes playing out in front.

The Family Rescued from Coyote

He walked directly into the hooghan and saw his wife sitting between his two sons, the elder to the left and the younger to the right. She looked up at him but said nothing and dropped her head. The place smelt like a coyote's den. Younger Brother sat down inside the door to the south and everyone was silent. Suddenly far off they heard the voice of the Coyote calling out, "Akazyiyánii (Gland Eater), come and take in the kill." (Coyote called the children of Younger Brother by this contemptuous name.) The older son got up and started to go out of the door at this call, but his father stopped him, telling him to sit still. Then the Coyote came closer, calling again, "Gland Eater, come out and bring in the kill!" The younger son started to obey but his father stopped him, and twice more he prevented his children from obeying the calls of the Coyote. Suddenly Coyote dashed in the door, very angry. When he entered he saw Younger Brother sitting there, and stopped at the doorway. He laid down the kill that he had brought with him, which was nothing but four field mice, and sat down on the opposite side of the door from where Younger Brother was sitting.

Younger Brother spoke and said to him, "You were very mean to send me up the rock after young eagles, which after all were only crows, and then to make the rock grow up into the sky where I suffered a great deal from loneliness and want of all earthly things." Coyote said nothing. Then Younger Brother said, "Do you like this place? Do you like to stay here?" And he said this four times. Coyote answered, "Yes, I do." Younger Brother said, "All right take this and swallow it," and he gave Coyote the star that was given him by Sǫ'tsoh, which he had wrapped up in some of the fat which was given him by the Blue Star in the sky. The Coyote was so anxious to stay that he took this lump of fat and ate it. Then he rushed out and began running around the hooghan, and they heard him going slower and slower until he fell dead as he came back to the door. As he fell, the star dropped out of his mouth and Younger Brother picked it up. (In the Evil-Chasing Chant, when the bull-roarer is swung by the assistant to ward off Spirits around the hooghan, he should not make a complete circle of the hooghan but retrace his steps and put it back in his medicine pouch.) Younger Brother then went out of the hooghan and found the two young Coyotes and killed them, and came back to the hooghan again, and sat silent. After a time he went off to quite a distance, built a fire and spent the night near it, and did not return to his own home.

Great Star Chant Performed Over the Family

Next day he built himself a hooghan nearby, made four pokers of pinyon, oak, cedar and hard oak, and put four branches of hard oak in the roof of the hooghan in four directions. By the time he brought in his medicine pouch it was evening. He went back to his wife and two boys and told them to come over to the new hooghan. They entered it, circling around the fire to the south, and sat down at the west side. He was going to give the ceremony that he had learned in the sky, and also some of the ceremonies that he had learned before going up above. The next day in the morning he made the ceremonial fire and made one small tsibąąs which was used in the purification ceremony. They then took the emetic and vomited through the small black hoop. Then they made five tsibąąs (ceremonial hoops) and set them up at the east of the hooghan outside, the black tsibąąs next to the hooghan as described before in the story. That night they held the wooltáád (untying of knots) ceremony with five bundles. Younger Brother built another hooghan and next morning they held the purification ceremony and mixed the emetic in a jet basket. As the patients were about to take the emetic, Haashch'ééłti'í(Talking God) ran in saying, "So you are a medicine man, my grandson; give me the basket." Younger Brother said, "Yes, if you will give me a song or two." Talking God answered, "I do not sing well, my mouth is not made for singing, but I will give you two songs," and he sang one song to the jet basket and one to the purifying medicine. Younger Brother said, "Come back when the ceremony is all over and I will give you your basket." Even after the first day of the ceremony the place still smelt like a coyote's den. After the purifying ceremony they made hoops and set them towards the south and passed through them with prayers and songs. They said the prayers when passing over the mountains, and sang when passing through the tsibąąs. That evening they had the wooltáád ceremony, with seven bundles. The next day he built another hooghan and they moved over to that, to carry on the ceremony, but this time the hoops were set up at the west of the hooghan, and the small hoop used for the purifying ceremony was yellow. But the hooghan still smelt of Coyote and they had the wooltáád ceremony at night, with nine bundles. On the fourth day he built another hooghan and they held the same ceremony, but with a white hoop for the purifying, and the tsibáás ceremony at the north of the hooghan. They had the wooltáád ceremony again at night with twelve bundles. Talking God came on that day for his basket and took it away. The next day Younger Brother built still another hooghan, the fifth. He took his medicine pouch and all the medicine to the hooghan. There he prepared saba kéet[29], which is a medicine to use after the ceremony of beating the basket, and tséiik'á, powdered rock, for sandpaintings. (All the ceremonies performed by Sǫ'tsoh and by the Black Winds, and the Black Snake, all those pertaining to the black color, are to be given to the older son of Younger Brother to learn. All the ceremonies pertaining to the blue color will be learned by the wife of Younger Brother, and all the ceremonies pertaining to yellow will belong to Younger Brother himself.)

That evening when Younger Brother was about to start the singing with the basket-drum, a ray of light appeared and grew brighter and brighter. The fourth time it appeared they saw that it was Sǫ' tsoh. "So you are acting as medicine man," he said, and Younger Brother answered, "Yes." Sǫ' tsoh said, "I will return on the fourth day, which is the last day of the ceremony." Younger Brother told Sǫ' tsoh that he had held this ceremony because of the killing of the Coyotes. The ceremony was needed to purify his family and himself. Sǫ' tsoh told him that the Coyotes had come to life again. The spirits of the bee, wasp, wind, stones and plants, of the wren, eagles, bat, snakes, and all sorts of living things which lived on the earth, and also those things which Younger Brother had brought down from the sky were protecting the Coyote, and had brought him back to life while this ceremony was going on. Then Sǫ'tsoh left and Younger Brother started the singing.

---

[29]This is in the transcription of M. C. Wheelwright.

Next morning, at dawn, Younger Brother took the nidii' á, the five ceremonial plaques, and he and his wife and two sons walked out of the hooghan to the east. They made a mound opposite the door and set up the plaques on this mound, facing the hooghan, with the plaque of Sǫ' tsoh in the center and, beginning at the south, placed the yellow, white, blue and all-colored plaques in this order. Then he sang and prayed and made offerings to the sacred plaques. After this they came back into the hooghan and ate. Younger Brother ate his star food and the others ate ordinary food. In this particular ceremony Younger Brother made this offering to the plaques. The patients are the ones who are supposed to make it, but in this ceremony all were learning as well as being cured, and so Younger Brother made the offering himself. Then they began the sandpainting with Sǫ' tsoh in the center, and four different-colored Star People around him, all dressed in flint clothing, and carrying lightning and rattles with their bows beside them. All the Star People had blue faces, and the medicine strings from their elbows were blue and yellow on all the figures, with black tassels and red tips and white borders. If the ceremony is Idiilkíísh, then the tassels are red and blue, and only on the last day are they yellow and blue. This ceremony being given is the Holy Ceremony, or Diyin k' ehgo Hatáál. When the painting was made they brought in the ceremonial plaques and placed them at the west side of the painting. They then treated the patient with the sandpainting, and that night they sang with the basket. Next day they placed the ceremonial plaques as before to the east of the door outside, and then made the second sandpainting, with the blue star in the center. Then they brought in the ceremonial plaques and treated the patient as before, and sang at night. On the third day the ceremonial was as before, the sandpainting of the yellow star in the center, and, with singing at night.

On the fourth day when they put up the ceremonial plaques they turned them around facing east. When they came back after placing them, and as Younger Brother was about to begin the sandpainting, his father, mother and older brother, his sister and her son, Earth Boy, all came in. As he had no one to help him he was very glad to see them and he appointed his older brother his assistant and sent him to get yucca root. Older Brother brought this and also some corn meal, for the family were asked to give that. Then Younger Brother asked his sister to make the yucca root soapsuds for the use of his wife's ceremonial bath. Older Brother fixed the bath for the eldest son of Younger Brother, and Earth Boy fixed the bath for the younger son. They spread sand and the baskets full of suds on it; his own family had brought the baskets which were needed. The bath for his older son was in a jet basket, for his wife in a turquoise basket, and for his younger son in an abalone shell basket. Then they all bathed with the suds, and were dried with corn meal.

Since he had had no help in the ceremony up to this time, his own wife and sons had made the sandpaintings, but on the fourth day his family made it, and neither he nor his sons nor his wife touched it. This painting was with the white star in the center, and while they were making it Younger Brother prepared ayeel and pollen for the shoes, and paints for the body. Meanwhile his mother and father were preparing food for all the rest. When the sandpainting was finished Younger Brother painted the body of his wife with the Blue Star Man on the front of her body, and painted the bodies of his two sons with Black Star Man on the front. Then when the body paintings were done Younger Brother held the rite of adziisįįh, pressing his limbs to their limbs, and his body to their bodies. Meanwhile Older Brother sang for him and they gave him the medicine gad ádin, a decoction of herbs which all the people drank. After that the rest was passed around and they all rubbed it on their bodies.

Food was brought in, meal and meat and other things, and they put four parts aside for the three patients and Younger Brother, who was the medicine man. They all ate together, and this was the first meal that Younger Brother had eaten with the Earth People. Then Younger Brother told them his whole story from beginning to end, and when he finished it was night and they ate once more before beginning to sing. Then a ray of light appeared, growing brighter and brighter and they heard someone at the door. It was Sǫ'tsoh Diłhił, the Great Black Star, with the other Stars, the Blue Star, the Yellow Star and the White Star, and the Star People ate with the people in the hooghan. Then they turned down the basket and sang in turn all through the night, and no one slept. At dawn they all went out and drew the light into their bodies, and as they did this Younger Brother, the medicine man, took off the prayer feathers tied to the heads of the patients, but left the turquoise and abalone.

The medicine man went back into the hooghan but the family stayed outside, and Sǫ'tsoh spoke to him and said, "You have given the Great Star Chant well. You can do it hereafter. When you have finished with this ceremony we will take the ceremonial plaque to the sky with us, because it is not right for Earth People to use what we have in the sky. In the future you must use yucca leaves woven in five strands for each plaque; there must be five plaques and they will all be painted red, with feathers tied to the tops of them. This is best for the Earth People because this can be easily replaced." Sǫ'tsoh also said to Younger Brother that his wife was to be his wife no longer, but only his relation, "And neither she nor your sons can ever have this ceremony given by you again; it is forbidden for it to be given by a medicine man over his mother or father, or wife, or son, or daughter, or brother or sister." He was told that the two stars that were given to him by the Star People should be given to his sons. The one with which he killed Coyote was to go to his older son, and the other to the younger son. The ceremonial fat was to be given to his wife, but the lightning arrows he was to keep. The Star People said to the family, "You have had this ceremony over you with no offering given to the medicine man. If you were able to give anything as an offering you would be able to keep Younger Brother on the earth, but you have given nothing for his help, so now we will have to take him back with us to the sky in exchange for this ceremony." The Star People had brought back flint armor for Younger Brother. They now dressed him in it and he looked just like one of them. They divided his medicine bundle between his former wife and his two sons equally, and told them that each would have to get for himself whatever else was needed in the ceremonies.

The Sacred Company Journey for Power

The father and mother and family now left, and Younger Brother and his older son and four Stars went off toward the east. Younger Brother's younger son and his former wife stayed in the place where the ceremony had been held. Younger Brother, his son and the Stars went to the home of the Coyote, for Younger Brother wanted to find out why everything was protecting him. As they approached, they saw the Coyotes running away. The travelers called out and said that they wanted to talk with them, so the Coyotes came back. Younger Brother asked Coyote why he had sent him up to the sky, also how he had come back to life, and said that if the Coyote would tell these things there would be peace between them in the future. Coyote was afraid and said, "If I tell you these things you must promise to use three songs of mine," and this was agreed. Coyote sang three songs and in these he put himself above everybody. When he had finished he said that he also must have an offering of ayeel and a k'eet'áán, and then he said the reason he agreed to tell about his behavior was because he wanted Younger Brother's wife again. When the Stars said to him, "You have not yet told why you behaved so," he said "I have already told you in the songs," but he had told nothing. Then the Star People made Coyote and Younger Brother agree that they would neither of them go back to the woman. The Star People told them that all the trouble began because of mixture of blood, for in the beginning the son of Tł'iishtsoh married their relation and then had come the mating of the woman and Coyote, and now Younger Brother was to be one of the Stars. They said there would always be these three kinds of people, Snake men, Coyote men, and Star men. They said that it always would be so, and that they must accept it, and they made peace between Younger Brother and Coyote.

Then the travelers went east from Coyote's home to where the earth and sky meet. There they found a hooghan called Darkness Hooghan and this place is also called Rainbow's End, for in it the rainbow was the light coming down to the center of the hooghan. They went in and found the son of Sǫ'tsoh, who lived there. The older son of Younger Brother had not yet learned all the songs and the medicine, but at this hooghan he learned the origin of the chant. Younger Brother's son had seen many sandpaintings and the ceremonial plaques, and all the medicine which his father used. He saw all this again here and everything was explained to him, and he learned that this place was the beginning of the Chant. They gave him three songs and a prayer, and the travelers left that evening and went back to the place where the ceremony had been.

Next day they went south, the Stars and Younger Brother and his younger son, leaving the older son with his mother in the hooghan. They went to the place where the sky and earth meet, called Yaasilá, and found the blue hooghan where Blue Star's son lived. The rays of the sun crossed in the middle of this hooghan, giving it light. There the younger son saw the ceremonial things that he was to use, and learned three songs and a prayer. The prayer they learned here was to all the Stars, saying, "You, in time of danger with your clothing of stone, protect me." There are four sections to this prayer. Then the travelers went back to the place where the ceremony was held. Next day Younger Brother, the medicine man, with the Stars and his wife, went west and came to where the sky and earth meet. They found a hooghan called Yellow Sunset Hooghan, which is also called the Thunder Bolt. This hooghan was lit by the lightning and the medicine man's wife saw everything there that she needed for her ceremonies. She learned four prayers, and then they went back to the ceremonial hooghan. Next day the medicine man, his older son and the Stars went north to a ledge on the sky and found a hooghan with the White Star's son in it. It was called White Ray of Light Hooghan. This was also called the Crystal Hooghan. This was lit by a ray of light and there the older son saw everything for his ceremony, and learned four prayers, after which they returned to the ceremonial hooghan.

The Second Journey for Power

The next day they went east again, the older son, the medicine man and the Stars, and came to the home of Tééhoołtsódii (Water Monster), who lives in the Great Sea. The older son was told that this was a dangerous place, but that Water Monster would give three songs and four prayers, and that there would be peace in the future with him. Then they went south to the home of the Water Horse, who lives at Tónahelįįh, the Crossing of the Rivers. He gave them three songs and four prayers, and there was peace between them. Then they went on to the west, to Holy Water, where lived Water Monster and older Water Monsters of a different kind.

Part of the Water Chant Story

Here is where part of the Water Chant story branches off. In this story there was a very large white male Butterfly, who had twelve wives. Someone killed the Butterfly, and threw all his wives into the sea. This was the origin of all the Water Monsters. The big white Butterfly had many bells with very pleasant tone with which he enticed women, and when the white Butterfly was killed the Hummingbird picked up the bells and hung them on himself. These Water Monsters who live in Holy Water were fighting among themselves, which made it very dangerous for anyone standing nearby. When the travelers came to this place they made peace between the Monsters, and the older son of the medicine man learned three songs and four prayers. Then they went on until the older son felt tired and wanted to rest. While he was resting he saw a Hummingbird flying overhead taking his food from the bee weed. The older son reached out and caught him and held him by the end of each wing. At that time the Hummingbird made no noise while flying. The Hummingbird said, "Why do you hold me?" and the older son said, "I want to ask you questions," and said that he had been to the west where the Water Monsters lived. Hummingbird said, "Oh, I know all about you," and the older son realized that the Hummingbird knew everything. The Hummingbird told the older son about the killing of the white Butterfly, and whence the Water Monsters came. Looking at the Hummingbird the older son noticed that he had bells hung on him and he asked Hummingbird where he got them. He said that he took them from the white Butterfly and begged the older son to let him go, saying that he would offer two songs for his freedom. So the older son learned these songs, and the Hummingbird gave him the bells. The older son looked at them, and then hung them around Hummingbird's shoulders like a medicine pouch, and let him go. From that day Hummingbird has made a ringing sound when he flies.

Part of the Hail Chant Story

Then the older son followed the Great Stars and his father and caught up with them, and they walked on to the north where they found the home of White Thunder, who lived in a hooghan of ice. He used hail as his weapon. Anyone trying to reach him was driven away by the hail.

As the travelers neared his home they saw Lightning and heard Thunder, then felt the hail, so they returned to their home and stayed over night. Next morning they summoned Jaa'abaní, the Bat, who lived at Tséyaat'i'í. When he came, they praised his courage and said they hoped that he would help them to reach White Thunder. The Bat said, "I am not afraid, I am willing to attack him." So they went back to the home of White Thunder, who is the thunder of winter. The Bat went forward and attacked him from above, while the rest attacked below. He was carrying hot water which he poured on the ice shield of White Thunder. The Star People shot their lightning arrows at the shield but only made marks on it, but the Bat poured down his hot water making many holes in it. Though the Bat was slow he managed to dodge the hail and brought the White Thunder closer to the Star People, calling to them for help for he was nearly exhausted. He knew that the hot water would finally melt the ice, and he said to the Star People, "Shoot now," and so they all shot at the shield and knocked it to pieces. Then they chased the White Thunder back into his hooghan. They followed him in and found him begging for mercy, saying that he would not make war on the people any more. He also said he would give five songs. Three of these songs are used on the last night of the ceremony, one in the cleansing ceremony, and another for the bull-roarer. He also gave two prayers, one for protection as a shield, called ách'ááh sodizin, and another prayer called ch'ééhóyátééh, "forcing-out-from-danger prayer." Then the travelers went back to their home and stayed all night.

The Third Journey for Power

The next day the Great Star People, the medicine man and his younger son went to the east, and came to Sisnaajiní[30] which is north of Taos. (It is a small white mountain and the black belt around it is the timber line.) On top of this mountain lived Black Wind and Black Thunder. There the people discussed the ceremonies with Black Wind and Black Thunder, and agreed that their ceremonies would be alike except for a small difference in the body painting and the sandpainting. The Black Wind and Black Thunder body paintings have a snake on the outside of the legs, as was described for the Great Star ceremony, but there they had lightning painted on the legs instead of snakes. This talk on Sisnaajiní (Black Belt Mountain) was between Sọ'tsoh, Black Wind and Black Thunder. The rest listened. Then they went south to Tsoodził, Mount Taylor, and went up to the top. There they met Blue Wind and Blue Thunder, who talked about the ceremony with the Blue Star and said that the ceremony should be the same as in the Great Star ceremony, except that there should be blue color where there had been black in the Black Star ceremony. Then they went west to Dook'o'oosłííd (San Francisco Peaks), and there the Yellow Star talked with Yellow Wind and Yellow Thunder about the ceremony.

---

[30]The four sacred mountains of the Navajo country are now mentioned: Sisnaajiní = Blanca Peak, Colorado; Tsoodziń = Mt. Taylor, New Mexico; Dook'o'oosłííd = San Francisco Peak, Arizona; Dibé Nitsaa = La Plata Peaks, Colorado.

On the same day they went north to Dibé Nitsaa and there they met White Thunder, who is the greatest of thunders, and found him angry. They could not get near him, so they went home. They called on the Bat to help them as he had before, but he refused and said, "Ask Tsénoolch'óshii (the Rock Wren) and he will help you." They went back home and next morning they went back to Dibé Nitsaa and the White Thunder began shooting ice arrows at them, so they asked Tsénoolch'óshii to lead them. He was carrying a stone shield and arrows, while White Thunder had a shield of ice. Tsénoolch'óshii began dodging and whirling about when the ice arrows were aimed at him, and he shot his stone arrows and hit the ice shield of White Thunder and chipped it, and kept on shooting until it was all cracked. The ice arrows did no harm to the stone shield of Tsénoolch'óshii. White Thunder retreated and the Wren chased him back into his ice house. Then the travelers entered and White Thunder offered them three songs and four prayers. and they gave him an offering of nitł'iz and biyeel. (That is why at present, medicine is always taken from where thunder has hit.)

Now the travelers went home. After a while they decided to have the whole family at a meeting, so they called them in and had a talk with the Star People. The Great Star said, "Younger Brother will not be much longer on the earth because we are taking him up to the sky again, as we told you we would do. The people of the sky will be known as Diyin Dine'é, Holy People, and the Earth People will be known as Nihookáá' Dine'é. You may see Younger Brother once more before we take him." The people were also told that Thunder and all the people in this story are protectors of the Earth People, because peace had been made between them and the people of the earth. Because of this peace the Earth People can travel through the earth, over the earth, through the sea, and over the sea, and through the air. They can hear and understand and talk with everything through Nítch'i Biyázhí, the Spirit Wind. If Earth People do not respect the laws that are made for them and break their agreements they will be punished, by accident, or falling, or killing themselves. They may be killed by wind or by water, or by lightning or fog. These accidents are punishments because the laws are not kept.

Now all the people were gathered together and Younger Brother and Older Brother were both there. This was the first time they had seen each other since Younger Brother had started out to get a medicine man for the ceremony over Older Brother. Sǫ'tsoh told the people that Older Brother need not worry even though the medicine man had never given that ceremony for him. The ceremonies that were held in the sky while Younger Brother was there were really for the benefit of Older Brother. Sǫ'tsoh said to Older Brother, "We are going to have one more ceremony over you when we return from a journey which we must take now."

The Fourth Journey for Power

They started the next day, the four star people, the medicine man and his two sons, but his wife and the rest of the family including Older Brother stayed at home. The four Star People, the medicine man and his two sons went toTséhołhót'ááyá where lived the Black Wind with Tsénoolch'óshii, and there they learned how the Black Wind ceremonies were performed.

From there they went to Coiled Mountain, where lived the Blue Wind with Tł'iishtsoh, the Great Snake, and there they were told how the Blue Wind ceremonies were performed. They went to Naadahas'éí. There, on the top, lived Yellow Wind with Gila Monster, and they there learned about the ceremonies of the Yellow Wind. From there they went to Yá'hóógai (Mountain of Light), which was vibrating rays like the aurora. There lived White Wind, and with him all sorts of pretty birds. This mountain is in the south where all the birds and insects go in the winter, and there are many flowers blooming there all the time. Here they learned how the White Wind ceremonies were performed.

Then they came back to the hooghan where the rest of the family were living. Here the two sons and the wife of the medicine man were told that they were to perform these different ceremonies of the Four Winds, and Star Chant. They were also to perform the ceremonies performed by the Snake and Talking God, and all the rest of the ceremonies given since the beginning of this story. In addition they were to go and see four more people, after which the Star People and Younger Brother were to go back to the sky.

The Fifth Journey for Power

They stayed there all night and the next day Younger Brother, the medicine man, his wife, his two sons and the Star People went north. They journeyed by Ashįįh Haagai, the salt lake south of Zuni, and on to Hadeeshtł'iizh, south of Manuelito. They went past Tsénáshchii', Round Circle Red Rock, south to St. Michael's, came on to the ridge of St. Michael's Mountain, and came down that mountain to a point at Ni'haldzis, the hollow in the earth now called Buell Park. This hollow in the earth at that time was full of water, and a salt crater was there. The Salt Woman had lived there long ago, but later went away down through where Buell Park now is, and so down the valley to the crater beyond Zuni.

This point on which the travelers stood was the top of the hooghan of the Salt Woman. It was protected by the Red Ants who lived at this time under the Black Rock at Red Lake. East of this place, and next to the mountain, is the forked black rock, Black Monster Rock, where lived the Black Ants. All these ants protected the home of the Salt Woman, for she did not want anyone to bother her. The ants were her guards, and when they saw travelers standing on top of the Salt Woman's hooghan they began shooting their arrows which were magic arrows, and were really poison shot from their minds. When the Star People found that the ants were shooting magic arrows, they blew at them, blowing the arrows back and killing the ants with them. Then the travelers came down from Salt Woman's home and found the ants scattered about, most of them dead, only a few alive. The survivors asked for mercy and begged the Star People to bring their people back to life. They said if the Star People would do this that they would give them ten songs and their arrows. This is the origin of the Akéé'-dahoodzoh ceremony, where the medicine man uses arrows to press on the body of the patient to cure him. The Star People used this ceremony to restore the Red Ants to life, and used the same rite to cure the Black Ants.

After this the travelers went on to Tódildǫ' (Whirling Water), where lived Tééhoołtsodii, the Water Monster.[31] This Monster, who was in the form of a man, could draw any person into the water by sending a wave over him. He tried blowing the water over the Star People but was not successful. It began to rise in a wave but it soon fell back, and the Water Monster called for mercy. At this time there were living on the east and west side of Whirling Water four great grey snakes who were protectors of the Water Monsters. Even today you can see a ridge of two grey hills on each side of the valley; these were the snakes of long ago. To the north and south of the valley were rock walls, and these grey snakes held the water in the valley.

The guardian snakes let the Star People and the travelers come in, and they went to the home of Tééhoołtsodii (Water Monster) in the center of Whirling Water. When he made peace he offered them a prayer called Hááhóyátééh.[32] This prayer is all-powerful: it can take you down under the earth, up to the sky, and back to the earth again. It is in two parts, one goes down to the Spirits under the earth, and one up to the sky. It is used when all else fails in a ceremony. Tééhoołtsódii gave four songs, and there were two sandpaintings connected with this, one for men and one women. This painting had a rock with a hole in it in the center called Hajíínéí.[33] It is where people came up to this world from below. The black surrounded with a white border is the sea, and to the east is a black mountain, Mountain-Where-They-Came-Up, which is at the eastern end of the La Plata Mountains. At the south of the sandpainting is a blue mountain, Ruler Mountain (Naats'ádziil), which is southeast of the La Plata Mountains. To the west is a yellow mountain, Rain Mountain (Niłtsądziil), which is to the west of the first black mountain, and to the north of the sandpainting is a white mountain, Corn Mountain (Naadą'ádziil), which is northwest of the black mountain. Covering the yellow mountain to the west is laid a buckskin with a painting on it made of pollen. The buckskin is laid with the head to the east and the pollen painting faces in the same direction. The painting is made of yellow pollen both for male and female patients. For a male patient the pollen figure has a small waist, with a different design on the head from the painting made for a female patient. On the sandpainting made for a female patient the sea around the central stone is blue instead of black. The design of the pollen painting for both the male and female patients is also used on the buckskin in the Ch'ééhóyátééh rite which brings back a person out of sickness and evil. This rite and prayer belong to the earth, and the Hááhóyátééh prayer not only goes down to the earth but up to the sky and back again. If this last prayer is not spoken correctly it will leave the patient as sick as before, if not worse, and this prayer the patient should repeat after the medicine man, word for word. The evil spirits live below and will draw you down in sickness. In that case this Hááhóyátééh prayer is used to draw their evil power away from them. It also draws down from the good powers above into the patient, and in that way brings the patient back to normal. So the evil from below is overcome with good from

[31]This is the most powerful of the Water Monsters. It was Tééhoołtsodii who pursued the people into this world from the previous one, in the Creation Myth.

[32]This is the prayer of invocation and liberation, see pages 59–67.

[33]See the creation story, Navajo Religion Series, Vol. I.

above. In this prayer we go down to the lower world and come up again and go to the top of Black, Blue, Yellow and White Mountains. From there we go up into the sky and back to earth again. (At this point the interpreter said, "This prayer lasts one day and one night and is known only to three or four men now.") All this ceremony of bringing back the person from sickness or evil was given by Tééhoołtsódii to the people.

Then the Star People and the travelers went on south a few miles to Hairy Mountain (Dził Ditł'oi). Many bears lived there, and at that time this was a very dangerous place to visit, but the travelers went directly to it. Upon reaching the foot of the mountain, the medicine man took out of his pouch a mixture of plants and rock and earth and put this in his mouth. There was a little tree growing there, and the medicine man stood at the east of it and blew into the tree. Then he blew into it from the south and west and north, and a heavy wind started to blow which moved rocks and blew down the trees. This frightened the bears very much and they took refuge in their den thinking that winter had come on. There they lay down and all of them went to sleep. The seven travelers came to the home of the bears and walked in, but the bears were all sleeping, and one of the travelers spoke and said, "Is everybody asleep?" That woke one bear, but instead of attacking he was frightened and went into a fit and fell over. One after another the others woke up and went into convulsions. That was where the jidiitłah[34] rite to cure nervous seizures, originated, and still happens sometimes in the ceremony. One bear begged to be restored and promised that all the bears would be friendly to the people. Then the medicine man gave the ceremony learned in the sky from the Star People over the bear, and the bear gave the medicine man a rattle of skin. Now he had two rattles, one which the Stars had given him, and one from the bears. The bear also gave the medicine man four mountains for the ceremonial hoop ceremony, and the footprints for this ceremony, and the prayers. In the ceremony that the medicine man performed over the bears he laid the patient down with his head to the north, facing east, and he used his rattle for making the marks on the earth leading from the body. First he made a mark from the patient's breast to the east, then from his feet to the south, from his back to the west, and from his head to the north, and then he made four straight marks in the reverse order.[35] The prayer given by the bear was called ách'ááh sodizin, "the protecting prayer which is like a shield."

The Final Ceremony Given Over Older Brother

All this time the medicine man's two sons had been receiving instructions on how to perform these ceremonies over people, and when this was finished they all returned home to the medicine man's wife. When they reached there they found the medicine man's nephew, Earth Boy, and he said that they were all invited to go to the ceremony being held over Older Brother this same day. He said that all the people they had met and from whom they had obtained

---

[34]See page 40.
[35]See page 25.

ceremonies since the beginning of this story would be present, and the travelers said that they would come. This was the last and most important day (bijí) of the ceremony, and it is the custom today that most people arrive on this day. The ceremony was at the place where Older Brother killed the Left-Handed Wind's son, and they all left to go to this place. There they found Older Brother ready for the ceremony, which was called "The Ceremony Given Once." It is called this because it is very seldom given. It is a combination of the four-day ceremonies of the Star Chant and the Wind Chant, all given in one day. In giving this today they decorate all the body with dots of white earth as in the Wind and Star ceremonies.

Now the ceremony was about to be given by Sǫ'tsoh, and everyone was there. Older Brother had been taught to give the Wind Chant and this was where it started. From him it passed to his sister, whose ceremony was called the Female Wind Chant. Her son learned the Male Wind Chant, and so the two Wind Chants were passed down from these two people. Older Brother's sister and her son learned these chants because they were to carry them in the future. Older Brother was told to be ready because he was to leave in the morning and live at Coiled Mountain among the Snake People.

Younger Brother, the medicine man, was also told that he was no longer to live on earth but would be taken to the sky. They were to be taken in exchange for the two ceremonies which were given to the Earth People. Younger Brother's wife learned to perform the ceremony of the Female Great Star. His older son learned the Male Great Star Chant, and his younger son learned the Evil-Chasing Great Star Chant. As they were preparing for the singing with the basket in the evening, they asked for food and in came the Gopher with a basket of wild potatoes. One of the people said, "We want better food than that. We are used to better things and can not eat potatoes. We want something different." So the Gopher said, taking out the potatoes, "I will bring it back again with white earth, which has some mineral in it to give the potatoes a taste. Then we will eat it with the white earth," but the Gopher never came back. She was offended and went to her own home. (That is why earth is used to clean wool and in purifying water. That was the time the Navajo learned to eat wild potatoes with white earth, boiling them and mixing them into a dough with the earth.) Next to come into the ceremony was Tóneinilí, the Water God, bringing water. Someone said to him, "There is plenty of water outside, we didn't call for water, we called for food." He also was offended and walked out with the water, saying "Water won't be plentiful any more, it is going to be scarce. (Both the Gopher and the Water God said of the things they brought, "This is my power," meaning that potatoes give strength to the Gopher and water strength to the Water God.) Next came in the Asdzáán Áshįįhí (Salt Woman) with a basket of salt. As she laid it down someone said, "We don't want salt but want food with it," and she said, "I will go and I will be far away; I won't live near here any more." Being offended she walked out with the salt and as she went said, "This is my power," for the salt was what gave her strength. Then came in Holy People, bringing in food such as meat and bread. The people ate, and prepared for the singing with the basket. The ceremony started, and they sang all night.

In the morning at early dawn the singing was finished. Older Brother was told to go out and breathe in the dawn four times, which brings new life into the body. Then he was told to go away from the hooghan until sunrise and then come back. They called for water to be brought in, but they found there was no water in the neighborhood, and they sent one of the people to one of the four water holes nearby but they found them dry. The messenger came back saying there was none. Then they sent another fast runner to go further to see if he could find water. Further and further he went in a circle but found no water, for Water God had hidden it all. Then the messenger went to the Salt Woman's home and found that she was gone and the salt was gone, and he saw the Salt Woman going far off to where her home is today. He returned and told all this to the others. When the sun rose, Older Brother, the patient, returned to the hooghan, and the life feather was taken from his head. He was told to be ready to go with the Wind People to Coiled Mountain where he would live and be one of the Snake People, for he was taken in exchange for the Wind ceremony. Then the rest of the people went home, the ceremony was finished, and the medicine pouch was taken out. Then Younger Brother was taken to the sky by the Stars.

The name of Older Brother is Nítch'i Diłhił Biye', "The Son of the Black Wind," or Tádídíín Yeeneeyánii, meaning "Reared in the Pollen, or Blessed with Pollen." The name of Younger Brother is Sǫ'tsoh Diłhił Biye', "Son of Black Star" (the Great Star), or Tádídíín Yeeneeyánii, "Blessed with Pollen." The other members of the family were Earth People and took their names from things on the earth. These names as given above of Older Brother and Younger Brother should never be used by people of the Earth.

PRAYERS OF THE GREAT STAR CHANT

Recorded by Father Berard Haile from the Medicine Man, Ayóó'áníɫnézí.

"This prayer, you see, is not spoken at every chant, but when a person asks for it at any time it is then said. And when it is to be said, a buckskin is laid down upon which a sandpainting is drawn with white corn meal for a man, yellow corn meal for a woman. It is called "the sandpainting at the field," and it is made circular with keystoneshaped clouds projecting at the four (cardinal) points. Inside, a standing figure is made of pollen, which is called Tádídíín Ashkii, the Pollen Boy, and, coming towards it, four footprints are made around the fire. For a woman, the same pollen is used in drawing the Aniɫt'ánii At'ééd, the Cornbeetle Girl. While the medicine man is singing, the patient steps into the footprints, following them to the sandpainting, and sits upon it. Then the singer places the talking prayersticks in the patient's hands, also the bull-roarer and the rock crystal, and begins to pray for him.

"The sandpainting need be made but once, when a prayer is to be said with a night intervening between its parts. It is then merely folded together and the skin laid aside. Then it can be spread out again when the prayer starts again. The footprints alone must be made over each time. When the prayer is interrupted they are shaken out at the patient's resting place and he spends the night sleeping on them.

"If it is decided to finish the prayer from the four directions in a single continuous recitation, it can be done so. It can likewise be said from just two directions. If a decision is reached to have it done with a night interrupting it, that too may be done.

"A person can also request that it be done for him without the chant and, if he request that it be added to a no-sleep ceremony, this too can be done. If this prayer is completed very nicely without an omission, it is very well, but if a person recites it with occasional slips here and there, that is not so good.

"Another version of this same prayer may also be employed in a Blessing Chant which the patient himself may decide to have. In these Blessing Prayers, Haashch'ééɫti'í and Haashch' ééwaan are always substituted for Naayéé' Neezghání and the line about lightning is always omitted. The red door guards are also left out in the Blessing Prayers.

"These Blessing Prayers cannot be separated from the Great Star Chant itself, unlike the

Evil-Chasing Prayers. In the story, Haashch'éélti'í frees Earth Boy from Tł'iishtsoh, so Haashch'éélti'í comes into the prayer right away instead of Naayéé' Neezghání.

"They look for a perforated stone (see page 54) for this sandpainting too. When a person finds one, he notices which side faces east when he picks it up. It is set down on the sand-painting in that identical position and when the ceremony and prayer are all over, he puts it back where he found it in exactly the same position it originally had, except that now pollen is scattered twice below it and twice on top of it.

"The sandpainting is rubbed out right where it is. It might be done by a person lying on it. It is never taken out in a blanket, and this is true of the mountains (see page 54), too.

"As a matter of fact, this Emergence Prayer can be used even outside of a chant. The two parts of the prayer must be kept together; the prayer must be said over these two times without an interruption. The no-sleep ceremony can also be combined with it.

"The Prayer for Protection can be said even without a chant, but if it is used during a chant it comes in the evening after all other ceremonies are over. If a person asks that the whole thing be said, that can be done, as well as if he asks only for any part. It can be done on a sandpainting, or it can be done without a sandpainting."

PRAYER OF INVOCATION AND LIBERATION FROM THE MYTH OF THE GREAT STAR

Part I

1. From the center of the earth, Naayéé' Neezghání[36], using his dark staff, comes into search for me; With lightnings flashing before him, with lightnings flashing behind him, he comes in to search for me; Using a rock crystal and a talking k'eet'áán[37] he comes in to search for me.

2. Below the east, he comes in to search for me, farther on, he comes in to search for me; Beyond that place, through a dark mountain, Naayéé' Neezghání, using his dark staff, comes in to search for me; With lightnings flashing before him, with lightnings flashing behind him, he comes in to search for me; Using a rock crystal and a talking k'eet'áán, he comes in to search for me. Farther on, he comes in to search for me; Beyond that place, through two blue mountains, Naayéé' Neezghání, using his dark staff, comes in to search for me; With light-nings flashing before him, with lightnings flashing behind him, he comes in to search for me;

---

[36]Naayéé' Neezghání, "Enemy Slayer," is the son of Changing Woman and the Sun. A deity of warlike connotation, helpful to man, his mission on earth was to rid the world of its dangerous monsters.

[37]k'eet'áán: a hollow reed about the size of a cigarette, filled with offerings such as tobacco, bits of shell, and other precious materials.

Using a rock crystal and a talking k'eet'áán, he comes in to search for me. Farther on, he comes in to search for me; Beyond that place, through three yellow mountains, Naayéé' Neezghání, using his dark staff, comes in to search for me; With lightnings flashing before him, with lightnings flashing behind him, he comes in to search for me; Using a rock crystal and a talking k'eet'aan, he comes in to search for me. Farther on, he comes in to search for me; Beyond that place, through four white mountains, Naayéé' Neezghání, using his dark staff, comes in to search for me; With lightnings flashing before him, with lightnings flashing behind him, he comes in to search for me; Using a rock crystal and a talking k'eet'áán, he comes in to search for me.

3. Farther on, he comes in to search for me; Beyond that place, through a dark cloud, Naayéé' Neezghání, using his dark staff, comes in to search for me; With lightnings flashing before him, with lightnings flashing behind him, he comes in to search for me; Using a rock crystal and a talking k'eet'áán, he comes in to search for me. Farther on, he comes in to search for me; Beyond that place, through two blue clouds[38] . . . Farther on, he comes in to search for me; Beyond that place, through three yellow clouds . . . Farther on, he comes in to search for me; Beyond that place, through four white clouds . . .

4. Farther on, he comes in to search for me; Beyond that place, through a dark mist, Naayéé' Neezghání, using his dark staff, comes in to search for me; With lightnings flashing before him, with lightnings flashing behind him, he comes in to search for me; Using a rock crystal and a talking k'eet'áán, he comes in to search for me. Farther on he comes in to search for me; Beyond that place, through two blue mists . . . Farther on, he comes in to search for me; Beyond that place, through three yellow mists . . . Farther on, he comes in to search for me; Beyond that place, through four white mists . . .

5. Farther on, he comes in to search for me; Beyond that place, through a dark moss, Naayéé' Neezghání, using his dark staff, comes in to search for me; With lightnings flashing before him, with lightnings flashing behind him, he comes in to search for me; Using a rock crystal and a talking k'eet'áán, he comes in to search for me. Farther on, he comes in to search for me; Beyond that place, through two blue mosses . . . Farther on, he comes in to search for me; Beyond that place, through three yellow mosses . . . Farther on, he comes in to search for me; Beyond that place, through four white mosses . . .

6. Farther on, he comes in to search for me; Beyond that place, through dark water, Naayéé' Neezghání, using his dark staff, comes in to search for me; With lightnings flashing before him, with lightnings flashing behind him, he comes in to search for me; Using a rock crystal and a talking k'eet'áán, he comes in to search for me. Farther on, he comes in to search for me; Beyond that place, through two blue waters . . . Farther on, he comes in to search for

---

[38]To save space and to help the reader gain a clear idea of the structure of the prayer, some of the straight repetition has been omitted. The rest of this verse is an exact repetition of that part of the first verse in stanza 3 which follows ". . . through a dark cloud . . ." Thus the omitted portion of any verse is an exact repetition of the analogous portion of the first verse of that stanza.

me; Beyond that place, through three yellow waters . . . Farther on, he comes in to search for me; Beyond that place, through four white waters . . .

7. Farther on, he comes in to search for me[39]; Beyond that place, at the door of the Darkness Hooghan, where a pair of red coyotes lie with heads reversed, Naayéé' Neezghání tosses these apart with his dark staff and thus he comes in to search for me; With lightnings flashing before him, with lightnings flashing behind him, he comes in to search for me; Using a rock crystal and a talking k' eet' áán, he comes in to search for me. Farther on, he comes in to search for me; Beyond that place, at the corners by the door of the Darkness Hooghan, where a pair of red bluejays lie with heads reversed . . . Farther on, he comes in to search for me; Beyond that place, at the fireplace of the Darkness Hooghan, where a pair of red hoot-owls lie with heads reversed . . . Farther on he comes in to search for me; Beyond that place, at the center of the Darkness Hooghan, where a pair of red screech-owls lie with heads reversed . . .

8. Farther on, he comes in to search for me; At that place, in the west corner of the Darkness Hooghan, behind the Traveler in Darkness, where my feet lie, where my legs lie, where my body lies, where my mind lies, where my voice lies, where my speech lies, where my power of movement lies; I came in, searching for all these. Farther on, he comes in to search for me; At that place, in the west corner of the Darkness Hooghan, behind the Whirling Darkness . . . Farther on, he comes in to search for me; At that place, in the west corner of the Darkness Hooghan, behind the Spreading Darkness . . .

9. "I came searching for you; you and I will begin our return, my grandchild. We two are now leaving, my grandchild," Naayéé' Neezghání says to me; With the talking k' eet' áán in his right hand, he encircles me with it, in a sunwise direction, and places it in my right hand; Encircling me, sunwise, with a rainbow, he turns me, sunwise, toward himself; "We two will now start back, my grandchild," he says to me; "We two are now leaving, my grandchild," he says to me as I return to stand upon the rainbow.

10. From the west corner of the Darkness Hooghan, Naayéé' Neezghání returns with me, whirling his dark staff about himself for protection; With lightnings flashing behind him, with lightnings flashing before him, he returns with me; As the rainbow returns with me and the talking k' eet' áán teaches me. Naayéé' Neezghání returns with me. Farther on, he returns with me; From the center of the Darkness Hooghan . . . Farther on, he returns with me; From the fireplace of the Darkness Hooghan . . . Farther on, he returns with me; From the corners by the door of the Darkness Hooghan . . . Farther on, he returns with me; From the door of the Darkness Hooghan . . .

11. Farther on, he returns with me; Through four white waters, Naayéé' Neezghání returns with me, whirling his dark staff about himself for protection; With lightnings flashing behind him, with lightnings flashing before him, he returns with me; As the rainbow returns with me and the talking k'eet'áán teaches me, Naayéé' Neezghání returns with me. Farther on, he returns with me; Through three yellow waters . . . Farther on, he returns with me; Through two blue waters . . . Farther on he returns with me; Through the dark water . . .

---

[39]The four verses of stanza 7 are omitted in "Holy Way" versions of the ceremony.

12. Farther on, he returns with me; Through four white mosses, Naayéé' Neezghání returns with me, whirling his dark staff about himself for protection; With lightnings flashing behind him, with lightnings flashing before him, he returns with me; As the rainbow returns with me and the talking k' eet' áán teaches me, Naayéé' Neezghání returns with me. Farther on, he returns with me; Through three yellow mosses . . . Farther on, he returns with me; Through two blue mosses . . . Farther on, he returns with me; Through the dark moss . . .

13. Farther on, he returns with me; Through four white mists, Naayéé' Neezghání returns with me, whirling his dark staff about himself for protection; With lightnings flashing behind him, with lightnings flashing before him, he returns with me; As the rainbow returns with me and the talking k' eet' áán teaches me, Naayéé' Neezghání returns with me. Farther on, he returns with me; Through three yellow mists . . . Farther on, he returns with me; Through two blue mists . . . Farther on, he returns with me; Through a dark mist . . .

14. Farther on, he returns with me; Through four white clouds, Naayéé' Neezghání returns with me, whirling his dark staff about himself for protection; With lightnings flashing behind him, with lightnings flashing before him, he returns with me; As the rainbow returns with me and the talking k' eet' áán teaches me, Naayéé' Neezghání returns with me. Farther on, he returns with me; Through three yellow clouds . . . Farther on, he returns with me; Through two blue clouds . . . Farther on, he returns with me; Through a dark cloud . . .

15. Farther on, he returns with me; Through four white mountains, Naayéé' Neezghání returns with me, whirling his dark staff about himself for protection; With lightnings flashing behind him, with lightnings flashing before him, he returns with me; As the rainbow returns with me and the talking k' eet' áán teaches me, Naayéé' Neezghání returns with me. Farther on, he returns with me; Through three yellow mountains . . . Farther on, he returns with me; Through two blue mountains . . . Farther on, he returns with me; Through a dark mountain . . .

16. Farther on, he returns with me; Farther this way, from the summit of Sisnaajiní[40], Naayéé' Neezghání returns with me, whirling his dark staff about himself for protection; With lightnings flashing behind him, with lightnings flashing before him, he returns with me; As the rainbow returns with me and the talking k'eet'áán teaches me, Naayéé' Neezghání returns with me. Farther on, he returns with me; Farther this way, from the summit of Tsoodził . . . Farther on, he returns with me; Farther this way, from the summit of Dook'o'oosłííd . . . Farther on, he returns with me; Farther this way, from the summit of Dibé Nitsaa . . .

17. Farther on, he returns with me; Farther this way, from the summit of Soft Stuffs Mountain, Naayéé' Neezghání returns with me, whirling his dark staff about himself for protection; With lightnings flashing behind him, with lightnings flashing before him, he returns with me; As the rainbow returns with me and the talking k'eet'áán teaches me, Naayéé' Neezghání returns with me. Farther on, he returns with me; Farther this way, from

---

[40]See footnote, page 51.

the summit of Jewel Mountain . . . Farther on, he returns with me; Farther this way, from the summit of Pollen Mountain . . . Farther on, he returns with me; Farther this way, from the summit of Cornbeetle Mountain . . . Farther on, he returns with me; Farther this way, from the summit of Old Age Mountain . . . Farther on, he returns with me; Farther this way, from Old Age Hooghan . . .

18. Farther on, he returns with me; From that place, from the center of the wide cornfield, Haashch'ééłti'í[41] returns with me, whirling his dark staff about himself for protection; Blue, small birds sing before me, Cornbeetle sings behind me, as Haashch'ééłti'í returns with me; As the rainbow returns to that place with me, and the talking k'eet'áán teaches me, Haashch'ééłti'í returns with me. Farther on, he returns with me; From that place, from the center of Pollen Boy's hooghan . . . Farther on, he returns with me; From that place, from the center of Cornbeetle Girl's hooghan . . .

19. Farther on, he arrives with me; From there to where my hooghan first comes in sight. Haashch'ééłti'í arrives with me, whirling his dark staff about himself for protection; Blue, small birds sing before me, Cornbeetle sings behind me, as Haashch'ééłti'í arrives with me; As the rainbow arrives at that place with me, and the talking k'eet'áán teaches me, Haashch'ééłti'í arrives with me; Farther on, he arrives with me; From there to the path to my hooghan . . . Farther on, he arrives with me; From there to the door of my hooghan . . . Farther on, he arrives with me; From there to the corners by the door of my hooghan . . . Farther on, he arrives with me; From there to the fireplace of my hooghan . . . Farther on, he arrives with me; From there to the center of my hooghan . . . Farther on, he arrives with me; From there to the west corner of my hooghan . . .

20. "This is your home, my grandchild!" he says to me as he sits down beside me; "I have returned with you to your home my grandchild!" he says to me as he sits down beside me; "Upon the pollen figure[42], I have returned to sit with you, my grandchild!" he says to me as he sits down beside me; "Your home is yours again . . . "Your fire is yours again . . . "Your food is yours again . . . "Your resting place is yours again . . . "Your feet are yours again . . . "Your legs are yours again . . . "Your body is yours again . . . "Your mind is yours again . . . "Your voice is yours again . . . "Your speech is yours again . . . "Your power of movement is yours again . . . "This enables you to live on in blessing . . .

21. "Whatever makes it blessed before me, that shall make it blessed before you, my grandchild!" he says to me as he sits down beside me; "Whatever makes it blessed behind me . . . "Whatever makes it blessed below me . . . "Whatever makes it blessed above me . . . "Whatever makes it blessed all around me . . . "Whatever makes my speech blessed, that shall make your speech blessed, my grandchild!" he says to me as he sits down beside me; "Whatever enables me to live long, that shall enable you to live long, my grandchild!" he says to me

[41]Haashch'ééłti'í; "Talking God," one of the principal Navajo deities. He frequently appears in time of trouble and instructs the people in the ceremonial means of solving problems.

[42]Pollen figure in the sandpainting.

as he sits down beside me; "Whatever enables me to live happily, that shall enable you to live happily, my grandchild!" he says to me as he sits down beside me; "Blessed again it has become, blessed again it has become!"

Part II

1. From the center of the earth, Tóbájíshchíní[43], using his blue staff, comes in to search for me; With lightnings flashing before him . . .

2. Below the south, he comes in to search for me . . .

3–7. (As in *Part I* except for substitution of "Tóbájíshchíní" and "blue staff" for "Naayéé' Neezghání" and "dark staff.")

8. Farther on, he comes in to search for me; At that place, in the west corner of the Darkness Hooghan, behind the Wind Traveler . . . Farther on, he comes in to search for me; At that place, in the west corner of the Darkness Hooghan, behind the Whirling Wind . . . Farther on, he comes in to search for me; At that place, in the west corner of the Darkness Hooghan, behind the Spreading Darkness . . .

9–17. (As in *Part I* except for substitutions as noted above.)

18. Farther on, he returns with me; From that place, from the center of the wide cornfield, Haashch'é'éwaan[44] returns with me, whirling his blue staff about himself for protection; Cornbeetle sings behind me, blue, small birds sing before me, as Haashch'é'éwaan returns with me . . .

19–20. (As in *Part I* except for substitutions as noted above.)

21. "Whatever makes it blessed behind me, that shall make it blessed before you, my grandchild!" he says to me as he sits down beside me; "Whatever makes it blessed before me . . . (The rest of the stanza as in *Part I*.)

Part III

(As in *Part I* except for stanza 2 where "west" is substituted for "east.")

Part IV

(Up to stanza 21, as in *Part II* except for stanza 2 where "north" is substituted for "south.")

---

[43]Tóbájíshchíní: "Born of Water." The twin brother of Enemy Slayer. He accompanies his brother on the journey to the home of the Sun in order to obtain power to rid the world of monsters. He complements Enemy Slayer in ritual poetry, balancing the harsh male with the gentler "female" quality.

[44]Haashch'é'éwaan: "Hooghan God," one of the principal Navajo deities. He is a balancing entity for Talking God, just as Born of Water is for Enemy Slayer.

20a. "Your maternal uncle is yours again, my grandchild!" he says to me as he sits down beside me; "Your mother is yours again . . . Your elder brother . . . Your younger sister . . . All your relatives . . . All your children . . . Your life's mate . . . All your neighbors are yours again, my grandchild!" he says to me as he sits down beside me.

20b. "Your soft stuffs are yours again, my grandchild!" he says to me as he sits down beside me; "Your jewels . . . Your horses . . . Your sheep . . . All your possessions . . . Your country . . . Your springs that flow . . . Your mountain ranges are yours again, my grandchild!" he says to me as he sits down beside me.

20c. "Your fields are yours again, my grandchild!" he says to me as he sits down beside me; "White Corn Boy is yours again . . . Yellow Corn Girl is yours again . . . Pollen Boy is yours again . . . Cornbeetle Girl is yours again . . . Old Age People are yours again . . . Long life is yours again . . . Happiness is yours again, my grandchild!" he says to me as he sits down beside me.

21. "Whatever makes it blessed behind me, that shall make it blessed behind you, my grandchild!" he says to me as he sits down beside me; "Whatever makes it blessed before me . . . Whatever makes it blessed below me . . . Whatever makes it blessed above me . . . Whatever makes it blessed all around me . . . Whatever makes my speech blessed . . . Whatever enables me to live long . . . Whatever enables me to live happily, that shall enable you to live happily, my grandchild!" he says to me as he sits down beside me; Blessed again it has become, Blessed again it has become, Blessed again it has become, Blessed again it has become!

BLESSING PRAYERS OF INVOCATION AND LIBERATION FOR CASES OF ILLNESS CAUSED BY LIGHTNING, THUNDER, BEARS, AND SNAKES

The Lightning Prayer

1. From the Pollen Hooghan, Haashch'ééłti'í, using his dark staff, comes in to search for me; Using a rock crystal and a talking k'eet'áán, he comes in to search for me.

2. Below the east, he comes in to search for me, farther on, he comes in to search for me; At that place, through a dark mountain, Haashch'ééłti'í, using his dark staff, comes in to search for me; Using a rock crystal and a talking k'eet'áán, he comes in to search for me. Farther on, he comes in to search for me; Beyond that place, through two blue mountains . . . Farther on, he comes in to search for me; Beyond that place, through three yellow mountains . . . Farther on, he comes in to search for me; Beyond that place, through four white mountains . . .

3. Farther on, he comes in to search for me; Beyond that place, through a dark cloud, Haashch'ééłti'í, using his dark staff, comes in to search for me; Using a rock crystal and a talking k'eet'áán, he comes in to search for me. Farther on, he comes in to search for me; Beyond that place, through two blue clouds . . . Farther on, he comes in to search for me; Beyond that place, through three yellow clouds . . . Farther on, he comes in to search for me; Beyond that place, through four white clouds . . .

4. Farther on, he comes in to search for me; Beyond that place, through a dark mist, Haashch'ééłti'í, using his dark staff, comes in to search for me; Using a rock crystal and a talking k'eet'áán, he comes in to search for me. Farther on, he comes in to search for me; Beyond that place, through two blue mists . . . Farther on, he comes in to search for me; Beyond that place, through three yellow mists . . . Farther on, he comes in to search for me; Beyond that place, through four white mists . . .

5. Farther on, he comes in to search for me; Beyond that place, through a dark moss, Haashch'ééłti'í, using his dark staff, comes in to search for me; Using a rock crystal and a talking k'eet'áán he comes in to search for me. Farther on, he comes in to search for me; Beyond that place, through two blue mosses . . . Farther on, he comes in to search for me; Beyond that place, through three yellow mosses . . . Farther on, he comes in to search for me; Beyond that place, through four white mosses . . .

6. Farther on, he comes in to search for me; Beyond that place, through a dark water, Haashch'ééłti'í, using his dark staff, comes in to search for me; Using a rock crystal and a talking k'eet'áán, he comes in to search for me. Farther on, he comes in to search for me; Beyond that place, through two blue waters . . . Farther on, he comes in to search for me; Beyond that place, through three yellow waters . . . Farther on, he comes in to search for me; Beyond that place, through four white waters . . .

7. (These "Evil-Chasing" verses are omitted since this is a "Holy Way" prayer.)

8. Farther on, he comes in to search for me; At that place, in the west corner of the Dark Cloud Hooghan, behind the dark thunder, where my feet lie, where my legs lie, where my body lies, where my mind lies, where my voice lies, where my speech lies, where my power of movement lies; I came in, searching for all these. Farther on, he comes in to search for me; At that place, in the west corner of the Blue Cloud Hooghan, behind the blue thunder . . . Farther on, he comes in to search for me; At that place, in the west corner of the Yellow Cloud Hooghan, behind the yellow thunder . . . Farther on, he comes in to search for me; At that place, in the west corner of the White Cloud Hooghan, behind the white thunder . . .

9. "I came searching for you; you and I will begin our return, my grandchild. We two are now leaving, my grandchild," Haashch'ééłti'í says to me; With the talking k'eet'áán in his right hand, he encircles me with it, in a sunwise direction, and places it in my right hand; Encircling me, sunwise, with a rainbow, he turns me, sunwise, towards himself; "We two will now start back, my grandchild," he says to me; "We two are now leaving, my grandchild," he says to me as I return to stand upon the rainbow.

10. From the door of the Dark Cloud Hooghan, Haashch'ééłti'í returns with me, whirling his dark staff about himself for protection; As the rainbow returns with me and the talking k'eet'áán teaches me, Haashch'ééłti'í returns with me. From the door of the Blue Cloud Hoog-

han . . . From the door of the Yellow Cloud Hooghan . . . From the door of the White Cloud Hooghan . . .

11. Farther on, he returns with me; Through four white waters, Haashch'ééłti'í returns with me, whirling his dark staff about himself for protection; As the rainbow returns with me and the talking k'eet'áán teaches me, Haashch'ééłti'í returns with me. Farther on, he returns with me; Through three yellow waters . . . Farther on, he returns with me; Through two blue waters . . . Farther on, he returns with me; Through a dark water . . .

12. Farther on, he returns with me; Through four white mosses . . . Farther on, he returns with me; Through three yellow mosses . . . Farther on, he returns with me; Through two blue mosses . . . Farther on, he returns with me; Through a dark moss . . .

13. Farther on, he returns with me; Through four white mists . . . Farther on, he returns with me; Through three yellow mists . . . Farther on, he returns with me; Through two blue mists . . . Farther on, he returns with me; Through a dark mist . . .

14. Farther on, he returns with me; through four white clouds . . . Farther on, he returns with me; Through three yellow clouds . . . Farther on, he returns with me; Through two blue clouds . . . Farther on, he returns with me; Through a dark cloud . . .

15. Farther on, he returns with me; Through four white mountains . . . Farther on, he returns with me; through three yellow mountains . . . Farther on, he returns with me; Through two blue mountains . . . Farther on, he returns with me; Through a dark mountain . . .

16. (Omitted.)

17. Farther on, he returns with me; Farther this way, at the summit of Pollen Mountain, Haashch'ééłti'í returns with me, whirling his dark staff about himself for protection; As the rainbow returns with me and the talking k'eet'áán teaches me, Haashch'ééłti'í returns with me. Farther on, he returns with me; Farther this way, at the summit of Cornbeetle Mountain . . . Farther on, he returns with me; Farther this way, at the summit of Old Age Mountain . . . Farther on, he returns with me; Farther this way, at Old Age Hooghan . . .

18. Farther on, he returns with me; From that place, from the center of the wide cornfield, Haashch'ééłti'í returns with me; whirling his dark staff about himself for protection; Blue small birds sing before me, Cornbeetle sings behind me, as Haashch'ééłti'í returns with me; As the rainbow returns to that place with me, and the talking k'eet'áán teaches me, Haashch'ééłti'í returns with me. Farther on, he returns with me; From that place, from the center of Pollen Boy's Hooghan . . . Farther on, he returns with me; From that place, from the center of Cornbeetle Girl's hooghan . . .

19. Farther on, he arrives with me; From there to where my Pollen Hooghan first comes in sight, Haashch'ééłti'í arrives with me, whirling his dark staff about himself for protection; Blue, small birds sing before me, Cornbeetle sings behind me, as Haashch'ééłti'í returns with me; As the rainbow returns to that place with me, and the talking k'eet'áán teaches me, Haashch'ééłti'í returns with me. Farther on, he arrives with me; From there to the path of my Pollen Hooghan . . . Farther on, he arrives with me; From there to the door of my Pollen Hooghan . . . Farther on, he arrives with me; From there to the corners by the door of my Pollen Hooghan . . . Farther on, he arrives with me; From there to the fireplace of my Pollen Hooghan . . . Farther

on, he arrives with me; From there to the center of my Pollen Hooghan . . . Farther on, he arrives with me; From there to the west corner of my Pollen Hooghan . . .

20. "This is your home, my grandchild!" he says to me as he sits down beside me; "I have returned with you to your home, my grandchild!" he says to me as he sits down beside me; "Upon the pollen figure I have returned to sit with you, my grandchild!" he says to me as he sits down beside me; "Your home is yours again . . . Your fire is yours again . . . Your food is yours again . . . Your resting place is yours again . . . Your feet are yours again . . . Your legs are yours again . . . Your body is yours again . . . Your mind is yours again . . . Your voice is yours again . . . Your speech is yours again . . . Your power of movement is yours again . . . "This enables you to live on in blessing . . .

21. "Whatever makes it blessed before me, that shall make it blessed before you, my grandchild!" he says to me as he sits down beside me; "Whatever makes it blessed behind me . . . "Whatever makes it blessed below me . . . Whatever makes it blessed above me . . . Whatever makes it blessed all around me . . . Whatever makes my speech blessed, that shall make your speech blessed, my grandchild!" he says to me as he sits down beside me; "Whatever enables me to live long, that shall enable you to live long, my grandchild!" he says to me as he sits down beside me; "Whatever enables me to live happily, that shall enable you to live happily, my grandchild!" he says to me as he sits down beside me.

22. "From the Dark Thunder Hooghan, kind feelings will come to you as you go about in life, my grandchild!" he says to me as he sits down beside me; "Guided by these things, you shall live on, respected everywhere, my grandchild!" he says to me as he sits down beside me; "Guided by these things, you shall find protection in all places as you live on, my grandchild!" he says to me as he sits down beside me; "Guided by these things, people everywhere will refuse to part with you, my grandchild!" he says to me as he sits down beside me,

20a. "Your maternal uncle is yours again, my grandchild!" he says to me as he sits down beside me; "Your mother is yours again, my grandchild!" he says to me as he sits down beside me; "Your elder brother . . . Your younger sister . . . All your relatives . . . All your children . . . Your life's mate . . . All your neighbors . . .

20b. "Your soft stuffs are yours again, my grandchild!" he says to me as he sits down beside me; "Your jewels . . . Your horses . . . Your sheep . . . All your possessions . . . Your country . . . Your springs that flow . . . Your mountain ranges . . .

20c. "Your fields are yours again, my grandchild!" he says to me as he sits down beside me; "White Corn Boy is yours again . . . Yellow Corn Girl is yours again . . . Pollen Boy is yours again . . . Cornbeetle Girl is yours again . . . Old Age People are yours again . . . Long life is yours again . . . Happiness is yours again, my grandchild!" he says to me as he sits down beside me; Blessed again it has become, Blessed again it has become, Blessed again it has become, Blessed again it has become!"

The Thunder Prayer

1. From the Pollen Hooghan, Haashch'é'éwaan, using his blue staff, comes in to search for me; Using a rock crystal and talking k'eet'áán, he comes in to search for me.

2. Below the south, he comes in to search for me, farther on, he comes in to search for me; At that place, through a dark mountain, Haashch'é'éwaan, using his blue staff, comes in to search for me; Using a rock crystal and a talking k'eet'áán, he comes in to search for me; Farther on, he comes in to search for me; Beyond that place, through two blue mountains . . . Farther on, he comes in to search for me; Beyond that place, through three yellow mountains . . . Farther on, he comes in to search for me; Beyond that place through four white mountains . . .

3–6. (Like stanza 2 above, but using "clouds," "mists," "mosses," and "water," instead of "mountains.")

7. (Omitted.)

8. (As in the Lightning Prayer.)

9. (As in the Lightning Prayer, except that "Haashch'é'éwaan" and "blue staff" are substituted for "Haashch'ééłti'í" and "dark staff.")

10. From the door of the Dark Cloud Hooghan, Haashch'é'éwaan returns with me, whirling his blue staff about himself for protection; As the rainbow returns with me and the talking k'eet'áán teaches me, Haashch'é'éwaan returns with me. From the door of the Blue Cloud Hooghan . . . From the door of the Yellow Cloud Hooghan . . . From the door of the White Cloud Hooghan . . .

11–15. (Stanzas 2–6 reversed.)

16. (Omitted.)

17–19. (As in the Lightning Prayer, except that "Haashch'é'éwaan" and "blue staff" are substituted for "Haashch'ééłti'í" and "dark staff.")

20. (As in Prayer I, stanza 20.)

21. (As in Prayer I, stanza 21, except that the last line is omitted.)

22. From the Blue Thunder Hooghan, kind feelings will come to you . . . (as in the Lighting Prayer.)

20a–20b. (As in the Lightning Prayer.)

20c. (As in the Lightning Prayer, but the following two lines are added:) Blessed again it has become, Blessed again it has become, Blessed again it has become, Blessed again it has become!

The Bear Prayer

1. From the Pollen Hooghan, Haasch'ééłti'í, using his dark staff, comes in to search for me; Using a rock crystal and a talking k'eet'áán, he comes in to search for me.

2. Below the west, he comes in to search for me, farther on, he comes in to search for me; At that place, through a dark mountain, Haasch'ééłti'í, using his dark staff, comes in to search for me; Using a rock crystal and a talking k'eet'áán, he comes in to search for me. Farther on, he comes in to search for me; Beyond that place, through two blue mountains . . . Farther on, he comes in to search for me; Beyond that place, through three yellow mountains . . . Farther on, he comes in to search for me; Beyond that place, through four white mountains . . .

3–6. (Like stanza 2 above, but using "clouds," "mists," "mosses," and "waters," instead of "mountains.")

7. (Omitted.)

8. Farther on, he comes in to search for me; At that place, in the west corner of the Dark Mountain Hooghan, behind the dark bear, where my feet lie, where my legs lie, where my body lies, where my mind lies, where my voice lies, where my speech lies, where my power of movement lies; I came in, searching for all these. Farther on, he comes in to search for me; At that place, in the west corner of the Blue Mountain Hooghan, behind the blue bear, . . . Farther on, he comes in to search for me; At that place, in the west corner of the Yellow Mountain Hooghan, behind the yellow bear, . . . Farther on, he comes in to search for me; At that place, in the west corner of the White Mountain Hooghan, behind the white bear, . . .

9. (As in Prayer I, stanza 9, except that "Haashch'ééti'í" is substituted for "Naayéé' Neezghání.")

10. From the door of the Dark Mountain Hooghan, Haashch'ééłti'í returns with me, whirling his dark staff about himself for protection; As the rainbow returns with me and the talking k'eet'áán teaches me, Haashch'ééłti'í returns with me. From the door of the Blue Mountain Hooghan . . . From the door of the Yellow Mountain Hooghan . . . From the door of the White Mountain Hooghan . . .

11–15. (Stanzas 2–6, reversed.)

16. (Omitted.)

17–21. (As in the Lightning Prayer.)

22. "From the Yellow Bear Hooghan, kind feelings will come to you," etc. (as in the Lightning Prayer).

20a–20c. (As in the Lightning Prayer.)

The Great Snake Prayer

1. From the Pollen Hooghan, Haashch'é'éwaan, using his blue staff, comes in to search for me; Using a rock crystal and a talking k'eet'áán, he comes in to search for me.

2. (As in the Thunder Prayer, except that "north" is substituted for "south.")

3–6. (As in the Thunder Prayer.)

7. (Omitted.)

8. Farther on, he comes in to search for me; At that place, in the west corner of the Dark Pollen Hooghan, behind the dark Great Snake, where my feet lie, where my legs lie, where my body lies, where my mind lies, where my voice lies, where my speech lies, where my power of movement lies; I came in, searching for all these. Farther on, he comes in to search for me; At that place, in the west corner of the Blue Pollen Hooghan, behind the blue Great Snake, . . . Farther on, he comes in to search for me; At that place, in the west corner of the Yellow Pollen Hooghan, behind the yellow Great Snake, . . . Farther on, he comes in to search for me; At that place, in the west corner of the White Pollen Hooghan, behind the white Great Snake.

9. (As in the Thunder Prayer.)

10. From the door of the Dark Pollen Hooghan, Haasch'é'éwaan returns with me, whirling his blue staff about himself for protection; As the rainbow returns with me and the talking k'eet'áń teaches me, Haashch'é'éwaan returns with me. From the door of the Blue Pollen Hooghan . . . From the door of the Yellow Pollen Hooghan . . . From the door of the White Pollen Hooghan . . .

11–15. (As in the Thunder Prayer.)

16. (Omitted.)

17–21. (As in the Thunder Prayer.)

22. "From the White Snake Hooghan, kind feelings will come to you as you go about in life, my grandchild!" he says to me as he sits down beside me. "Guided by these things, you shall live on, respected everywhere, my grandchild!" he says to me as he sits down beside me; "Guided by these things, you shall find protection in all places as you live on, my grandchild!" he says to me as he sits down beside me; "Guided by these things, people everywhere will refuse to part with you, my grandchild!" he says to me as he sits down beside me.

20a–20c. (As in the Thunder Prayer, where the following two lines are added:) Blessed again it has become, Blessed again it has become, Blessed again it has become, Blessed again it has become!

PRAYER OF EMERGENCE FROM THE LOWER REGIONS

Part I

1. From the center of the earth, Naayéé' Neezghání, using his dark staff, comes in to search for me; With lightnings flashing before him, with lightnings flashing behind him, he comes in to search for me; Using a rock crystal and a talking k'eet'áán, he comes in to search for me.

2. At Emergence Place, he comes in to search for me, farther on, he comes in to search for me; Beyond that place, through a dark earth, Naayéé' Neezghání, using his dark staff, comes in to search for me; With lightnings flashing before him, with lightnings flashing behind him, he comes in to search for me; Using a rock crystal and a talking k'eet'áán, he comes in to search for me; Farther on, he comes in to search for me; Beyond that place, through two blue earths, Naayéé' Neezghání, using his dark staff, comes in to search for me; With lightnings flashing before him, with lightnings flashing behind him, he comes in to search for me; Using a rock crystal and a talking k'eet'áán, he comes in to search for me; Farther on, he comes in to search for me; Beyond that place, through three yellow earths, Naayéé' Neezghání, using his dark staff, comes in to search for me; With lightnings flashing before him, with lightnings flashing behind him, he comes in to search for me; Using a rock crystal and a talking k'eet'áán, he comes in to search for me. Farther on, he comes in to search for me; Beyond that place,

71

through four white earths, Naayéé' Neezghání, using his dark staff, comes in to search for me; With lightnings flashing before him, with lightnings flashing behind him, he comes in to search for me; Using a rock crystal and talking k'eet'áán, he comes in to search for me.

3. Farther on, he comes in to search for me; Beyond that place, through a dark rock, Naayéé' Neezghání, using his dark staff, comes in to search for me; With lightnings flashing before him, with lightnings flashing behind him, he comes in to search for me; Using a rock crystal and a talking k'eet'áán, he comes in to search for me. Farther on, he comes in to search for me; Beyond that place, through two blue rocks . . . Farther on, he comes in to search for me; Beyond that place through three yellow rocks . . . Farther on, he comes in to search for me; Beyond that place, through four white rocks . . .

4. Farther on, he comes in to search for me; Beyond that place, through a dark wood, Naayéé' Neezghání, using his dark staff, comes in to search for me; With lightnings flashing before him, with lightnings flashing behind him, he comes in to search for me; Using a rock crystal and a talking k'eet'áán, he comes in to search for me; Beyond that place, through two blue woods . . . Farther on, he comes in to search for me; Beyond that place, through three yellow woods . . . Farther on, he comes in to search for me; Beyond that place, through four white woods . . .

5. Farther on, he comes in to search for me; Beyond that place, through a dark grass, Naayéé' Neezghání, using his dark staff, comes in to search for me; With lightnings flashing before him, with lightnings flashing behind him, he comes in to search for me; Using a rock crystal and a talking k'eet'áán, he comes in to search for me. Farther on, he comes in to search for me; Beyond that place, through two blue grasses . . . Farther on, he comes in to search for me; Beyond that place, through three yellow grasses . . . Farther on, he comes in to search for me; Beyond that place, through four white grasses . . .

6. Farther on, he comes in to search for me; Beyond that place, through a dark moss, Naayéé' Neezghání, using his dark staff, comes in to search for me; With lightnings flashing before him, with lightnings flashing behind him, he comes in to search for me; Using a rock crystal and a talking k'eet'áán, he comes in to search for me. Farther on, he comes in to search for me; Beyond that place, through two blue mosses . . . Farther on, he comes in to search for me; Beyond that place, through three yellow mosses . . . Farther on, he comes in to search for me; Beyond that place, through four white mosses . . .

7. Farther on, he comes in to search for me; Beyond that place, through a dark cloud, Naayéé' Neezghání, using his dark staff, comes in to search for me; With lightnings flashing before him, with lightnings flashing behind him, he comes in to search for me; Using a rock crystal and a talking k'eet'áán, he comes in to search for me. Farther on, he comes in to search for me; Beyond that place, through two blue clouds . . . Farther on, he comes in to search for me; Beyond that place, through three yellow clouds . . . Farther on, he comes in to search for me; Beyond that place, through four white clouds . . .

8. Farther on, he comes in to search for me; Beyond that place, through a dark mist, Naayéé' Neezghání, using his dark staff, comes in to search for me; With lightnings flashing before him, with lightnings flashing behind him, he comes in to search for me; Using a rock crystal and a talking k'eet'áán, he comes in to search for me. Farther on, he comes in to search

for me, Beyond that place, through two blue mists . . . Farther on, he comes in to search for me; Beyond that place, through three yellow mists . . . Farther on, he comes in to search for me; Beyond that place, through four white mists . . .

9. Farther on, he comes in to search for me; Beyond that place, through a dark water, Naayéé' Neezghání, using his dark staff, comes in to search for me; With lightnings flashing before him, with lightnings flashing behind him, he comes in to search for me; Using a rock crystal and a talking k'eet'áán, he comes in to search for me. Farther on, he comes in to search for me; Beyond that place, through two blue waters . . . Farther on, he comes in to search for me; Beyond that place, through three yellow waters . . . Farther on, he comes to search for me; Beyond that place, through four white waters . . .

10. Farther on, he comes in to search for me; Beyond that place, at the Muddy Water Hooghan at the cross streams, where a pair of red coyotes lie with heads reversed, Naayéé' Neezghání tosses these aside with his dark staff, and thus he comes inside to search for me; With lightnings flashing before him, with lightnings flashing behind him, he comes in to search for me; Using a rock crystal and a talking k'eet'áán, he comes in to search for me. Farther on, he comes in to search for me; Beyond that place, at the corners by the door of the Muddy Water Hooghan, where a pair of red bluejays lie with heads reversed, Naayéé' Neezghání . . . Farther on, he comes in to search for me; Beyond that place, at the fireplace of the Muddy Water Hooghan, where a pair of red hoot-owls lie with heads reversed, Naayéé' Neezghání . . . Farther on, he comes in to search for me; Beyond that place, at the center of the Muddy Water Hooghan, where a pair of red screech-owls lie with heads reversed, Naayéé' Neezghání . . .

11. Farther on, he comes in to search for me; At that place, in the west corner of the Muddy Water Hooghan, behind the Traveler in Darkness, where my feet lie, where my legs lie, where my body lies, where my mind lies, where my voice lies, where my speech lies, where my power of movement lies, I came in, searching for all these. Farther on, he comes in to search for me; At that place, in the west corner of Muddy Water Hooghan, behind the Whirling Darkness, where my feet lie . . . Farther on, he comes in to search for me; At that place, in the west corner of the Muddy Water Hooghan, behind the Spreading Darkness, where my feet lie. . .

12. "I came searching for you; you and I will begin our return, my grandchild. We two are now leaving, my grandchild," Naayéé' Neezghání says to me; With the talking k'eet'áán in his right hand, he encircles me with it, in a sunwise direction, and places it in my right hand; Encircling me, sunwise, with a rainbow, he turns me, sunwise, towards himself; "We two will now start back, my grandchild," he says to me; "We two are now leaving, my grandchild," he says to me as I return to stand upon the rainbow.

13. From the west corner of the Muddy Water Hooghan, Naayéé' Neezghání returns with me, whirling his dark staff about himself for protection; With lightnings flashing behind him, with lightnings flashing before him, he returns with me; As the rainbow returns with me and the talking k'eet'áán teaches me, Naayéé' Neezghání returns with me. Farther on, he returns with me; From the center of the Muddy Water Hooghan . . . Farther on, he returns with me; From the fireplace of the Muddy Water Hooghan . . . Farther on, he returns with me; From the

corners by the door of the Muddy Water Hooghan . . . Farther on, he returns with me; From the door of the Muddy Water Hooghan . . .

14. Farther on, he returns with me; Farther on, past the door of the Muddy Water Hooghan, through four white waters, Naayéé' Neezghání returns with me, whirling his dark staff about himself for protection; With lightnings flashing behind him, with lightnings flashing before him he returns with me; As the rainbow returns with me and the talking k'eet'áán teaches me, Naayéé' Neezghání returns with me. Farther on, he returns with me; Through three yellow waters . . . Farther on, he returns with me; Through two blue waters . . . Farther on, he returns with me; Through a dark water . . .

15. Farther on, he returns with me; Through four white mists, Naayéé' Neezghání returns with me, whirling his dark staff about himself for protection; With lightnings flashing behind him, with lightnings flashing before him, he returns with me; As the rainbow returns with me and the talking k'eet'áán teaches me, Naayéé' Neezghání returns with me. Farther on, he returns with me; Through three yellow mists . . . Farther on, he returns with me; Through two blue mists . . . Farther on, he returns with me; Through a dark mist . . .

16. Farther on, he returns with me; Through four white clouds, Naayéé' Neezghání returns with me, whirling his dark staff about himself for protection; With lightnings flashing behind him, with lightnings flashing before him, he returns with me; As the rainbow returns with me and the talking k'eet'áán teaches me, Naayéé' Neezghání returns with me. Farther on, he returns with me; Through three yellow clouds . . . Farther on, he returns with me; Through two blue clouds . . . Farther on, he returns with me; Through a dark cloud . . .

17. Farther on, he returns with me; Through four white mosses, Naayéé' Neezghání returns with me, whirling his dark staff about himself for protection; With lightnings flashing behind him, with lightnings flashing before him, he returns with me; As the rainbow returns with me and the talking k'eet'áán teaches me, Naayéé' Neezghání returns with me. Farther on, he returns with me; Through three yellow mosses . . . Farther on, he returns with me; Through two blue mosses . . . Farther on, he returns with me; Through a dark moss . . .

18. Farther on, he returns with me; Through four white grasses, Naayéé' Neezghání returns with me, whirling his dark staff about himself for protection; With lightnings flashing behind him, with lightnings flashing before him, he returns with me; As the rainbow returns with me and the talking k'eet'áán teaches me, Naayéé' Neezghání returns with me. Farther on, he returns with me; Through three yellow grasses . . . Farther on, he returns with me; Through two blue grasses . . . Farther on, he returns with me; Through a dark grass . . .

19. Farther on, he returns with me; Through four white woods, Naayéé' Neezghání returns with me, whirling his dark staff about himself for protection: With lightnings flashing behind him, with lightnings flashing before him, he returns with me; As the rainbow returns with me and the talking k'eet'áán teaches me, Naayéé' Neezghání returns with me. Farther on, he returns with me; Through three yellow woods . . . Farther on, he returns with me; Through two blue woods . . . Farther on, he returns with me; Through a dark wood . . .

20. Farther on, he returns with me; Through four white rocks, Naayéé' Neezghání returns with me, whirling his dark staff about himself for protection; With lightnings flashing behind him, with lightnings flashing before him, he returns with me; As the rainbow returns with me and the talking k'eet'áán teaches me, Naayéé' Neezghání returns with me. Farther on, he

returns with me; Through three yellow rocks . . . Farther on, he returns with me; Through two blue rocks . . . Farther on, he returns with me; Through a dark rock . . .

21. Farther on, he returns with me; Through four white earths, Naayéé' Neezghání returns with me, whirling his dark staff about himself for protection; With lightnings flashing behind him, with lightnings flashing before him, he returns with me; As the rainbow returns with me and the talking k'eet'áán teaches me, Naayéé' Neezghání returns with me. Farther on, he returns with me; Through three yellow earths . . . Farther on, he returns with me; Through two blue earths . . . Farther on, he returns with me; through a dark earth . . .

22. From Emergence Place Naayéé' Neezghání returns with me, whirling his dark staff about himself for protection; With lightnings flashing behind him, with lightnings flashing before him, he returns with me; As the rainbow returns to that place with me and the talking k'eet'áán teaches me, Naayéé' Neezghání returns with me.

23. Farther on, he returns with me; Farther this way, from the ladder's first rung, Naayéé' Neezghání returns with me, whirling his dark staff about himself for protection; With lightnings flashing behind him, with lightnings flashing before him he returns with me; As the rainbow returns to that place with me and the talking k'eet'áán teaches me, Naayéé' Neezghání returns with me. Farther on, he returns with me; Farther this way, from the ladder's second rung . . . Farther on, he returns with me; Farther this way, from the ladder's third rung . . . Farther on, he returns with me; Farther this way, from the ladder's fourth rung . . . Farther on, he returns with me; Farther this way, from the ladder's fifth rung . . . Farther on, he returns with me; Farther this way, from the ladder's sixth rung . . . Farther on, he returns with me; Farther this way, from the ladder's seventh rung . . . Farther on, he returns with me; Farther this way, from the ladder's eighth rung . . . Farther on, he returns with me; Farther this way, from the ladder's ninth rung . . . Farther on, he returns with me; Farther this way, from the ladder's tenth rung . . . Farther on, he returns with me; Farther this way, from the ladder's eleventh rung . . . Farther on, he returns with me; Farther this way, from the ladder's twelfth rung . . .

24. Farther on, he returns with me; Farther this way, at the Emergence Rim, Naayéé' Neezghání appears with me, whirling his dark staff about himself for protection; With lightnings flashing behind him, with lightnings flashing before him, he appears with me; As the rainbow returns to that place with me and the talking k'eet'áán teaches me, Naayéé' Neezghání returns with me. Farther on, he returns with me; Farther this way, from the summit of Emergence Mountain . . . Farther on, he returns with me; Farther this way, from the summit of Chief Mountain . . . Farther on, he returns with me; Farther this way, from the summit of Rain Mountain . . . Farther on, he returns with me; Farther this way, from the summit of Corn Mountain . . . Farther on, he returns with me; Farther this way, from the summit of Pollen Mountain . . . Farther on, he returns with me; Farther this way, from the summit of Cornbeetle Mountain . . . Farther on, he returns with me; Farther this way, from the summit of Old Age Mountain . . . Farther on, he returns with me; Farther this way, from Old Age Hooghan, Naayéé' Neezghání returns with me, whirling his dark staff about himself for protection; With lightnings flashing behind him, with lightnings flashing before him, he returns with me; As the rainbow returns to that place with me and the talking k'eet'áán teaches me, Naayéé' Neezghání returns with me.

25. Farther on, he returns with me; Farther this way, from the center of the wide cornfield, Haashch'éélti'í returns with me, whirling his dark staff about himself for protection; Blue, small birds sing before me, Cornbeetle sings behind me, as Haashch'éélti'í returns with me; As the rainbow returns to that place with me and the talking k'eet'áán teaches me, Haashch'éélti'í returns with me. Farther on, he returns with me; Farther this way, from the center of Pollen Boy's hooghan . . . Farther on, he returns with me; Farther this way, from the center of Cornbeetle Girl's hooghan . . .

26. Farther on, he arrives with me; From there to where my hooghan first comes in sight, Haashch'éélti'í arrives with me, whirling his dark staff about himself for protection; Blue, small birds sing before me, Cornbeetle sings behind me, as Haashch'éélti'í arrives with me; As the rainbow arrives at that place with me, and the talking k'eet'áán teaches me, Haashch'éélti'í arrives with me. Farther on, he arrives with me; From there to the path to my hooghan . . . Farther on, he arrives with me; From there to the door of my hooghan . . . Farther on, he arrives with me; From there to the corners by the door of my hooghan . . . Farther on, he arrives with me; From there to the fireplace of my hooghan . . . Farther on, he arrives with me; From there to the center of my hooghan . . . Farther on, he arrives with me; From there to the west corner of my hooghan . . .

27. "This is your home, my grandchild!" he says to me as he sits down beside me; "I have returned with you to your home, my grandchild!" he says to me as he sits down beside me; "Upon the pollen figure I have returned to sit with you, my grandchild!" he says to me as he sits down beside me. "Your home is yours again . . . Your fire is yours again . . . Your food is yours again . . . Your resting place is yours again . . . Your feet are yours again . . . Your legs are yours again . . . Your body is yours again . . . Your mind is yours again . . . Your voice is yours again . . . Your speech is yours again . . . Your power of movement is yours again . . . This enables you to live on in blessing . . .

28. "Whatever makes it blessed before me, that shall make it blessed before you, my grandchild!" he says to me as he sits down beside me; Whatever makes it blessed behind me . . . Whatever makes it blessed below me . . . Whatever makes it blessed above me . . . Whatever makes it blessed all around me . . . Whatever makes my speech blessed, that shall make your speech blessed, my grandchild!" he says to me as he sits down beside me; "Whatever enables me to live long, that shall enable you to live long, my grandchild!" he says to me as he sits down beside me; "Whatever enables me to live happily, that shall enable you to live happily, my grandchild" he says to me as he sits down beside me; "Blessed again it has become, blessed again it has become!"

Part II

Like Part I, except that "Tóbájíshchíní" and "blue staff" are substituted for "Naayéé' Neezghání" and "dark staff" throughout. In Stanza 2: "sky" is substituted for "earth." In Stanza 25: "before me" and "behind me" are reversed.

The additional stanzas, 20a, 20b, and 20c, in the fourth part of Prayer I may be included here, and the prayer ended with the four repetitions of "Blessed again it has become!"

PRAYER FOR PROTECTION

1. Dark great snake, arise to protect me with your dark flint shoes! Arise to protect me with your dark flint leggings! Arise to protect me with your dark flint garment! Arise to protect me with your dark flint hat! With your dark bow, your dark arrow, your dark flint knife, with these you shall arise to protect me! Then I can arise behind you, then I shall be recovered behind you, then I am fully restored behind you! Dangerous beings have not found me, dangerous beings have not found me! Blue great snake, arise to protect me with your blue flint shoes! Arise to protect me with your blue flint leggings! Arise to protect me with your blue . . . Yellow great snake, arise to protect me with your yellow flint shoes! Arise to protect me with your yellow flint leggings! Arise to protect me with your yellow . . . White great snake, arise to protect me with your white flint shoes! Arise to protect me with your white flint leggings! Arise to protect me with your white . . .

Dangerous beings have not found me, dangerous beings have not found me! Dangerous beings have not found me, dangerous beings have not found me![45]

2. Dark great bear, arise to protect me with your dark flint shoes! Arise to protect me with your dark flint leggings! Arise to protect me with your dark flint garment! Arise to protect me with your dark flint hat! With your dark bow, your dark arrow, your dark flint knife, with these you shall arise to protect me! Then I can arise behind you, then I shall be recovered behind you, then I am fully restored behind you! Dangerous beings have not found me, dangerous beings have not found me! Blue great bear, arise to protect me with your blue flint shoes! Arise to protect me with your blue flint leggings! Arise to protect me with your blue . . . Yellow great bear, arise to protect me with your yellow flint shoes! Arise to protect me with your yellow flint leggings! Arise to protect me with your yellow . . . White great bear arise to protect me with your white flint shoes! Arise to protect me with your white flint leggings! Arise to protect me with your white . . .

Dangerous beings have not found me, dangerous beings have not found me! Dangerous beings have not found me, dangerous beings have not found me!

3. Dark thunder, arise to protect me with your dark flint shoes! Arise to protect me with your dark flint leggings! Arise to protect me with your dark flint garment! Arise to protect me with your dark flint hat! With your dark bow, your dark arrow, your dark flint knife, with these you shall arise to protect me! Then I can arise behind you, then I shall be recovered behind you, then I am fully restored behind you! Dangerous beings have not found me, dangerous beings have not found me! Blue thunder, arise to protect me with your blue flint shoes! Arise to protect me with your blue flint leggings! Arise to protect me with your blue . . . Yellow

---

[45]Here the patient blows his breath out, saying "Puh!" This is done at the end of each stanza.

77

thunder, arise to protect me with your yellow flint shoes! Arise to protect me with your yellow flint leggings! Arise to protect me with your yellow . . . White thunder, arise to protect me with your white flint shoes! Arise to protect me with your white flint leggings! Arise to protect me with your white . . .

Dangerous beings have not found me, dangerous beings have not found me! Dangerous beings have not found me, dangerous beings have not found me!

4. Dark wind, arise to protect me with your dark flint shoes! Arise to protect me with your dark flint leggings! Arise to protect me with your dark flint garment! Arise to protect me with your dark flint hat! With your dark bow, your dark arrow, your dark flint knife, with these you shall arise to protect me! Then I can arise behind you, then I shall be recovered behind you, then I am fully restored behind you! Dangerous beings have not found me, dangerous beings have not found me! Blue wind, arise to protect me with your blue flint shoes! Arise to protect me with your blue flint leggings! Arise to protect me with your blue . . . Yellow wind, arise to protect me with your yellow flint shoes! Arise to protect me with your yellow flint leggings! Arise to protect me with your yellow . . . White wind, arise to protect me with your white flint shoes! Arise to protect me with your white flint leggings! Arise to protect me with your white . . .

Dangerous beings have not found me, dangerous beings have not found me! Dangerous beings have not found me, dangerous beings have not found me!

5. Dark great star, arise to protect me with your dark flint shoes! Arise to protect me with your dark flint leggings! Arise to protect me with your dark flint garment! Arise to protect me with your dark flint hat! With your dark bow, your dark arrow, your dark flint knife, with these you shall arise to protect me! Then I can arise behind you, then I shall be recovered behind you, then I am fully restored behind you! Dangerous beings have not found me, dangerous beings have not found me! Blue great star, arise to protect me with your blue flint shoes! Arise to protect me with our blue flint leggings! Arise to protect me with your blue . . . Yellow great star, arise to protect me with your yellow flint shoes! Arise to protect me with your yellow flint leggings! Arise to protect me with your yellow . . . White great star, arise to protect me with your white flint shoes! Arise to protect me with your white flint leggings! Arise to protect me with your white . . .

Dangerous beings have not found me, dangerous beings have not found me! Dangerous beings have not found me, dangerous beings have not found me!

6. Let the dark flint which always arises to protect you, always arise to protect me! Let that which causes you to be invisible also cause me to be invisible! Let that which conceals you also conceal me! Let that which conceals you in darkness also conceal me in darkness! Let that which conceals you in haze also conceal me in haze! Let that which conceals you in glare also conceal me in glare! Behind these I am not found, behind these I am not found! Let the blue flint which always arises to protect you, always arise to protect me! Let that which causes you to be invisible also cause me to be invisible! Let that which conceals . . . Let the yellow flint

which always arises to protect you, always arise to protect me! Let that which causes you to be invisible also cause me to be invisible! Let that which conceals . . . Let the white flint which always arises to protect you, always arise to protect me! Let that which causes you to be invisible also cause me to be invisible! Let that which conceals . . . Behind these I am not found, behind these I am not found! Behind these I am not found, behind these I am not found!

COMMENTARY ON THE SǪ'TSOH (GREAT STAR) MYTH AND PRAYERS

by David P. McAllester

The story concerns a family in remote times when the Navajos subsisted largely on seeds, fruits and small game. They cooked their meat on crude spits and had such meager clothing they could hardly keep warm.

A young man appears. He has magical deer-hunting powers and supplies the family with venison. In gratitude they offer him a wife. He gets permission from his parents and, after the marriage, reveals that he is the son of Tł'iishtsoh, the Great Snake. Now he lives with his wife's family and teaches them the art of preparing buckskin and making clothing. At his suggestion, they trade venison and buckskins with a neighboring tribe in exchange for pottery and jewelry.

When a child is born, the family sets out to visit Tł'iishtsoh and his wife to show them their grandchild. The son of Tł'iishtsoh goes on ahead and disappears from the story. The family follow his tracks but lose the trail at a round lake bordered with rushes. They camp at the lake and search in vain for the son-in-law's tracks. But they also spend a good deal of time playing games and while they are thus diverted the baby disappears. Dǫ'tsoh, the messenger between men and gods, appears and informs them that they are to blame for the baby's loss. Though they received many presents at the time of the daughter's marriage, they did not return presents to the son of Tł'iishtsoh's family.

With supernatural help, the mother of the baby and Older Brother enter a round opening in the center of the lake and come into a beautiful underworld full of flowers and many colored songbirds. But they come upon a threatening figure, a great snake, and the Messenger Wind tells them that Tł'iishtsoh knows where the baby is and must be propitiated with offerings. With the help of Talking God and the Winds, they make offerings and perform a ceremony, the origin of the Wind Chant. In this ceremony, Tł'iishtsoh is passed through ceremonial hoops (tsibąąs) and turns into a youth who was the baby four days before!

The Winds instruct Older Brother, his sister, and the recovered youth in ceremonial procedures and in various strict hunting and dietary taboos. Then the reunited family return to their home.

This part of the myth seems to tell of the transition from primitive hunting and gathering to large-scale hunting. It also tells of the beginnings of intertribal trade - the larger human interdependence. The theme of interdependence is underlined by the punishment for failure to reciprocate wedding gifts, and in the ceremony which recovers the lost baby, heavy responsibilities are laid upon the people in the form of laws of behavior and of diet. A richer life has been gained, not only in material things but also in the ceremonial knowledge whereby man can be restored and recreated, but this gain has been at the cost of a kind of primal innocence and irresponsibility.

This introduction is followed by a series of episodes in which the pattern is always the same. Life is easier but now there are many dangers to be avoided. When instructions and warnings are disregarded, drastic illness results. Supernatural aid is sought and obtained, often with considerable difficulty, after which the patient is cured and a new ceremonial has been brought to mankind.

Older Brother and Younger Brother have so far been unsuccessful hunters. Now Older Brother does kill a deer, but breaking a taboo, he eats intestine which changes into a snake and causes his stomach to swell terribly. With the help of Do'tsoh, the messenger fly, Younger Brother learns the very complicated way to make a proper offering and persuade the Winds to come and cure his brother.

Next, Older Brother kills and eats a snake and is himself turned into a snake. At this time, the youth whose father was the son of Tł'iishtsoh, the Great Snake, is revealed, by Do'tsoh, to be "Nourished-by-the-growth-of-the-Earth Boy." With the earth-wisdom inherited from his snake kin, Earth Boy leads a group of supernatural powers to the cave hooghan of Tł'iishtsoh. Fire God and Water God force Tł'iishtsoh to give back Older Brother and restore him to human shape. By the rites of restoration, mankind learns the Evil-Chasing ceremony. And with this ceremony come further responsibilities and laws.

Again Older Brother breaks a taboo and kills a woodrat. For this transgression he is injured in the ankle by one of the wind powers. Earth Boy suggests Yellow Wind as the healer this time and from the ceremonial, further knowledge, including the power of divination, and further laws and restrictions come to the people.

But Older Brother "was the ancestor of those who never do what they are told, and always do what they are told not to do." He now breaks another taboo: he shoots a left-turning whirlwind that got in his way and thereby he incurs the wrath of the great Níyoltsoh, the Cyclone. Older Brother realizing his danger, is frightened and begs for help, but Earth Boy tells him that now no one can save him but himself. As the roaring Cyclone approaches, the embodiment of the new and frighteningly dangerous world, Older Brother at last finds courage and resourcefulness. He performs various rituals and goes to meet the Cyclone alone.

The Cyclone is stopped at zigzag and straight lines drawn in the earth with a flint. The great wind changes into a man who says, "I was not so big after all. You have more power than I have. Now if you will restore my son whom you have killed, I will teach you three ceremonial songs."

Now for the first time, Older Brother appears in the role of ceremonial practitioner. He restores Left-turning Wind to life. He has finally faced the result of his rashness and found maturity and power. This part of the story is the source of the larger Wind Chant Myth[46]

---

[46]Collected in the 1920s from Hasteen Klah (Hastiin Tł'aai)— by Mary C. Wheelwright.

where the hero undergoes a similar prolonged series of experiments in healing the after-effects of lawlessness.

In the present story, so far, we have seen the awakening of man to greater possibilities and responsibilities. The basic vital force portrayed by the snake world has started man on his way, and we see Older Brother struggling through a world made complicated and difficult. Learning by experience he begins to know the ceremonies and laws that give him control of his universe and himself. Older Brother represents man's control of animal vitality but this is as far as Older Brother goes. We are to see man betrayed by animal vitality and moving on to still another plane of awareness and control.

Younger Brother Visits the Sky

The story now shifts to Younger Brother. At first he begins preparations for a large ceremony to be given over Older Brother to remove the harmful influences of the latter's many misfortunes. A mysterious stranger keeps visiting Younger Brother's wife, ostensibly to inquire for him. The stranger and Younger Brother meet and the stranger, who is revealed as Coyote, suggests that they go eagle hunting. He promises to donate eagle plumes for the ceremony and help find a suitable medicine man, always a major worry in arranging ceremonies. When Younger Brother climbs a steep rock to the eagles' nest it turns out that he has been tricked by Coyote. The birds are crows painted with white earth to look like young eagles and as Coyote mocks Younger Brother, "How pretty your eagles are going to be!" the rock grows upward until it reaches a circular opening in the sky. Now Coyote returns to Younger Brother's home and appropriates his wife and family.

In a nice balance of motif, Younger Brother enters a new world, the sky, as Older Brother and his sister earlier entered a new world, the underworld, via a dramatic sexual symbolism. But instead of a nature world of flowers and songbirds, we now have a sky world very highly charged with danger and peopled with hostile birds of prey and infinitely powerful Star People. The focus of this world is on two concentric circles of long hooghans in the sacred colors. The inner circle is inhabited by hawks and eagles and the outer circle is inhabited by the Star People. In the black hooghan of the Black Star People lives Sǫ'tsoh, the Great Star, who becomes the teacher of Younger Brother. And now begins a long apprenticeship in ceremonial learning.

At first Younger Brother makes a false start. He disregards warnings and revisits the hole by which he entered the sky. He feels lonely. Perhaps at this moment there is the danger that he will try to abandon his arduous enterprise. Suddenly he is pinned down by a great rock. He has been trapped by the Tsénoolch'óshii. Only the efforts of his friends, the Star People, can persuade the Wren to let him go, and then only on condition that he learn certain ritual songs to be used in future ceremonials.

But after this adventure, Younger Brother moves to a higher plane of learning than the mistake-punishment-lesson sequence followed by Older Brother. In four dramatic episodes, he learns the power of bees, wasps, the rock wren and the Left-turning Wind by observation and the intervention of his own power. Though he is warned of danger in each case by his friends, the Star People, he insists on accompanying the eagles and hawks on raids against the four powers named above. Even the unfriendly birds warn him of extreme danger, indeed certain death, and refuse to allow him on their war parties. But each time, Younger Brother follows the raiders, observes the power of the bees, wasps, the rock wren and Left-turning Wind as they defeat the eagles and hawks, and then by magic or medicine, conquers these powers after the birds have fled. He restores the slain birds by the same means and then shows the warring factions that there is no need for conflict between them.[47]

In most cases he finds a beneficent use for the conquered power. The bees, with their deadly stings removed, are dropped down to earth and bee medicine is bequeathed to the world. So also are wasp medicine and rock medicine. From the restored eagles and hawks he takes prized downy feathers which are to be used in later ceremonials. And all of this time, back on earth, his nephew, Earth Boy, knows what is happening and knows why Younger Brother disregards warnings and has these adventures. The Star People are testing him, so as to prepare him for initiation into their wisdom. The Spirit Wind (symbol of inspiration), all unknown to Younger Brother is prompting him to seek out these experiences.

Now Sǫ'tsoh, the Great Star, is revealed in his role as medicine man and teacher. He instructs Younger Brother in the ceremonial use of the various plants used in the encounters with the four powers and teaches him the additional properties and rites which comprise the Great Star Chant.

He tells Younger Brother that when he returns to earth the Spirit Wind will enter his body and speak to him in dreams. He will also receive warnings to pay attention and wait for council by means of certain symptoms such as nervous twitchings and hiccups. In dreams the Spirit Wind can make us hear, but when we are awake our own thoughts get in the way so that we require these warnings. Then for four years Younger Brother helps in the performance of the Great Star Chant given for the sick Bird People, first by the Black Star, then the Blue Star, then the Yellow Star, and finally by the White Star. In each case the apprenticeship lasts for a full year.

Younger Brother Returns to Earth

Younger Brother's return to earth is a portrayal of rebirth enacted amidst impressive manifestations of the powers of nature. The Star People give him clouds of the sacred colors, lightnings, sacred fat for ceremonial use and stars for use in divination. Dressed in their flint armor, all the stars assemble for Younger Brother's departure from the sky. Sǫ'tsoh lets fall a black cloud which hovers just below the hole in the sky. Then Blue Star, Yellow Star and White Star drop clouds of blue, yellow, and white. These clouds constitute four stages reaching from the sky to the earth. Younger Brother leaves the sky and travels from stage to stage on three kinds of lightning and the rainbow while all the stars shake down powder to form a mist and conceal Younger Brother's arrival from the people of the earth.

---

[47]This emphasis on peace and conciliation is unusual in Navajo mythology.

He lands near the place of his departure four years before. He looks for his family at his old home but finds it deserted. The fire poker falls from over the door and tells him to seek his family to the south. This Younger Brother does, and then goes south again, then west, then north, and finally to the east. In each direction he finds a deserted hooghan and each time is directed on by the fire poker,[48] until he finds his wife and two sons in the hooghan to the east.

When he enters and sits down, his family are too overwhelmed to speak. The place smells like a Coyote den. Soon they hear Coyote calling contemptuously and vaingloriously from a distance, "Gland Eater, come and take in the kill!" Younger Brother prevents his sons from obeying the insulting demands of Coyote.[49] Coyote dashes in angrily, carrying four field mice. At the sight of Younger Brother he lays down the mice and sits down without a word.

Now it is Younger Brother's turn to repay the mocking question of Coyote. He asks, "Do you like this place? Do you like to stay here?" Coyote, can only answer, "Yes," and he swallows the ceremonial fat Younger Brother hands him. But now the trickster is tricked. The fat was wrapped around the star given Younger Brother by Sǫ'tsoh and Coyote rushes out of the hooghan and dies in agony.[50] Younger Brother then kills the two younger coyotes and withdraws to an uncontaminated place where he camps for the night. Thus Coyote, the personification of the unstable, half-divine vitality of the earth is overcome by sky-force. In a sense it is self-destruction since it was Coyote himself who sent Younger Brother up to the sky to obtain this power.

The Realization of Sky Power

The remainder of the myth tells of the long process of making the sky power a reality of earth. This is accomplished by the performance of a series of ceremonies which are learned and preserved for the people by Younger Brother's family. First comes the purification from the influence of Coyote. There are four days of preparation, including the building of a sacred hooghan, the use of emetics and the construction of sacred tsibąąs. On the fourth day, Sǫ'tsoh appears and tells the people the Coyote and his sons have come to life again, through the agency of the power in the living creatures of the earth, and also with the help of those creatures which Younger Brother had rendered beneficent and sent down to earth from the sky. Thus, it might be said, animal vitality maintains itself and coexists with the more highly organized vitality of man, the sky-instructed. Sǫ'tsoh tells Younger Brother he will return on the fourth day of the Great Star Chant and now this ceremony is given for the first time on earth. In this first performance Younger Brother's wife and two sons are the patients, but they

---

[48]This is the reason that medicine men always begin a ceremony today by preparing a fire poker. The poker is a symbol of daily necessity to man and is therefore considered almost human.

[49]The humble role of Younger Brother's two sons is an interesting recapitulation of the ignominy of Younger Brother and Older Brother four years before when they were unsuccessful hunters and carried in the kill for their nephew, Earth Boy.

[50]By Navajo customs, death must take place outside of the hooghan, if possible.

are also assistants and learners. For the first three days, ceremonial plaques are set up and the sandpaintings of Black Star (Sǫ'tsoh), the Blue Star and the Yellow Star are made. On the culminating fourth day, all Younger Brother's family arrive. The elaborate construction of the White Star sandpainting and the painting of the bodies of the patients takes place with the family's help. At the evening meal Younger Brother eats earth food with the others for the first time. Until now he has eaten apart and has taken only sky food that he had brought with him. By the purification and ceremony the people as a whole have been raised to a level near enough to that of sky-force so that this force in Younger Brother can no longer be weakened or contaminated.[51]

Now Sǫ'tsoh and the other Star People arrive and join all night in the singing. On the next day, Sǫ'tsoh in his role of father to Younger Brother[52] instructs the people in the responsibilities that go with the new power. By virtue of giving his wife ceremonial treatment, Younger Brother is now related to her and may not approach her again as a wife. Never again may a medicine man give a ceremonial for a member of his immediate family. The two divining stars brought by Younger Brother from the sky are to be given to his sons and the ceremonial fat is to be given to his former wife.

As in the case of the marriage of the son of Tł'iishtsoh at the beginning of the story, the principle of reciprocity is involved. Since there was nothing to give to the medicine man in payment for the ceremony, Younger Brother is to be taken back to the sky. He is now dressed in flint armor and takes on the physical appearance of the Star People.

The Sacred Company Journey for Power

The Star People, Younger Brother and his older son now journey to the east to the home of Coyote. Coyote gives them power and, irrepressible, announces that he wants the woman back again. The Star People announce that there must always be three kinds of people, Snake Men, Coyote Men and Star Men, and that only trouble would come from the crossing of these classes. Here the three kinds of vital forces are clearly stated and one realizes that this, after all, is the meaning of the entire myth. The Snake is the awakening, the Coyote is man's animality and the Star is man's spirituality.

Now the sacred company journeys in the four directions and further ceremonial knowledge is acquired. Younger Brother's older son learns the origin of the Great Star Chant and reviews all the ritual under the tutelage of Sǫ'tsoh's son, in the east. Next the younger son is taken to the south where he learns about ceremonial equipment and is taught a prayer and three songs. Younger Brother's former wife is taken to the west and learns ceremonies and prayers. The older son is then taken to the north and learns prayers and ceremonial detail at the Crystal Hooghan.

---

[51]This suggests the food laws of India.

[52]The medicine man usually assumes a kinship relationship to his apprentice, and also to his patients, in present-day Navajo practice.

In this second journey for power the Star People and Younger Brother take only the older son. The powers are obtained from water beings and the quest culminates in a battle with White Thunder who lives in an Ice Hooghan in the north. The myth of the Hail Chant has its origin in this part of the story.

The third journey for power is for the benefit of the younger son. He is taken to the four sacred mountains and learns ceremonial detail from the Winds and Thunders living there. Again there is trouble with White Thunder in the north, but he is conquered and yields his power. On the return, Sǫ'tsoh tells the people that the Thunders are now friendly and will not harm mankind so long as the laws are kept.

On the fourth journey for power, both of Younger Brother's sons go. They travel in the four directions and learn ceremonies from the four Winds and their animal associates: Black Wind and Rock Wren; Blue Wind and Tł'iishtsoh, the Great Snake; Yellow Wind and Gila Monster; White Wind and all sorts of pretty songbirds. On their return they are told that there is one more journey to be made.

On the fifth and last journey for power, both sons and their mother go with the sacred company. First they visit Salt Woman in the north. They have to fight her guards, the red and black ants; from the defeated ants they learn power and ceremonials. Next they try to visit Tééhołtsódii (Water Monster) but first have to defeat his grey snake guards. Then they learn from Water Monster the great prayer of invocation and liberation. This prayer which requires a day and a night for its recitation, "takes you down under the earth, up to the sky and back again," and thus recapitulates the over-all theme of the Myth of the Great Star. From Water Monsters they also learn songs and the details of a sandpainting for men and another for women. In the south the sacred company visit the Hairy Mountains and have to fight the bears living there. From the defeated bears they learn further ceremonial detail and receive paraphernalia.

In this part of the myth, mankind seems to be receiving a ratification of the sky power from all the vital sources on earth. The trouble-making animal power of Coyote and the related animal power of ants, songbirds, snakes and bears, are tamed and made available for beneficent use. The Ends of the Earth, the Waters, the Mountains, Winds, Thunders, are all visited and all contribute willingly or are vanquished and forced to relinquish their power for the good of the people. The prayer of invocation and liberation seems deliberately designed to take care of any powers that have been overlooked in the rest of the myth. It is used when every other resource fails in a ceremony.

Now in the last scene, the awakening power that brought so much trouble to Older Brother is finally controlled by spiritual power won by Younger Brother and world-ratified, world-acknowledged, world-reinforced. On the very spot where Older Brother faced the Cyclone, all the characters in the story are brought together for the first time in a ceremony called, "Ceremony Given Once," a combination of the two four-day ceremonies, the Wind Chant and the Great Star Chant, all given in one day.[53]

---

[53]This is sometimes done nowadays and in this case the patient's body is decorated with white dots, representing stars, as in the Wind Chant and the Great Star Chant.

The Wind Chant part is done by Older Brother himself and this is followed by the Female Wind Chant performed by his sister. Her son, Earth Boy, learned the Male Wind Chant from his maternal uncle, Older Brother, and this comes down to the people. The former wife of Younger Brother performs the Female Great Star part of the ceremony, the older son does the Male Great Star part, and the younger son does the Evil-chasing Great Star part.

"In the morning at early dawn the singing was finished. Older Brother was told to go out and breathe in the dawn four times, which brings new life into the body."

The ceremony is over. A new dawn has come in the awakening of an awareness of spiritual power. The vital forces of the earth and sky exist in readiness to help recreate that power in time of need.

The Prayers

These are the prayers won by the sacred company of Star People from Tééhoołtsódii, the greatest of the water monsters. The myth states that this great prayer (and its variations), called "Hááhóyátééh," is all-powerful.

"It can take you down under the earth, up to the sky, and back to the earth again. It is in two parts, one goes down to the Spirits under the earth, and one up to the sky. It is used when all else fails in a ceremony." (See page 54.)

In the first prayer, the Prayer of Invocation and Liberation, the powerful figure of Naayéé' Neezghání, Enemy Slayer, comes to "search for me." As in much of Navajo ceremonial poetry, the pronoun is general. It refers to the medicine man who sings, to the patient for whose sake this power is summoned, to the audience, friends and family who are present at the ceremony. Everyone who hears the prayer shares in the power of the invocation. Perhaps they all share the role of Earth Boy, the grandson of Tł'iishtsoh, the Great Snake. It was Earth Boy who was imprisoned in the underworld and then released by the gods through the rites which were thus learned by the people and became part of the Great Star Chant.

So, in the invocation part of the prayer, it is to the Earth Boy in all of us that Naayéé' Neezghání makes his impressive descent. With his dark staff and the dread evil-chasing power of lightning, he descends through mountains, mists, mosses, and finally water. In the seventh stanza, he flings aside guardians of evil power (coyotes and owls are, particularly, creatures of ill omen to the Navajos) and in the eighth stanza he passes behind three powers of darkness, perhaps the Winds which helped to free Earth Boy, to arrive at the side of his "grandchild."

This affirmation of kinship is of the greatest importance in a culture where clan ties are the paramount bonds between human beings. Now to the protective forces of the dark staff and the lightning are added the healing, supporting powers of the rainbow and the talking k'eet'één which teaches the "grandchild," all of us, how to emerge safely from the time and place of great danger.

The second movement of the prayer begins. We return through the waters, mosses, mists, clouds and mountains. But this is not the end of the return. As Ayóó'ánííłnézí said, the prayer "takes you up to the sky." The return goes on to each of the sacred mountains of Navajo mythology (stanza 16) and then to a general blessing of sacred things and the promise of old age. Perhaps here we have a reflection of Younger Brother's ascent to the sky where he learned the power to help the people to all good things and a safe journey through this life to the Old Age Hooghan.

In the third movement, "back to earth," the analogy to the three movements in the myth is completed. Naayéé' Neezghání is replaced by Haasch'ééłti'í, the god who actually assisted the brothers in the Great Star Myth. We come down to the good things of this earth: cornfields, the sacred parts of the hooghan, symbol of safe homecoming, back to fire, food, a resting place and a restored body. There is an enumeration which symbolizes the body-mind unity of Navajo philosophy:

> "Your feet are yours again . . .
> "Your legs are yours again . . .
> "Your body is yours again . . .
> "Your mind is yours again . . .
> "Your voice is yours again . . .
> "Your speech is yours again . . .
> "Your power of movement is yours again . . .
> "Your power to live is yours again . . . ."

The concluding stanza bestows blessing, behind, below, above, all around. And the final blessing is on speech, the essential human act which makes possible not only the transference of power but also the establishment of community itself.

As in much Navajo ritual poetry, the first prayer is in four parts, all balancing and complementing each other. Naayéé' Neezghání with his dark staff in parts 1 and 3 is balanced in parts 2 and 4 by his twin brother Tóbájíshchíní with a blue staff. Black and blue are the colors of north and south, male and female, ill omen and happiness. In stanza two, the direction changes: east, south, west, north, the usual enumeration of the sacred cardinal directions. In stanza eight, Traveler in Darkness and Whirling Darkness alternate with Wind Traveler and Whirling Wind, giving the reader grounds for thinking that these figures of darkness may have some connection with the Winds, in the myth, who helped release Earth Boy from the underworld. In the last stanza, "Whatever makes it blessed behind me," alternates with "Whatever makes it blessed before me."

In part 4, three new stanzas occur before the concluding stanza of general blessing. No. 20a adds an enumeration of relatives to whom the patient has been restored; no. 20b adds precious fabrics, jewels, livestock, springs and mountain ranges to the good things restored to the patient; no. 20c lists the restoration of fields, the powers of fertility, long life and happiness. One sees that the sacred, to the Navajos, is that which is good on this earth. Property, the countryside, and above all, the family—all these are holy, integrated with the supernatural powers which bestowed them, maintain them, and can restore them when they have been lost.

The second prayer is a blessing version of the first, with specific references to thunder, lightning, snakes and bears. It may be used to heal illness caused by any of these forces and it differs from the first prayer chiefly in the deletion of such evil-chasing aspects as the enemy-slaying twins Naayéé' Neezghání and Tóbájíshchíní, lightning protection, and the red guardians of the underworld. This prayer cannot be used apart from the Great Star Chant as can the first prayer. Haashch'éélti'í, who was the principle help in delivering Earth Boy from the power of Tł'iishtsoh, is the chief deity invoked in the prayer.

The third prayer, the Emergence Prayer, is again very much like the first. It, too, is an evil-chasing prayer, and so Naayéé' Neezghání and his twin, the lightning power and the red guardians of the underworld are all included. The journey is more complicated: it includes a wood, the Muddy Water Hooghan, a twelve-rung ladder, and more mountains that must be traversed. But the three great movements are the same—this prayer is simply a variation on the first.

The fourth prayer which Ayóó'áníłnézí associated with the Great Star Chant is quite different from the other three. This is the Prayer for Protection. It is quite short and stresses weapons, armor, concealment and escape.

Tł'iishtsoh is invoked, to protect the patient with his flint garments, his bow and arrows and his knife. Bears, thunder, winds, and stars are similarly invoked and then the prayer calls flint, darkness, haze and glare to hide the supplicant from dangerous beings. The positive powers, the strength and the homecoming of the first three prayers are missing here. The Prayer for Protection seems to belong to the descent portion of the myth before ceremonial knowledge has been learned. The plea is for safety and escape and suggests that the means have not yet been provided for coping with a dangerous world.

CEREMONIAL PROCEDURE
OF THE GREAT STAR CHANT

*Given October 12, 1932 at Newcomb
by Sǫ'tsohjí Hataałii from Ch'ínílí (Chinle)*

FIRST EVENING

The hooghan was blessed by the medicine man. He touched each wall with pollen and then circled the hooghan, on the outside, whirling a bull-roarer to ward off evil influences.

SECOND MORNING

A sweating rite was held. Four stars were marked around the fire in the four directions, and, west of the fire, a round hollow was made in the earth. A small hoop about a foot wide was set up at the west of the hollow with an eagle feather hanging down into the hollow. The hoop was set upright in the earth. There were five small hoops or tsibąąs used in the treatment of the patient. These were pressed to his body while prayers were recited. After the emetic had been taken, women carried out the vomit in bags of sand and left them at the north of the hooghan. Then the assistant came out of the hooghan with the bull-roarer in his hand. He whirled it as he circled outside the hooghan to the east, southwest and north; then he went again to the west, to the south and back to the east and went into the hooghan again. Meanwhile, inside the hooghan they were singing.

Tsibąąs Rite

After the hooghan had been cleaned out and cooled they made five big hoops (tsibąąs), each made of five twigs about 2½ feet long tied butt to tip with two cords of split yucca. They used a claw of a mountain lion to split this yucca. The yucca has to be wound from the root towards

90

the tip. Each hoop when finished was about 3½ feet across. At the top, the last butt and tip was tied with only one cord leaving the ends of the sticks projecting, and the tip was cut off slanting. The first hoop was made of soft oak, colored black; the second hoop was of ma'iidą́ą́', coyote bush, colored blue; the third was of hard oak, colored yellow; the fourth of cedar, colored white; the fifth of rose, which was naturally red.

Four bunches of herbs each containing ch'ildiilyésii, tsé'azhiih, tł'oh nástasii and tóyiką́ą́ł were tied to the upper half of each hoop with yucca fibre; and a long wool wooltą́ą́d string was tied round the upper crossed sticks of each hoop. On the tip of the black hoop a face was painted in white with yellow across the chin; on the blue hoop a yellow face; and on the yellow hoop a blue face with yellow chin; and on all the hoops but the rose hoop, four pairs of stripes were painted on each side of the top in the opposite colors from the hoops. The colors were thus black on white, yellow on blue, and so on.

Outside the hooghan to the east, a path three feet wide and fifty feet long was smoothed flat. At the east end of this path they made four small oval mountains a pace apart; the one to the east was a black mountain edged with a white line which had an opening to the west. West of the black mountain was a blue mountain, with a yellow stripe around it; then a yellow mountain edged with blue; then a white mountain edged with black. In each case the stripe around the mountain had an opening to the west. At the east of the black mountain they made two square black bear tracks with claws pointing to the right, and next to the blue mountain, two rounded blue tracks of the bear with claws pointing to the left; next to the yellow mountain were two yellow square tracks with claws to the right, and next to the white mountains were two rounded tracks with claws to the left. All the tracks were edged with the opposite colors. Then they stuck the black hoop upright, a pace to the westward of the mountains; next they stuck up the blue hoop; next the yellow; then the white and the red hoop. Next along the path to the hooghan they laid two tiny medicine bows, and two prayer wands. Then they made four small mounds and in each stuck two crossed eagle wing feathers. Then still nearer the hooghan they made four more mounds and stuck two bluebird feathers in the top of each mound. Then they made four mounds and stuck two yellowbird feathers on the top of each mound.

Beginning at the easternmost of the mounds with bluebird feathers in them, they scattered a path of white meal over the mounds toward a hooghan and into it, and round the fire to the south ending in a square patch of meal west of the fire. There were four white footsteps on the path leading to this patch of meal.

The patient came in and sat on this white patch of meal and the medicine man put on him cinctures made of skin strings with bear paws hung on them, also two bracelets of the same materials. Then he tied a prayer plume in his hair. The patient came out of the hooghan and went to the eastern end of the path, east of the black mountain, and the medicine man gave him a bunch of prayer sticks to hold, while he himself held a basket and a bunch of eagle feathers. The patient stood on the easternmost bear tracks and said a prayer antiphonally with the medicine man. Then the patient stepped with his left foot over the first mountain and on the next bear tracks, where another prayer was said. Then he stepped over the next mountain, said another prayer, and then over the last mountain and said another prayer. Then the patient stooped under the first of the big hoops and as he did so the assistant put over his head a new piece of cotton cloth, while the medicine man untied the wooltáád cord on the hoop over the patient's head and the assistant pulled down the cotton cloth to the patient's shoulders. The medicine man now sang of the blue hoop and the same procedure was held with the assistant pulling the cotton cloth down to the patient's waist as he untied the wooltáád string over his head. The same procedure was held while passing under the yellow hoop, and the white hoop, and the red. When the patient passed the red hoop the cotton cloth was thrown aside, typifying his shedding his old skin and getting a new body. The patient next stepped, alone, over the two little medicine bows and wands and over the mounds of the eagle feathers, bluebird feathers and yellowbird feathers and walked into the hooghan along the white path. Meanwhile, as soon as the prayers had ended, the assistant whirled the bull-roarer around, as the patient passed west into the hooghan. After him came a woman with a child in her arms and with a big pouch over her shoulder. Then, all the assistants and the medicine man, still singing, and the assistant following with the bull-roarer, went into the hooghan. The patient stepped on the white footsteps, which were rubbed out after his passing, and then he sat down on the white patch west of the fire, while several songs were sung. The medicine man put pollen on the patient's feet, hands, body and head, twice blessing him, gave him pollen to eat and blessed the path to the hooghan. Then he handed his pouch of pollen to us and we blessed ourselves, eating it and touching our heads, and then all the others did likewise.

At about four p.m., a sandpainting of the four star people was begun, and finished just after sunset. There was no rainbow around it and no guardian. Then everyone ate supper.

Wooltáád Rite

In the evening there was a rite of seven wooltáád. The patient sat next to the fire, next to the sandpainting. The bundles around which the wooltáád strings were tied were made of tsé'azhiih, ch'ildiilyésii and tł'oh nástasii and an eagle wing feather, also the two little medicine bows and two reed prayer sticks, which had been used in the morning. After the usual treatment was over, the medicine man took a bunch of eagle wing feathers and touched the ashes in four directions around the fire. Then he waved the feathers over the big bowl of medicine infusion containing fir twigs and other ingredients, chopped up fine, singing as he did this. Then he gave the bowl to the patient, who drank. Everyone else in the hooghan did so too. Then the assistant sprinkled the hooghan and the patient rubbed the infusion over his body.

Then they held the Spruce Dress Rite, tying a long string of yucca fibre with spruce twigs tied to it to each of the patient's big toes, and then winding them sunwise up his legs (two men did this) and crossing the strings on his body twice, then over his shoulders and winding down his arms, ending by tying them to each thumb.

They put over his face a flat mask of spruce, and on the crown of his head tied a bundle of the holy plants and a reed. They stuck an eagle feather upright in the loop over each toe. Then the two assistants were given stone knives and went out of the hooghan. There was singing all this time.

The assistants came in representing Naayéé' Neezghání, and Tóbájíshchíní and the first named cut the strings of spruce off the patient, beginning at his mask and finishing at his feet, while Tóbájíshchíní held the string. Then they cut all the spruce strings into small pieces and Tóbájíshchíní held a bunch of spruce on the patient's head while Naayéé' Neezghání took some ashes and put them on the patient's head and brushed them off with eagle feathers. Tóbájíshchíní did the same and then brushed all the spruce off the patient and the two gods went out carrying the blanket full of spruce. Each person in the hooghan was given an eagle feather, which he held out in front of him, and on each feather was placed a pinch of ashes. The medicine man sang five verses of a song and at a certain phrase towards the end of each verse, everyone in the hooghan blew the ashes on his feather up towards the sky.

At midnight, when the moon was overhead, the patient sat on the north figure of the sandpainting, the medicine man crouched next to him, and four prayers were said to the four directions. They rested between the prayers. Then the sandpainting was erased and taken out.

THIRD DAY

The sweating rite was given as before. After this the big hoops (tsibą́ą́s) were made as before and the same rite was held outside the hooghan as on the day before, except that the path went to the south instead of to the east.

In the afternoon they made the sandpainting of the four star people. The medicine man said that this particular painting should be made on the last day of the ceremony, but on this occasion the order was confused because, when the medicine man arrived, the family of the patient, not knowing the ceremony, had no helpers ready to work on the sandpainting. He gave as the order of sandpainting, first day large star, second day stars, third day star people, and fourth day star people.

In the evening they had the Wooltáád Rite with nine wooltáád bundles, and the Spruce Dress Rite as before, except that instead of using two long strips they used small sections of string. The patient sat on the sandpainting at midnight and prayers were said.

FOURTH DAY

The sweating rite was given as before, followed by the Tsibáás Rite outside at the west of the hooghan. In the evening, twelve wooltáád bundles were used as before and the Spruce Dress Rite was given as before.

FIFTH DAY

The sweating rite was given and the tsibą́ą́s path was constructed at the north side of the hooghan in the morning. At about ten p.m. they began to get ready for the rite of painting the patient. The assistant was a man nearly blind, who carried on his functions by feeling. First, he kneaded some dough in a bowl, while the father of the patient burned some tse' azhiih and other medicine plants and made a good deal of charcoal. This the blind man kneaded into pellets of the dough. The singer who acted as assistant to the medicine man was Asdzáán Hataałii, the woman singer, from Two Grey Hills. She knew the songs well, and carried on the ceremony alone when the medicine man was too busy to sing.

They spread a new cotton cloth at the west of the side of the fire and on it put knives, wooltáád strings, the two medicine cinctures and bracelets made of sinew and animal and eagle claws, the bull-roarer and head plume, and a bowl of medicine infusion. Then they called in the patient, who took off his clothes, and sat facing the east at the north of the cotton cloth with his mother near him. The medicine man began to sing and sent the blind man to whirl the bull-roarer around the outside of the hooghan. Then the medicine man took his bunch of eagle feathers, touched the ashes to the four sides of the fire and waved the feathers over the bowl of infusion, singing as he did so. He went over to the patient and tapped him twice on the soles of his feet with the eagle feathers, and then made a motion upward as if wafting the trouble in his feet away. He performed the same action to his palms, his body, his shoulders, and his head. Afterwards he motioned with his feathers round the south side of the hooghan, and then tapped toward the east, then did the same at the north of the hooghan. Then he treated the patient again in the same way with the feathers, and waved them up and down, to the right and left of him, and then motioned over his head in an ascending spiral towards the sky. He went through this last treatment five times. Then the assistant gave the patient and all in the hooghan the infusion to drink and they rubbed the infusion on their bodies.

The assistant took the pellet of dough and charcoal and made a stripe across the patient's chin. Then he gave some to the mother and other women, who marked their chins in the same way. The assistant then touched the patient on the soles of his feet, palms, body, shoulder, and head. Next he rubbed some dough all over the patient, afterwards rubbing charcoal all over him until he was entirely black from head to foot, while the medicine man was singing. The medicine man then marked the patient all over the body and face with white spots (not as in other ceremonies with double spots, close together). Then he put the medicine cinctures and bracelets of sinew and animal claws on the patient and tied a prayer plume on his head. The assistant put pollen in the patient's shoes and he put them on. He also put on a coral necklace.

At midnight, when we left, they were singing many bear songs and probably treated him later with the wooltáád and medicine bows and other medicine articles during the all-night singing. This was the last night of the ceremony.

THE
COYOTE CHANT

THE MYTH OF MA'II NA'OOLJIŁJÍ
THE COYOTE CHANT

This myth was collected by Mary C. Wheelwright in 1931. It was given by Yoo'íijí Hataałii, who lived near Ganado at that time. He learned the myth from Hastiin Nééz, who lived, until his death in 1919, near Rainbow Bridge. Yoo'íijí Hataałii learned the Coyote Chant from Hashkeh Nani[54] of Keams Canyon, Arizona.

The Myth of The Coyote Chant

Creation of the White Corn People and the Yellow Corn People.
The Separation.
The Leader of the Yellow Corn People becomes a god.
The Leader's nephew guides the people.
The Story of the Hunter (The Leader's Grandnephew Brings Corn
    and the Coyote Chant to the People).
He Follows Coyote tracks to a Sacred Lake.
He enters the Underworld Country of the Coyotes.
He goes to the White House of the Coyote People.
He goes to the Yellow, Blue and Black Houses of the Coyote People.
He Brings Corn and the Coyote Chant to the people.

THE MYTH OF THE COYOTE CHANT

Creation of White Corn People and Yellow Corn People

The story begins on an island in the western ocean[55] when Asdzáán Nádleehé decided to make more people. This was after her sons Naayéé' Neezghání and Tóbájíshchíní had killed the monsters who were destroying mankind. She bathed herself in a white shell and dried

---

[54]This is the transcription of M. C. Wheelwright.
[55]Santa Cruz Island off the coast of Santa Barbara, California.

herself with white corn and yellow corn. Then she took the water in which she had washed and emptied it into the sea. A fog arose, and the white shell and white corn drifted together and made people. They were called Hazlį́į' ("Made Now") and their name was the Yoo'ii Dine'é or Bead People from the white shell out of which they were made. The first two men were made of white corn, and the first two women of white corn; then were made two men of yellow corn and two women of yellow corn; after this were made two white corn boys and girls, and two yellow corn boys and girls. Asdzáán Nádleehé told these people that they must go eastward. The Yellow Corn People traveled on the black cloud and the White Corn People on the gentle rain. The black cloud and the gentle rain guided them across the sea until they got to Naadá'ádziil, or Corn Mountain, where they spent the night. Then they went on to Dził Łahdilt'éhé, Mountain-by-Itself, and spent a second night there. Afterwards they traveled to the second mountain, Dził Nidilt'éhé, then to the third mountain, Dził Tált'éhé, and the fourth mountain, Dził Dįlt'éhé, and spent a night at each mountain. On the fourth mountain the white corn First Man woke at dawn and said that he had had a dream. He told his people that it was a holy dream, and that it was the beginning of his ceremony. On this same night the yellow corn First Man had a dream and told his people about it and said that he knew something was going to happen. The dream of the white corn man was that he was flying with wings, and he was the originator of the Yoo'iijí Hatáál, or Bead Chant. The yellow corn man dreamed that he turned into a white coyote, and that his power came from Náátsʼíílid, the rainbow. After they had told their dreams, the people went on to Níłtsą'dziil, Rain Mountain, and slept there, and then to another Naadą'ádziil, Corn Mountain, and then to Nanise'dziil, which means Everything-that-grows-on-earth Mountain. Then they traveled on the Tá-dádííndziil, Pollen Mountain. There the white corn man dreamed again, and at dawn told his people that he had dreamt of being very high up near a sky world. Yellow corn man dreamed that he was walking toward the east with four rainbows around him, and he said he thought everything would be all right on the journey.

They traveled on and came to Yoo'ídziil, Bead Mountain, and slept there. Then to Nitł'izdziil, Jewel Mountain and then to Tsin Bíil'á, Trees-growing-on-the-side-of-mountain, and there they talked about their dreams and wondered why the dreams came to them. "Does it mean that we must go back, or that we should make offerings to the gods?" And they decided to have the ceremony of Hózhóónjí, or Blessing, over some offerings of turquoise, jet, abalone and white shell. They all made these offerings to Asdzáán Nádleehé and had the Blessing Ceremony over them. They also gave the Blessing Ceremony over the two head men, the white corn man and the yellow corn man. This was the beginning of this ceremony and after they had finished it they were not worried any more about their dreams and felt that all would be well on their journey. All the songs used at that ceremony belonged to Nahasdzáán or Mother Earth.

Then they went on and came to Dook'o'oosłííd (the San Francisco Peaks), and went up to the top whence they could see in every direction. At the north they saw rain far off and at the east a rainbow. The white corn man wanted to go towards the rain at the north and yellow corn man towards Náátsʼíílid, the rainbow. At this place they began to differ in their plans and yellow corn man gave white corn man his ceremonial name and white corn man did the same for yellow corn man. Yellow corn man spoke to white corn man calling him Tsah Oshkinzh,[56] which means "Whatever-he-throws-down-spreads-out-flat" (vomit), and he said, "I think we should go towards the rainbow at the east for if we take this road we would have abundance." White corn man then spoke to yellow corn man and said, "I never thought that you would disagree with me, Tsinh Hodekloch[57] ("He-whose-stomach-trembles-with-hunger").

After this the people went towards the rain at the north and came to Dził Łabáí, Grey Mountain, and found there many kinds of bushes with berries: haashch'éédąą' (coyote bush), also tł'ohts'ósí and tł'ohtsoh and nidídlídii which has seeds good to eat. White corn man told his brother, "We were right in taking this path to the north, if we had taken your path we would have had nothing to eat." Then they decided to get on to Dził Diłhiłii, Darkness Mountain. When they came there, there were many animal people there: all members of the lion and cat families, Násdóíłtsoí, the Mountain Lion and his people. White corn man dreamed in this place that he was to be one of these lion people and yellow corn man dreamed that he was to be one of the Ma'ii or coyote family. Then they went on to Tónaneesdizí, "Where-the-water-goes-round-and-round" (Leupp), where there is a peak, and there they found more animal people of the lion and coyote families, and went on to Naastíín'tsoh, a peak near Black Mountain, where they met more animal people. The people lived on the seeds of plants on their journey.

Then they went to Naatsis'áán, Navajo Mountain, and they stayed four years on the top of the mountain. There were all kinds of food there to eat: didze', didlídii, tsiiłchin, klichee,[58] nahtezh,[59] tł'ohtsoh, tł'ohts'ósí, nidídlídii, and tł'ohlichi'ii. Some of the people went hunting to the north for deer, mountain sheep and other animals. They found they had to go a long way to get the meat, and finally decided to move on further and went along a ridge to a place later called Aghaa'łá. They stayed in this place four years and hunted, and towards Denihootsoh they found antelope and drove them into traps in the canyons. They named this place Aghaa'łą from aghaa' ("wool," or "woolly"), because after cleaning the skins there was much hair and wool accumulated in that place. They made clothes for themselves there.

The Separation

Finally the game began to grow scarce and they decided to move on again. So they went towards Black Mountain to Tódíníishzhee' and from there to Báálók'aa' north of White Cone, Arizona. There they looked about, and they could see at the northeast the Lók'ajígai mountains, and the white corn man said he was going in that direction to follow the rain in valleys. Then they looked towards the east and saw a rainbow towards Tséyi' Canyon (Canyon de

---

[56]This is in the transcription of M. C. Wheelwright.
[57]This is in the transcription of M. C. Wheelwright.
[58]This is in the transcription of M. C. Wheelwright.
[59]This is in the transcription of M. C. Wheelwright.

Chelly) and yellow corn man said he would go that way. So at this place the brothers separated. Yellow corn man, the younger brother, spoke to his older brother and said, "You go your way to Tséít'eezh and take your family with you," and the older brother told his younger brother that he should follow his own way with his family towards Tséyi' Canyon.

The white corn man and his family came to a place called Taahyilk'id, Ridge-which-goes-into-the-water (ten miles north of Chinle), and these people were the originators of the Bead Chant. The People of the Yellow Corn went to a place called Tsé Biná'ez'élí at the mouth of Tséyi' Canyon, and found there many bushes full of berries growing up the canyon, and also there were many bears among the bushes. The White Corn People who went to the north found a lot of seed plants also, and at about sundown they came to Taahyilk'id. There they ground up the seeds and made bread and balls of ground seeds. They ate these before dark and set some before the leader. Also just before dark the Yellow Corn People in the canyon gathered seeds particularly from Ma'iidą́ą́, or coyote bush, and ground this to meal and set the food before their leader. The white corn man said as his food was set before him, "I wonder what my brother is doing tonight. If he were with us he would have plenty to eat, but I am afraid at this time his stomach-is-trembling-with-hunger." At the same time his younger brother was making the same remark about him. So the White Corn and Yellow Corn People separated. Each went their own way and they did not meet again.

The Leader of the Yellow Corn People Becomes a God

The leader of the Yellow Corn or Coyote People and his wife made their fire at a distance from the camp of their family. That evening the Coyote People began to wonder why their leader had not told them where to go the next day and they said, "He does not seem to care for us." They supposed their leader was asleep, though his fire was still burning. Just as they were dropping asleep they heard their leader singing, the first Coyote song. The family talked about this song, as they did not know it, and said, "All through our journey we have never heard him sing before, and he would always build his fire apart with his wife and never told us that he could sing." No one dared go to the leader, and they finally went to sleep. Early in the dawn the people woke and looking towards Tsé Biná'ez'élí they saw a Yé'ii (god) standing facing east. Then they realized that it was their leader and they said, "What is he doing there so early in the morning? Why is he acting like a child?"

Just then he jumped off the rock and came back to his fire from another direction. No one had spoken a word to the leader but now they went to him and asked him why he had sung and why he had been up on the rock. They said, "Are you a child to behave so? You might fall off, you must not do this, but take care of us and be our leader." He said, "My children, I am not behaving like a child. The place where I was at dawn was a holy place. I left my footprints on top of the rock and in time to come our people will pray there and make offerings when they are in distress or need. Help will be given them, and will never fail. I did this for you and for our people to come."

The people talked this over and said they wanted to go on, for they were afraid that their leader might do something strange again. He had brought with him something given by Asdzáán Nádleehé called Tł'iish k'aa', or Snake Arrow, and he carried this as they went up the canyon to a place called Tsénanootł'iizh where there are now zigzag white marks on the rocks. They made camp opposite this place. They built two fires, one for the leader separate from the rest. He came to their fire that night and they talked about where to go and where to get food. They asked his advice. He said, "My children, I am leaving it to you. Up to this time I have been leading you but I have something else now that I must do." Then he went back to his own fire and the people talked together. When they were ready to go to sleep they heard the leader singing again.

When they woke at dawn they saw him climbing on the cliff opposite. He made the zigzag marks there and sang a song of the Yé'ibicheii, and then came back to his own fire as before. The people went to him and asked him why he behaved in this way, and he said, "My children, the place is holy and I left my marks on it, and I left also all that Asdzáán Nádleehé gave me. In time to come when people are in trouble and need rain they should make offerings at this place and they will get what they need. This is why I have done it." But the people did not seem to understand and were suspicious, and talked about where they wanted to go, and said, "If he keeps on doing these things we might lose him."

Then they went along up the canyon and came to a place now called Ch'óhazt'i', "Fir-trees-growing-in-a-row-at-mouth-of-canyon." They camped opposite this place, and made two fires as before. The people went to the leader's fire and asked him what he was going to do now, and he said, "My children, I am not doing these things of my own accord. Since we left Asdzáán Nádleehé to go on our journey I have been given these things to do and my actions come to me from a holy place." In the night the people talked it all over and said, "During our journey from the island we never heard him sing, but at various times he had dreams. From these dreams we have already had a Blessing ceremony and have given offerings, but it did not seem to do us any good." They said to the leader again, "You must take care of us," and they asked him again what made him behave in this way. He said, "My children, I cannot behave differently because I have given myself up to the Holy Ones already." The people talked half the night and heard the leader singing as before, and at dawn they saw him standing on a cliff across the little canyon. They heard him give a song of Haashch'éélti'í, the Talking God, and then he jumped down into the canyon. Where he stepped, fir trees sprang up in his footprints and this gave the name to this place. Then the leader came back to his fire and they questioned him again, and he said, "Don't you believe what I told you before? I have given myself to the Holy People and I won't be long with you. I am doing this for you and the people to come. In the future I will be with you always and will appear in different forms. You have been talking about me for three nights, but after this fourth night you will see me no more."

He told them now for the first time that he was selected by the Holy Ones to give the Coyote Chant, and said, "In the future, when there are lots of people on earth, if they do not give the Coyote Chant they will not live happily. My dreams told me this. In the future when there is drought the White Coyote of the east will howl, for then all the Coyotes over the earth will howl, calling the rain for the people." Then they went on their journey in the canyon and came to Tséniteel and camped nearby, and everything happened as before except that the leader did not sing that night. Early at dawn they saw him again on the top of the cliffs and this time he was dressed as Haashch' éélti' í. He sang and then jumped off the cliff and came up to their fire and pulled off his mask to that they could see that it was their leader. He said, "This is the last time you are going to see me now. I am going to stay in this canyon forever. You children can go on your way and take care of yourselves and go where you like." After these words he turned around and walked toward Tséniteel and as he went he sang Ye' ibicheii songs. Then he walked into the rock.

The Leader's Nephew Guides the People

The people took another leader, the nephew of the first leader, and went up to Lók' ajígai Mountain and spent the night there. They talked about the first chief, saying that he had gone to a holy place. His wife was with them. Next day they picked seeds for food and crossed the mountain and went down to Tsélichíí' Dah' azkání, a tall rock now called "Cheedi" in Red Rock Valley. Then they went toward the San Juan River to Taahdootł' izhi, "Blue-land-goes-into-river," where the Animas and San Juan Rivers meet in the direction of Dziłna' ooditii (Huerfano Peak). They came to that blue land and stopped to pick seeds and spend the night. From there they went on by a ridge leading to Dibé Nitsaa (La Plata Mountains) and spent the night there, and passed by Tónits' ósíkooh, "Narrow-water-canyon," where there were people living in the cliffs. If they had seen them the story would have been different.

Then they went on top of Dibé Nitsaa and spent the night there and at midnight a rainbow appeared over them which was a sign that they should follow it and in the morning it went towards the east. When the first leader left he told them that he would always be with them and when this rainbow appeared they knew that he was with them for the leader had told them that this was the first sign that he would show them. The rainbow went before them to Ch' óyáázh Ashkii at the east of the La Plata Mountains. They stayed there four years, and there the nephew of the present leader married the first leader's wife and their children began another family. They had eight children, four boys and four girls, and they were all born two years apart.

THE STORY OF THE HUNTER
(THE LEADER'S GRANDNEPHEW BRINGS CORN
AND THE COYOTE CHANT TO THE PEOPLE)

He Follows Coyote Tracks to a Sacred Lake

The oldest of these boys when he grew up liked nothing but hunting. He learned the ways of hunting deer, rabbits, mountain sheep, squirrels and antelope, and he was so keen about hunting that he hardly slept. His only weapons were bows and arrows and he spent his nights making them, and putting pinyon gum on the bows and polishing the arrows. He started at dawn on the mountains and at sundown would bring in the game, for his father was growing quite old and depended on him more and more. For four years he hunted.[60]

One night in Nílch'itsoh, the Great-Wind-month (December), about an inch of snow fell. The young man stayed up all night for he wanted to start very early to go trapping, and he left for the hunt before dawn. He went towards Dibé Nitsaa but could not find game. He got lost, and when night came he went into a little cave and took cedar boughs to cover him. Very early in the morning he started again and came to Tsen-koh-oltsin[61] just before sun-up, and saw a coyote track and followed it.

Meanwhile his parents were very much worried because he usually came home every night. They thought he must have frozen or had been eaten by some beast and they did not sleep. His father started in the early morning to try and track him down but as the sun rose the snow melted and there were no tracks. His father searched for him four days and then gave it up as hopeless, but his son was alive.

After the hunter found the coyote track he followed it because he hoped that the coyote might have chased a rabbit into a hole and he would be able to catch it. After a time he stopped and decided to back-track the coyote and came to a canyon where he saw a coyote coming down the other side of the canyon. He went down into the canyon at about sunrise and at the bottom he found the coyote's sign or spoor. Looking at it closely he saw that it was fresh and that there was a kernel of hard white corn in it, and he wondered where this came from in the middle of winter. He went on back-tracking the coyote until he came to a flat place where there was a round pond covered with ice with bulrushes growing round it, and he saw that the tracks of the coyote came out of this pond on the east side. He tried to find where the coyote had lain down or where he had come from so he went all around the pool of ice but only found tracks coming out of it. Then he circled the ice again in a bigger circle and on the west side he found another track leaving the ice, and following this track he found another piece of hard yellow corn in the spoor. He went back to the ice again and found tracks coming out of it at the south, and following this track found blue corn in the spoor. He went back to the ice again and took his bow and searched in the bulrushes. He found other tracks at the north with black corn kernels in the spoor.

He Enters the Underworld Country of the Coyotes

Then he stood at the east of the pool and took his bow and tried to lift up the ice, but it would not move. He tried it from the west, the south and the north, but he could not move it. So he

---

[60]Up to this point, the myth is similar to the version collected earlier from Tsegi-ruhe by Mary C. Wheelwright. Tsegi-ruhe is in the transcription of M. C. Wheelwright.

[61]This is in the transcription of M. C. Wheelwright.

tried again at the east side and the ice lifted. He saw a ladder sticking out of the water underneath.

He wanted to go down the ladder but thought he would freeze; it seemed so cold. Then Níłch'i Biyázhí (who was the first leader in the form of the Messenger Wind) spoke to him and said, "The water is just a covering to the hole. Blow with your breath on it and you can go down." So the hunter blew four times on it and the water went away to one side, and he looked and saw there were four ladders one below the other leading down. So he climbed down the four ladders and as soon as he arrived at the bottom the water closed up overhead.

He turned to the east and saw fields of white hard corn, and turned to the west and there were fields of yellow corn. At the south there were blue cornfields and at the north, black. At the east there was a long white house, at the west a yellow one, at the south a blue one, and at the north a black one. And he saw smoke coming out of the houses and heard the sound of children's voices coming from all of them. He said to himself, "What is this world that I am in? I wonder if these people will be kind enough to feed me?" And he did not know which house to go to. He listened and at the east he heard what the people were saying. The children were roasting corn, and as it popped the children said, "Ma'ii idiizts'ąą'" ("the coyote heard it"), for they were the Coyote People, and then he heard these same words coming from all directions.

He Goes to the White House of the Coyote People

So he went to the white house at the east and on entering it he saw a man colored white who said, "Where did you come from, son-in-law, here is no place for earth people." The hunter told him his story and that he came to find out where the corn had been found in the winter. The Coyote man said, "The tracks that you saw were those of my son going out hunting and it is nearly dark now and he will come back soon. We have heard about your people who came from the island of Asdzáán Nádleehé, and we also know about the first dream that your chief had and this dream was about our Coyote People. The White Coyote that your first chief dreamed about was my son."

Then they made a place for the hunter at the west side of the house and the Coyote man began to tell the hunter the story of the Coyote People, saying that they came from Asdázán Nádleehé long ago. He also said, "Now I see that you come from her also and that you are Yoo'ii Dine'é (Bead People)." Then the Coyote man told the hunter the story of the journey of his own people and about how the first chief had spoken to the hunter in the form of Níłch'i Biyázhí, the Messenger Wind, and had led him to the Coyote People. He said that when the first chief was going to leave his people he told them that he would be with them in different forms. The hunter did not know these things. The Coyote man told the hunter about his people and everything that had happened to him since his birth, and said when he finished, "Now I will make you holy."

At midnight one of the Coyote's sons who had been out hunting toward the west came into the house. He had small game of different kinds with him and they placed it spread out on a sacred doeskin placed on the ground with the head to the east. He said to the hunter, "My son-in-law, you must watch closely what we are going to do now." The young Coyote man who had brought in the game took a small object from his belt and laid it on the skin and said to the hunter, "This is what we get when we go hunting on the earth, and the Earth people pursue us because of this." Then they spread a buckskin on the top of the game with the small object on it, and they all stood at the east of the skin and stepped over it to the west and back again, meanwhile making coyote sounds. The hunter watched carefully and saw that the buckskin began to move. Then the Coyote People stood at the west side and stepped over the skin towards the east and back again, and the buckskin rose higher. Then the Coyote People stood at the south and stepped to the north and back, and the skin rose higher still. Then they stood at the north and stepped toward the south and back and by this time the hunter could see what was underneath the skin. It was a mass of fat. The Coyote man told the hunter that this had grown from the tiny piece of fat which was brought back by the Coyote hunter, and that this fat came from all the food animals belonging to the Earth People and made lean by the pursuit of coyotes. Then the Coyote People uncovered the fat which came from the deer and other game, and all the other Coyote People that lived in the blue, yellow and black houses came and ate some of the fat and then went back to their own homes. The Coyote man told the hunter that this was the way in which they ate and for this reason Earth People do not like coyotes.

He said, "We will give you something to eat also." So he sent two of his beautiful daughters into the cornfield toward the east. They brought home four ears of corn and roasted three on the fire and set them before the hunter. He ate the three ears of corn and kept one. The Coyote man said, "When you get back to the earth take that ear of corn with you and plant it and you will always be able to live on it and increase." After the hunter had eaten this corn they told him again the story of the journey of his own people, and the Coyote man said, "Now you have eaten and learned the history of your people. And now you can sleep, and I will give you both of my daughters." The hunter and the Coyote girls slept together.

At dawn next morning the girls left the hunter and he could overhear their talk with their father in the next room. The father asked whether the hunter had been good to them and they said he was a good Nihookáá' Dine'é or Earth Man. Later in the morning the Coyote man told the hunter not to go too far away to hunt and to take care of his two wives. He said to be careful, as there were lots of bad people about. And he said, "After you have been with us a while longer you can go your own way."

He Goes to the Yellow, Blue, and Black Houses of the Coyote People

The hunter disregarded the warning and went a long way off to the yellow house at the west, and there he found the Yellow Coyote people. They asked him to spend the night there. The chief said that one of his sons was out hunting and was about to come back, and that he wanted the hunter to see what his son would bring. Then Yellow Coyote man told the hunter about the history of his family. After dark the son came in, and they had the same feast of fat as in the east house and also the hunter was given four ears of yellow corn. He ate three ears and kept one to be planted on the earth. He married two Yellow Coyote girls there and in the morning they told their father that he was a fine man.

The Yellow Coyote man warned him not to go further and to take care of his daughters, but again he wandered away and spent the next night at the Blue Coyote's house in the south, where they had the same ceremony of eating the fat. Then he was given four ears of blue corn and kept one to plant on the earth, and he also married two Blue Coyote girls.

The next day he went to the black house at the north, where the same things happened: the eating of the fat, his eating of the corn and keeping one ear to plant on earth, and the marrying of two Black Coyote girls. He also learned how to make images of the coyote for offerings.

Later he went to the yellow, blue and black houses and learned their k'eet'áán offerings there. He also learned the wooltáád ceremony in each of the houses. After he had learned about the ceremonies the Coyote man said, "You have learned everything that we know and before you go we should like to give you the medicine and the pouch for it." So at the east house a five-night ceremony was given for the hunter; this consisted of k'eet'áán offerings but no sandpaintings were made. For five nights they painted the hunter red, spotted him with double white spots all over, and tied a feather to his hair. The Yellow Coyote man at the western house gave a nine-night ceremony for him which included the sweating ceremony inside the hooghan every morning for four days and afterwards sandpaintings for four days. Nowadays on three nights in this ceremony the patient is treated in the wooltáád ceremony by someone wearing a Ye'íbicheii mask. On the last night the patient stands on a buckskin holding ground meal in a basket and three gods, Haasch'éélti'í, Ma'ii, and Haashch'éé Bi'áadii[62] come to the patient and Haasch'éé Bi'áadii holds a shell with corn pollen in it and four eagle tail feathers radiating from the center.

After this ceremony the Blue Coyote man in the south house gave a five-night ceremony over the hunter like the one in the east house. Then the Black Coyote man of the north gave a nine-night ceremony over him, and after this they all gave him their masks and medicine, and gave him his ceremonial name, Nakoholdehe,[63] which is a holy name.[64] After this he was ready to leave and they told him that when he got back to his people he must teach one of his brothers everything that he had seen and learned. They said, "You must have a ceremony over your brothers and from now on all the Earth People should have these ceremonies."

The four ears of corn that he had kept he took with him for the Earth People, and out of this corn they made the images of four coyotes and one dog that are used in the ceremony. There are eight white k'eet'áán for the east, eight blue for the south, eight yellow for the west, and eight black for the north, and one image of coyote for each direction. At the north is a black image of a dog and a black k'eet'aan. The dog is called Łééchąą'í, and at his left a pellet of biyeel (sacred offering) should be placed. There should be four yellow-headed blackbird feathers radiating in the four directions. All these offerings are to be made in the hooghan and then taken out and placed outside of it, and they should be made before the first fire is made each day.

---

[62]Talking God, Coyote and Female God.

[63]This is in the transcription of M. C. Wheelwright.

[64]There never was a public dance at the end of the Coyote's ceremony.

He Brings Corn and the Coyote Chant to the People

After he had learned all this, the hunter went back to his people and gave the corn to his father and mother. He had thought that he had been away a very short time but found that he had been gone four years. Then the Earth People began these ceremonies and the hunter gave all his knowledge to his younger brother. He gave a ceremony over him and told the people not to forget what they had learned and to always give the ceremonies. He said, "I am going to leave you, you're seeing me for the last time." Then he went back to his wives and the Coyote People.

COMMENTARY ON THE COYOTE MYTH

by David P. McAllester

Throughout Navajo mythology, Ma'ii the Coyote is a figure of central importance. In the last part of the myth of the Great Star Chant, when the sacred company are journeying for power, they go first to Coyote. It is Coyote, the manifestation of animal vitality, who separated Younger Brother from his family and caused him to go to the sky where he learned Star wisdom and finally became one of the Holy People through a long process of testing and instruction.

Ma'ii was one of the first powers to emerge in the beginning of things. In the black world, the first and lowest in the order of creation, he brought fire to men. Characteristically, he stole it from the Fire God. Later in the creation myth Coyote endangered the world by stealing the child of Tééhooltsódii, the water monster. As the avenging floods rose, the people were forced to climb to safety in the present white world through a long hollow reed. But the waters followed and would have flooded this world as well if Coyote's trickery had not been found out. He was forced to give back the child and the floods receded.

Though Coyote is tricky, his power is great. In the Emergence Myth collected by Father Berard (Navajo Religion Series, Vol. III) he curbs the sun and understands the process of creation. He has much of the quality of Prometheus, or of Maui in New Zealand mythology. Like Loki, he is mischievous but useful. He bears a striking resemblance to the fox spirit of Japan and Korea and, in fact, the fox figure in mythology and folklore all across the Old World. Everywhere he is tricky, troublesome, hard to control, but sometimes, helpful to man.

Every conception of his character combines mischief and rebellion with wisdom. In the Navajo Ats'o'osii, or Feather Myth, he symbolizes uninhibited lust in the lower world, but becomes more controlled and useful when he emerges into the present world and is given control of rain. It is characteristic of Navajo myths that when the stories leave the magic period of creation and a hero is chosen and trained to be the transmitter of ceremonial knowledge and power, Coyote has a special role in this training. He is there to act as frustrater and goad to the hero if the latter shows signs of weakness or vacillation.

Ma'ii can triumph over the strong, but when he is vain, arrogant, greedy, libidinous, he is foiled, often killed. But he comes to life again, irrepressible, and unchanged. As the Great Star tells the hero in the Star Myth, we must accept the fact that there will always be different kinds of people in the world, and among them there will always be Coyote People.

The connection of Ma'ii (Coyote) with fertility, rain and water is clearly established in the myth of the Coyote Chant. The story begins in the ocean. The first people are created by Asdzáán Nádleehé, Changing Woman, the great mother who can grow old and then young again as she chooses. She is a nature figure, symbolic of the changes of the seasons. She is bathing in a great white shell and she dries herself with finely powdered meal of white corn and of yellow corn. When she empties the shell into the sea, the water, fog, corn and sacred shell come together, and people are formed.

There are two kinds of people. The first part of the myth establishes their differences in nature and destiny. The White Corn People embody masculinity, spirituality, the sky, and are destined to originate the Bead Chant. The Yellow Corn People represent the female principle, fertility, the earth, the rainbow and Coyote. They are to bring agriculture and the Coyote Chant to mankind.

The clues to these differences seem unmistakable. In Navajo ritual poetry there is usually a balance of complementary concepts. It is often a two-part balance in which male symbols dominate the first half and female symbols the second: Pollen Boy—Pollen Girl; male rain—female rain; and white corn—yellow corn. Coyote often represents the power of sex in its trouble-making ungovernable aspect. The rainbow is a symbol of fertile rain. The leader of the White Corn People dreams of a sky world and the leader of the Yellow Corn People dreams of walking on earth surrounded by rainbows. He also dreams that he will be of the Coyote family.

The differences of the two families are shown in the ceremonial names given to their leaders when they disagree. The White Corn leader's name refers to vomit, ceremonial purification, in a sense to the rejection of earthly things. The Yellow Corn leader's name is "He-whose-stomach-trembles-with-hunger." This is fitting for the people who are to bring forth from the earth man's first security against hunger.

As in the Myth of the Great Star Chant, these people are living at a hunting and gathering subsistance level. They must wander continually in search of game and wild fruits. In both myths there is a place named for the piles of hair heaped up where the people scrape hides in order to make clothes.

When the two families separate we follow the fortunes of the Yellow Corn, or Coyote, People. They are no sooner on their own than their leader begins to show signs of strangeness. He appears in various forms, creates landmarks which are to be sacred places hereafter, and finally reveals that he has given himself to the Holy People and that this family is to bring the Coyote Chant to the world, with his help. After this, in the form of Talking God, he disappears into the rock wall of Canyon de Chelly (Tséyi').

Now comes another period of wandering, this time under the guidance of the former leader's nephew. Led by a rainbow, a manifestation of the departed leader, they travel to a new place and there the nephew eventually marries his uncle's wife and has eight children.

The oldest boy in this family is the hero of the major part of the myth. A peerless hunter, he is destined to bring agriculture to his people: the best representative of the old culture leads the way to the new. And now, through his skill as a tracker and hunter, actual contact with the Coyote People is made. The hunter gets lost, follows coyote tracks, and is surprised to find kernels of fresh corn, even though it is midwinter, and comes to "a round pond covered with ice with bulrushes growing round it."

This is in close analogy to the pond in the Great Star Myth where that hero and his family find their lost child, the grandson of Tł'iishtsoh, the Great Snake, in a fertile underworld. In both instances the sexual symbolism of a round lake, entrance to the womb of the earth, is impressively and vividly drawn. In the Coyote Myth, the hunter forces an entrance through the lake with his bow, and, prompted by the former leader of the Yellow Corn People, in the guise of the Messenger Wind, goes down into an underworld where cornfields stretch in every direction. In four hooghans, one in each of the cardinal directions and colored with the sacred color of that direction, Coyote People are cooking corn. Here we have a reduced version of what Younger Brother found in the sky in the Star Myth. It is the microcosm of the Navajo country with its four sacred mountains, in the four directions, often equated with hooghans in myth and in sandpaintings.

In an earthly parallel to Younger Brother's adventures and instruction in the sky, the young hunter visits each of the hooghans in turn. He learns the magic of the White, Blue, Yellow and Black Coyote People. He is made holy, is given corn of the four sacred colors, and in keeping with the fertility motif of this myth, marries two coyote girls in each of the hooghans.

An interesting detail in the Coyote magic that the hunter witnesses is the increase of animal fat. A small portion is placed under deerskins and there is made to grow enormously until there is enough to feed all the Coyote People. This seems to be an analogy from the hunting world of the enormous proliferating power of agriculture where one seed reproduces itself many times over. The incident seems to provide a bridge to give rationality to the role of the carnivorous Coyote as giver-of-corn.

As in the Star Myth, the learner is cautioned against bad people about, but disregards these warnings of danger and thus goes on to further instruction and training. In the world of the coyotes, however, the danger is not very great. It is never explicitly described nor is it experienced by the hunter. We are dealing with a much simpler order of power than in the case of the Great Star Myth, and the attendant danger is correspondingly less.

As in Navajo life today, the chant is learned by becoming a patient. Four times, the young hunter is "the one sung over," once in each of the four hooghans of the Coyote People. He is told the mystery of the origin of his own people and he learns the Wooltáád Rite and how to make k'eet'áán offerings. In alternating five-night and nine-night ceremonies he learns the masks, the body paintings, the sandpaintings and the other ritual of the Coyote Chant. Now he is given a ceremonial name, "Nakoholdehe." And he learns how to make images of the Coyote moulded in corn meal of the appropriate color for each of the four directions. At the north, in addition, he learns to make a black corn meal image of a dog. Again the connection between corn and Coyote is affirmed.

In a brief ending, the hunter returns to the upper world. He is surprised to learn that he has been gone four years. He teaches the Coyote Chant to his younger brother. As in the Star

Myth the ritual must be taught to a relative and the hero who transmits it, now too sacred to live again in the ordinary world, must leave and take up his life in the other world whence the sacred knowledge was derived. The hunter gives corn to the people and then, his tasks accomplished, returns to the Coyote country and his wives. It is typically Navajo that the main emphasis on what is brought from the underworld is clearly on the ceremony rather than the corn. Though vital to the welfare of the people, the corn is merely a by-product of the all-important ritual which will keep man safe from harm and in proper balance with the great forces of the universe.

SOME NOTES GIVEN BY YOO'IJÍ HATAAŁII ON CEREMONIAL PROCEDURE IN THE COYOTE CHANT

They make a number of images and k'eet'áán in the hooghan before the first fire is kindled each day. After these are made, they are placed outside the hooghan.

Using corn, they make four coyote images and one of a dog. They use one of the coyote images for each of the cardinal directions, and for each of the directions there are eight k'eet'áán. For the east, these are white, for the south, blue, for the west, yellow, and for the north, black.

At the north, they place a black image of łééchąą'í, the dog, and at his left they place a pellet of biyeel (medicine) on which four feathers of the yellow headed blackbird (ch'agiiłtsooí) have been arranged to point in the four directions.

This chant is said to have originated near Rainbow Bridge.

THE
SANDPAINTINGS
AND
OTHER ILLUSTRATIONS

DESCRIPTION OF SANDPAINTINGS OF THE GREAT STAR CHANT

SECOND DAY SANDPAINTING OF THE SǪ'TSOHJÍ
(GREAT STAR CHANT)

The central figure is the great White Star with four Ii'ni', or Thunder Birds, around it. Lightning and rain bundles are dropping from their wings, and their tails are edged with points of thunder. Their feet are cloud symbols. Above their heads are bows and arrows.

Medicine Man: Ayóó'aníłnézí. Collected by Mrs. Newcomb.[1] Place: Sawmill, Arizona. Date: 1930. Drawn and painted by Mrs. Newcomb. Portfolio 14.

SANDPAINTING OF THE FOUR CEREMONIAL MOUNDS OF THE SǪ'TSOHJÍ

Made outdoors at the east, south, west and north of the ceremonial hooghan on four consecutive days of the Sǫ'tsohjí Ceremony. They represent mountains with arrow points on them. Bear tracks face them. They are made for the Tsibąąs Rite of the hoops.

Medicine Man: Ayóó'aníłnézí. Collected by Mrs. Newcomb. Place: Sawmill, Arizona. Date: 1930. Drawn and painted by Mrs. Newcomb. Portfolio 14.

WHITE FIVE-POINTED STAR AND BLUE-BIRD SANDPAINTING OF THE SǪ'TSOHJÍ

Made by Hasteen Klah (Hastiin Tł'aai) for Mary C. Wheelwright. Five Spirit Rays shoot out from it, and arrows are shown around it.

---

[1]The following people assisted the former Museum of Navajo Ceremonial Art in recording and reproducing these sandpaintings: Mrs. A. J. Newcomb, formerly at the Newcomb Trading Post north of Gallup; Mrs. Joan Wetherill, of Wetherill Trading Post, Kayenta, Arizona; Mr. Colville, (former assistant at the Wetherill Trading Post); Mr. Lloyd Moylan, (former curator of Museum of Navajo Ceremonial Art); Mrs. Laura Adams Armer, (former assistant of the Museum of Navajo Ceremonial Art); Mrs. Isabell Campbell, (former assistant of the Museum of Navajo Ceremonial Art). *The sandpaintings described here can be viewed at the Wheelright Museum of the American Indian* (in Santa Fe, New Mexico).

SǪ'TSOHJÍ SANDPAINTING

Central figure is the Black Star, who was the teacher of the hero of the myth. Four warriors in black flint armor carry bows, arrows and rattles and represent Naayéé' Neezghaní, the Slayer of Monsters. The surrounding rainbow has feathered ends and smaller stars are at its angles. Guardians at the east are two Dǫ'tsoh, or Messenger Flies.

Medicine Man: Ayóó'aniłnézí. Collected by Mrs. Newcomb. Place: Sawmill, near Crystal, Arizona. Date: 1930. Drawn and painted by Mrs. Newcomb. Portfolio 14.

SANDPAINTING OF THE SǪ'TSOHJÍ HÓCHÓ'ÍJÍ (STAR TRAIL CEREMONY)

The Star Trail is made to banish evil. It shows four mountains built in relief, with a pollen path leading to the door of the hooghan. Before each mountain is a pair of Bear footprints. The door guards are a couple of bears (the bear being both a mountain and a sky symbol of power and wisdom). The brown circle is the extent of the hooghan floor, and the trail leads to the yellow corn meal altar on which sits a basket of white corn meal crossed with yellow pollen. Rainbow spots guard this and a line of corn meal outlines three sides. Hawk feathers are erected at the west. Four white crosses at the north and at the south show where the medicine man and helpers sit. A yellow and a white star with red crosses hold the coals of the fire, and bear tracks lead out after the guards and the mountains have been erased.

Medicine Man: Black Mustache. Place: Sulphur Springs near Newcomb. Date: 1928. Collected by Mrs. Newcomb. Painted by Mrs. Newcomb. Portfolio 14.

SANDPAINTING OF THE SǪ'TSOHJÍ CEREMONY—THIRD PAINTING

The human spirits are those who live among the stars. These spirits taught Dilyéhé how to heal his people, after he awoke from his sleep. The spirits of the stars are clothed in arrow-point armor. The four groups of seven stars represent the tracks made by Dilyéhé when he came back to heal his people. They are still in the heavens and are called "the boy chasing an arrow."

Collected by Mrs. Wetherill. Place: Kayenta. Drawn and painted by Mr. Colville. Portfolio 15.

SECOND SANDPAINTING OF THE SǪ'TSOHJÍ CEREMONY

The central figure represents mixed clouds, the blue lines, moss, the yellow line, pollen, the white one is foam, and the black one is the "cat-o-nine-tails." The star people stand on the rainbow bars which whirl around the center. They are also Náhookǫs, the Dipper Constellation.

Collected by Mrs. Armer. Place: Black Mountain. Date: 1929. Checked by Father Berard Haile. Redrawn and painted by Lloyd Moylan. Portfolio 15.

FIRST SANDPAINTING OF THE SǪ'TSOHJÍ CEREMONY

The blue central water has yellow pollen edged with the fringed border representing the glitter of the stars and with white lines leading to the rainbow bars on which the four Star People stand and whirl about the central earth water. They are Náhookǫs, the stars that whirl about, or the Dipper. At the east entrance where the black cloud symbols end the surrounding rainbow are two white baskets and two footprints of yellow corn meal.

Collected by Mrs. Armer. Place: Black Mountain. Date: 1929. Checked by Father Berard Haile. Redrawn and painted by Lloyd Moylan. Portfolio 15.

FIRST[2] SANDPAINTING OF THE SQ'TSOHJÍ CEREMONY

Center figure a spring with moss growing around the water. The triangles around it are clouds. The circles are sunlight showing on the water and making lights like the rainbow. The interlaced lines forming diamonds from the corners of the clouds are heat lightning. The long bars running from the center figure is the pivot on which the sun turns, from north to south and from east to west. The crosses are the seven stars. The male figure is the boy who wandered around in all directions, carrying his bow to shoot rabbits and birds for food. The blue points of the border represent the sky, the red points the earth, the black line in the border is the water surrounding the earth. This was before he was taken to the skies.

Collected by Mrs. Wetherill. Place: Kayenta. Drawn and painted by Mr. Colville. Portfolio 15.

FOURTH SANDPAINTING OF THE SQ'TSOHJÍ CEREMONY

The interlaced lines forming diamonds on the eastern skies of the sandpainting represent the breath of the summer and winter coming together as the summer merges into winter. The square in the center is the opening beyond the stars. The circle of stars to the south of this opening are the seed basket. The stars in the form of a shepherd's crook is the staff of the old man who carries the seed basket. The group to the south of the staff is Atsé'ats'ózí, the group to the west is Atsé'atsoh. The seven stars are Dilyéhí. The four stars just to the north of Dilyéhí are the rabbit tracks. The big white star between Dilyéhí and the rabbit tracks is the evening star. That to the east of the rabbit tracks is the "Goddess of the Night." The Dipper is the "God of the Night." The red star between the God and Goddess is the North Star, their camp fire. The two stars together are Sǫ'ahóts'i'í. They represent two women who got into a quarrel over a gambling game and they have their hands fastened in each others hair. This is the heaven Dilyéhí told the people about after his return from the skies.

This chant was used to cure bad dreams, nervousness and worry.

Collected and described by Mrs. Wetherill. Place: Kayenta. Drawn and painted by Mr. Colville. Portfolio 15.

SECOND SANDPAINTING OF THE SQ'TSOHJÍ CEREMONY

The figures on each side are the son and daughter of the heat. The center figure is the son of the rain. The heat figures are sending forth heat from their hands, and the rain figure is retaining the rain in times of drought. The body of the central figure is composed of cloud figures.

Collected by Mrs. Wetherill. Place: Kayenta. Drawn and painted by Mr. Colville. Portfolio 15.

---

[2]There are many versions of the sandpaintings of this ceremony.

THIRD SANDPAINTING OF SQ'TSOHJÍ CEREMONY

The central figure is the darkness with a border of dawn, which is the home of the Big Star. The black and yellow figures are the male Star People and the blue and white, the females, and all are dressed in different colored flint garments. They have bows and arrows of jet, turquoise, abalone, and dawn, and a talking k'eet'áán is tied to each bow. The encircling rainbow ends in cloud symbols.

If the patient asks for it, a prayer may be said for him on this painting.

Collected by Mrs. Armer. Place: Black Mountain. Date: 1929. Checked by Father Berard Haile. Redrawn and painted by Lloyd Moylan. Portfolio 15.

FIRST SANDPAINTING OF THE SQ'TSOHJÍ CEREMONY

Big yellow star in center, fringed with red, yellow, black, white and blue bars. Four rainbow bars at cardinal points. Surrounded by curved rainbow, ending in clouds.

Collected by Mrs. Armer. Place: Black Mountain. Date: 1929. Drawn and painted by Mrs. Armer. Portfolio 15.

SECOND SANDPAINTING OF THE SQ'TSOHJÍ CEREMONY

Big white star in center, fringed with red, yellow, black, white and blue. Four rainbow bars at cardinal points. Surrounded by curved rainbow, ending in clouds.

Collected by Mrs. Armer. Place: Black Mountain. Date: 1929. Drawn and painted by Mrs. Armer. Portfolio 15.

THIRD SANDPAINTING OF THE SQ'TSOHJÍ CEREMONY

Big blue star in center, fringed with red, black, yellow, white and blue. Four rainbow bars at cardinal points. Surrounded by curved rainbow, ending in clouds.

Collected by Mrs. Armer. Place: Black Mountain. Date: 1929. Drawn and painted by Mrs. Armer. Portfolio 15.

FOURTH SANDPAINTING OF THE SQ'TSOHJÍ CEREMONY

Big black star in center, fringed with red, black, yellow, blue and white. Four rainbow bars at cardinal points. Surrounded by curved rainbow, ending in clouds.

Collected by Mrs. Armer. Place: Black Mountain. Date: 1929. Drawn and painted by Mrs. Armer. Portfolio 15.

FIFTH SANDPAINTING OF THE SQ'TSOHJÍ CEREMONY

Four big snakes of which the black and yellow are males, the blue and white are females. The black is a garment of darkness, blue, skyblue, yellow, the evening twilight, white, the dawn. Their horns were lent to them by the Deer-bird People of the Life Way (Flint Way Chant). Their bodies are spotted with all kinds of stars. The red spot between the eyes of the males, and the yellow spot on the females, represent the ring on their heads. The thin black streaks between the figures represent thin clouds. No border is mentioned. Rainbow spots at tongues and tails are omitted, also a white and black big pointed star should have been shown as entrance guards. Male patient sits on the yellow snake, the female patient on the blue snake.

Collected by Mrs. Armer. Place: Black Mountain. Date: 1929. Drawn and painted by Mrs. Armer. Portfolio 15.

TWO SANDPAINTINGS OF THE STAR GAZING CEREMONY

The blue oblong patch in the west represents Spruce Hill, the bear tracks representing those of the male and female bear living there. The mountain is surrounded by dawn (white). The rainbow lying along the length of footprints indicates the traveling means of the bear. The two rainbows lying towards the east show the entrance guards of bear dens represented in the two rainbows in the west of the hill. The white candle-like bar in the center represents the rock crystal through which star gazing is done, the four cones in white at the cardinal points are dawn mountains with live plumes. The large black and blue stars are the so-called "main stars," their fire or igniter being shown by the red cross in the center. Any star selected for gazing is called the "main" star. The four white crosses surrounding the main stars are so-called "never-ending month" stars. The black star holds a dark bow and tail-feathered arrow, the blue holds a mahogany bow and a yellow tail-feathered arrow. Each bow has red wing feathers attached to the bow grip and three round beads are strung on the bowstrings.

In front of Spruce Hill lying before the bear tracks, two bears should have been shown facing each other—a black one on the left, a white one on the right side (as you face the hill from the east).

The second painting is identical, showing the dawn home of bears in Spruce Knoll. The red crosses in the white and yellow stars are the "igniters," or fire of Ursa Major and Cassiopeia. A yellow and blue bear should replace the black and white ones of the first painting. In addition two flint knives, white and black, are omitted here, as such are used in cutting up the spruce garlands of the patient on this painting. No border or entrance guards are required for these two paintings. They are used mainly in star gazing and "testing one's nerves," and for treating the patient thereon with "mouth-put" medicine.

Collected by Laura Adams Armer. Checked and revised by Father Berard Haile. Repainted by Isabel Campbell. Date: June 29, 1939. Portfolio 15.

SANDPAINTING OF THE LITTLE STAR CEREMONY

Black Star Prayer Painting. This is made early in the morning to complete the Little Star Ceremony, and could be used with any similar group of star paintings. It is also used in the Hozhǫ'nii Bi'áád and in the Wind Chant. Hataałiiłchíí' and Ats'o'sii Biye' both used this sandpainting for the Hozhǫ'nii Ceremony, and Long Mustache used it in a Star Chant.

Medicine Man: Hasteen Klah (Hastiin Tł'aai), who learned it from Tséts'ósí. Collected by Mrs. Newcomb. Place: Close to Beautiful Mountain, near Newcomb. Date: 1931-32. Painted by Mrs. Newcomb. Portfolio 15.

SMALL PRAYER PAINTING OF THE SǪ'TSOHJÍ CEREMONY (1)

Small prayer painting which divides the star into four colors. Four arrows point from it southeast, southwest, northwest, northeast. The central red cross signifies fire—the light which makes the star shine. Trail of spirit steps enter the eastward opening of a black and white mist which encircles the star ending in k'oshchíín (a cloud and water emblem).

Medicine Man: Táchii'nii of Tanner Springs, Arizona. Collected by Mrs. Newcomb. Place: Newcomb. Date: 1929 – 30. Painted by Mrs. Newcomb. Portfolio 14 B.

SANDPAINTING OF THE SǪ'TSOHJÍ CEREMONY (2)

This painting shows the sky in the form of a big black star with a cross in the center, upon which the red cross represents fire (or life or spirit). This black star sky has a border of white dawn light edged with rays of all colors. Four stars are contained in this black sky, the sparkling or "winking" star at the east, edged with pink rays, the Blue Star to the south, Yellow Star to the west, and the White Star to the north. The fire symbol in the center of each star and the whole painting is guarded by shafts of light and darkness; light at the south and west, darkness at the north and east.

Medicine Man: Táchii'nii of Tanner Springs, Arizona. Collected by Mrs. Newcomb. Place: Newcomb. Date: 1929-30. Painted by Mrs. Newcomb. Portfolio 14 B.

SANDPAINTING OF THE SǪ'TSOHJÍ CEREMONY (3)

This painting is identical with No. 2, except that the sky background is blue instead of black. It would be used for a woman patient, whereas No. 2 would be used for a man.

Medicine Man: Táchii'nii of Tanner Springs, Arizona. Collected by Mrs. Newcomb. Place: Newcomb. Date: 1929-30. Painted by Mrs. Newcomb. Portfolio 14 B.

SANDPAINTING OF THE SǪ'TSOHJÍ CEREMONY (5)

This sketch was drawn by Táchii'nii and is the fifth of a set of five which he uses when he holds a five-day ceremony. The black star in the center has a fire symbol in the center, and black rays emanate from the edge. Four arrow points lead out to the southeast, southwest, northwest and northeast. The usual arrangement of four stars surrounds the central one, each with a red cross in the center showing that their light comes from fire.

Medicine Man: Táchii'nii of Tanner Springs, Arizona. Collected by Mrs. Newcomb. Place: Newcomb. Date: 1929-30. Painted by Mrs. Newcomb. Portfolio 14 B.

BLACK STAR, SNAKES AND ARROWS SANDPAINTING
FROM THE SǪ'TSOHJÍ CEREMONY (A)

This sketch was drawn by Hoskay Begay, during the five-day Star Chant which was held near the Sheep Dip, by Níłch'ijí Hataałii Biye', with Hoskay Begay as helper. The ceremony was held during the hours of darkness and the medicine man came part of each day. They drew several Star Chant sandpaintings for me and I took notes on the remainder of each set. These are not especially large paintings and can be used singly for one-night chants or in the full set of four for a five-night ceremony. These are all Hóchǫ'íjí pictures for the banishing of evil.

Medicine Man: Níłch'ijí Hataałii Biye'. Collected by Mrs. Newcomb. Place: Newcomb. Date: Fall of 1936 or 1937. Portfolio 14 B.

YELLOW STAR, SNAKES AND ARROWS SANDPAINTING
FROM THE SǪ'TSOHJÍ CEREMONY (B)

This is a variation of the Black Star painting and was drawn by Hoskay Begay. He made the Black Star completely and outlined the yellow, white, and blue that could be used with it, or separately. Yellow and white seems to be used for female patients, while the blue and black were used for male patients.

Medicine Man: Hoskay Begay. Collected by Mrs. Newcomb. Place: Newcomb. Date: 1937. Painted by Mrs. Newcomb. Portfolio 14 B.

BLUE STAR, SNAKES AND ARROWS SANDPAINTING
FROM THE SǪ'TSOHJÍ (GREAT STAR) CEREMONY (C)

This is another variant of the Black Star painting, and is often used in spring and summer chants when the nights are not really black. Sometimes these paintings are divided. The central star being made in sand inside the hooghan is the usual place for sandpaintings while the bow-and-arrow and the snakes are made on a tan sand mat outside, to the east, south, west and north. When it is painted in this manner there is no set of tracks or "trail" leading up to the door.

Medicine Man: Hoskay Begay. Place: Newcomb. Date: 1937. Painted by Mrs. Newcomb. Portfolio 14 B.

WHITE STAR, SNAKES AND ARROWS SANDPAINTING
FROM THE SǪ'TSOHJÍ CEREMONY (D)

This painting was drawn from a description given to me by Nílch'ijí Hataałii Biye' as a variant for the painting with a pink star in the center. The pink star seems to be more powerful, but if the ceremony is not for an especially important cause, then other colors may be used. The season of the year and the condition of the patient are also factors in determining which set of paintings is to be used at that particular time. The White Star is surrounded by white and yellow serpents and bows accompanied by arrows. These are not large paintings and can be used to banish evil influences from the fields and flocks, as well as from human beings.

Medicine Man: Nílch'ijí Hataałii Biye'. Place: Newcomb. Collected by Mrs. Newcomb. Date: 1937. Painted by Mrs. Newcomb. Portfolio 14 B.

THE PINK STAR SANDPAINTING FROM THE SǪ'TSOHJÍ CEREMONY

This is the third painting belonging to a set of four made by Nílch'ijí Hataałii Biye'. It shows the sparkling (pink) star shining with more power and importance than the stars which surround it. Crossed snakes which are the symbol of trouble are faced toward the star, while on four sides are ordinary evening stars. The painting is guarded by four serpents and all have red tongues, denoting that they are poisonous. Snake poison, poisoned arrows, and the pink stars seem to form a powerful combination to ward off evil.

Medicine Man: Nílch'ijí Hataałii Biye'. Collected by Mrs. Newcomb. Place: T'iis Názbąs. Date: 1935. Drawn and Painted by Mrs. Newcomb. Portfolio 14 B.

STAR AND MOUNTAIN SANDPAINTING FROM THE SǪ'TSOHJÍ CEREMONY

This is the fourth painting of a five-day Star Ceremony by Nítch'ijí Hataałii Biye', in which all of the sandpaintings were made at night. The sparkling star was again the important central design, but none of its evil power is apparent. There are no poison-tipped arrows or red-tongued serpents. At each point are mountains, raised five or six inches high. The eastern mountain is black with bear foot-prints; the southern mountain is blue, with mountain lion foot-prints; the western mountain is yellow with wolf foot-prints; and the northern mountain is white with eagle foot-prints. The pollen trail leads the patient to his seat on the star.

Medicine Man: Nítch'ijí Hataałii Biye'. Collected by Mrs. Newcomb. Place: T'iis Názbąs. Date: 1935. Drawn and painted by Mrs. Newcomb. Portfolio 14 B.

TWO STAR SANDPAINTING FROM THE SǪ'TSOHJÍ CEREMONY

This is from a five-day Hochǫ'íjí Chant held by Nítch'ijí Hataałii Biye', who lived near Tsénást'i'. It could be held to banish any sort of bad luck, and the one I saw was held after a rock shelf had fallen and killed some sheep. It seems to begin with the largest sandpainting and end with a small one which has the pollen trail. There are two 'sparkling' (mixture of colors, mostly red) stars in the center guarded by four sets of serpents, male and female: black to the east, blue to the south, yellow to the west, and white to the north. The male bows and arrows are to the east and west, while the female bows and arrows are on the south and north. Only the general indication is that the bows and arrows are never female even when the color seems to point to such a distinction.

Medicine Man: Nítch'ijí Hataałii Begay. Collected by Mrs. Newcomb. Place: T'iis Názbąs. Date: 1935. Drawn and painted by Mrs. Newcomb. Portfolio 14 B.

THE BLACK STAR SANDPAINTING OF THE SǪ'TSOHJÍ CEREMONY

This is a single painting used by Na'ał'oijí Hataałii for the banishing of evil dreams and fear of darkness. This great black star refused to have a light to cover its face and it refused to travel a given path. So, it roams whenever it pleases and it sends out little imps with arrows on their heads to annoy people who are out of doors on a 'black' night. Black is for a male patient. This is also Klah's version of the painting.

Medicine Man: Na'ał'oijí Hataałii. Place: Newcomb. Date: 1930. Collected by Mrs. Newcomb. Drawn and painted by Mrs. Newcomb. Portfolio 14 B.

YELLOW STAR PAINTING OF THE SǪ'TSOHJÍ CEREMONY (HOCHǪ́'ÍJÍ)

This sketch was outlined for me in 1928, by Black Mustache when he held a three-night Star Chant over Irene at Little Sulphur Springs, not far from the Trading Post. The yellow star is the evening star of the harvest season and the blue figure is that of the Corn Maiden. The prongs are all colors indicating the change of seasons. The black sky of fall and winter is dotted with the variously colored stars which surround the yellow star. The spear points, one white quartz and one of pink agate (petrified wood) guard the east. A bar of white dawn-light shows in the east and the rainbow-guard ends in the k'oschíín symbol. A bow and arrow of mountain mahogany are laid down to guard the eastern opening. There are only four star sandpaintings which show the Pollen Boy and the Corn Maiden. These seem to take the place of the Sun and Moon paintings which belong to other chants.

Medicine Man: Black Mustache. Collected by Mrs. Newcomb. Place: Sulphur Springs near Newcomb. Date: 1928. Drawn and painted by Mrs. Newcomb. Portfolio 14 B.

WHITE STAR PAINTING OF THE SǪ'TSOHJÍ CEREMONY (I)

The white star in the center with star rays spreading from it represent light and power. On each corner stand female cloud people, from whose elbows and wrists hang rain bundles; rain or cloud bundles of shá'bitł'óól or rain ribbons. Faces are covered with brown wind masks. The crosses on their bodies are stars. On one side of each figure is a bow, and on the other, an arrow point.

Medicine Man: Hasteen Klah (Hastiin Tł'aai). Collected by Mrs. Newcomb. Place: Near Newcomb. Date: 1931-32. Drawn and painted by Mrs. Newcomb. Portfolio 14 B.

BLACK STAR PAINTING OF THE SǪ'TSOHJÍ CEREMONY (4)

This is similar to No. 3, except that the star center is black. They may both be used when the patient is a man or boy, and any of these can be made separately for a small ceremony, or in a set of four for a longer one. Usual length is five nights. All these chants are given at night, and even the fire pit by the door is dimmed by sprinkled ashes. The only light should be from the stars through the roof opening.

Medicine Man: Hasteen Klah (Hastiin Tł'aai), who learned it from Tséts'ósí. Collected by Mrs. Newcomb. Place: Near Newcomb. Date: 1931-32. Drawn and painted by Mrs. Newcomb. Portfolio 14 B.

ILLUSTRATIONS OF THE STAR CHANT AND THE COYOTE CHANT

The Star Chant ceremonies are used mostly for divination and the casting out of evil influences, so are called Sǫ'tsohjí Hóchǫ'íjí and are often held at night. The last three Star Chant paintings are not evil-chasing. The Coyote Chant has few sandpaintings but plastic figures of animals are used.

M. C. WHEELWRIGHT

I

Star Trail

"Star trail for banishing evil," a form of Tsibąąs Rite of passing the patient over a holy path and usually through four hoops. This is the trail for the man patient, and one with yellow and white bears is for the woman. The patient comes into the hooghan over the four mountains which represent the Navajo world, and as he leaves each mountain it is erased by the medicine man. Then he enters the hooghan and the ceremony is performed while he sits on the sandpainting. I have come to the conclusion that these trails and sandpaintings can be as simple or as complicated as the patient wishes to pay for. It seems to depend on how much bad luck has pursued the patient and how badly frightened he has been.
Medicine Man: Black Mustache. Collected by A.J. Newcomb. Place: Sulphur Springs near Newcomb. Date: 1928.

II

Great Star Chant, Evil-Chasing Ceremony
Star Gazing Sandpainting

The blue oblong patch at the west of the sandpainting represents Spruce Hill, and the tracks on it are those of the male and female bears living there. The mountain is surrounded by a line of white dawn. The rainbow bars paralleling the bears' tracks are what the bears travel on. The two rainbow bars at the west of Spruce Hill represent the bears' dens and the rainbow bars at the east are the entrance guards of the bears' dens. The white candle-shaped figure at the east of Spruce Hill is the rock crystal used in star gazing. The four cone-shaped white figures at the cardinal points are dawn mountains with white "live feathers" on their tops. The large blue and black four-pointed stars are the so-called "main stars," their fire shown as red crosses in the center. Any star selected for star gazing is a "main star." The small white crosses close to the "main stars" are the "never-ending month" stars. The black star has a dark bow and arrow near it, and the blue star has a mahogany bow and a yellow-feathered arrow. The bows have red wing feathers attached to the bow grip and three round beads strung on the bowstrings. The two large ceremonial knives between the bows and one in the center are the kind used in cutting up the spruce wreaths which are put on the patient in the rite.
Medicine Man: Not recorded. Collected by Laura Adams Armer.
Place: Black Mountain. Described and checked by Father Berard Haile. Date: 1939.
Painted by Isabel Campbell.

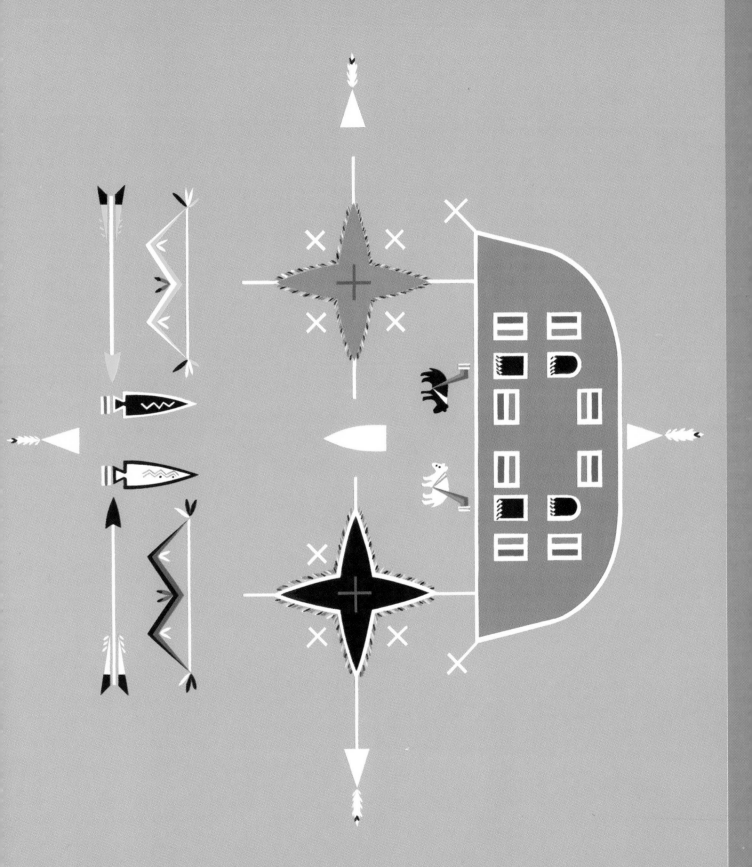

III

Great Star Chant—Evil-Chasing Ceremony
The Great Blue Star

This Blue Star version is held for a woman, and is a companion painting for the Great Black Star. It is used in an evil-chasing rite held at night. All stars are more or less evil, but these are feared most of all as they cannot be seen as they move through the sky. To them is attributed all the sickness, accidents and frights that occur to people who are abroad at night. Those who have no trouble when they travel often at night are suspected of being guarded by evil spirits.
Medicine Man: Hataałii Biye'. Collected and painted by F. J. Newcomb. Place: Newcomb. Date: 1930.

IV

Great Star Chant—Evil-Chasing Ceremony
Description of Four Sandpaintings of the Five-Day Ceremony

The big black circle is the round black house in the sky visited by the hero of the myth, with the five Great Star People sitting inside it. The Black Star is next to the entrance at the black point which is towards the east. The zigzag line on it is the path into the house connected with the big ceremonial knife belonging to Black Star, the different-colored knives are connected by their paths to the house and the direction of the different stars that use them. The hero sat in the center and was taught by the stars their songs and prayers.

The similar painting, No. 2, of the second day's ceremony shows a blue house. The only other variation is in the circles of color around the house. No. 3 shows the painting for the third day, and No. 4, for the fourth day's ceremony.

Medicine Man: Edward Martin. Collected by M. C. Wheelwright. Place: Near Crown Point. Date: 1942. Painted by Lloyd Moylan.

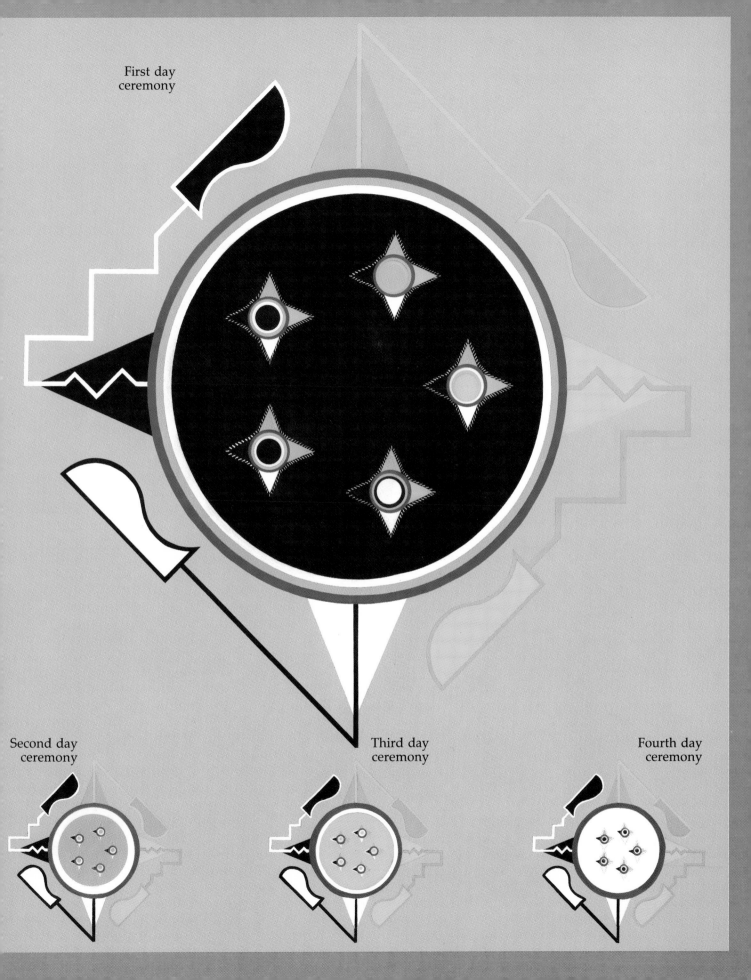

First day
ceremony

Second day
ceremony

Third day
ceremony

Fourth day
ceremony

V

Great Star Chant—Evil-Chasing Ceremony
The Little Star (I)

This painting comes from the Little Star Chant, which is a two- or three-night evil-chasing ceremony. The first night there is a trail outside the hooghan and a sandpainting inside. On the second night this white star painting is used for a man patient, and on the third night is the painting of the body of the patient and the chanting which lasts until dawn. This large white star with many-colored prongs is the star which shines brightest just before dawn. The yellow pollen boy stands on its face. The blue sky is the sky of spring and summer and is dotted with all the stars that surround the white star: black to the east, blue to the south, yellow to the west, and white to the north. The two spear points that guard the eastern opening are made of black obsidian and blue flint. A streak of white-dawn light appears in the east and is guarded by a bow and arrow made of mountain ash. The rainbow guards three sides and ends in the k'oschíín symbol. This is said to be a very powerful evil-chasing painting.

Medicine Man: Black Mustache. Collected and painted by Mrs. F. J. Newcomb. Place: Sulphur Springs, near Newcomb. Date: 1950.

VI

Sǫ'tsohjí Hóchǫ'íjí (Evil-Chasing) Chant

This is the second Hóchǫ'íjí painting by Niłch'iji Hataałii Biye' and has one large sparkling star in the center. This painting emphasizes the importance of the black and red bows and arrows, made of mountain mahogany. These arrows seem to be tipped with poison, but it has been two or three generations, according to the Navajo medicine men, since they used snake poison to ward off the evil spirits. The black snakes guard the arrows, and the blue snakes guard the painting.
Medicine Man: Niłch'iji Hataałii Biye'. Collected and painted by Mrs. F. J. Newcomb. Place: T'iis Názbąs. Date: 1935.

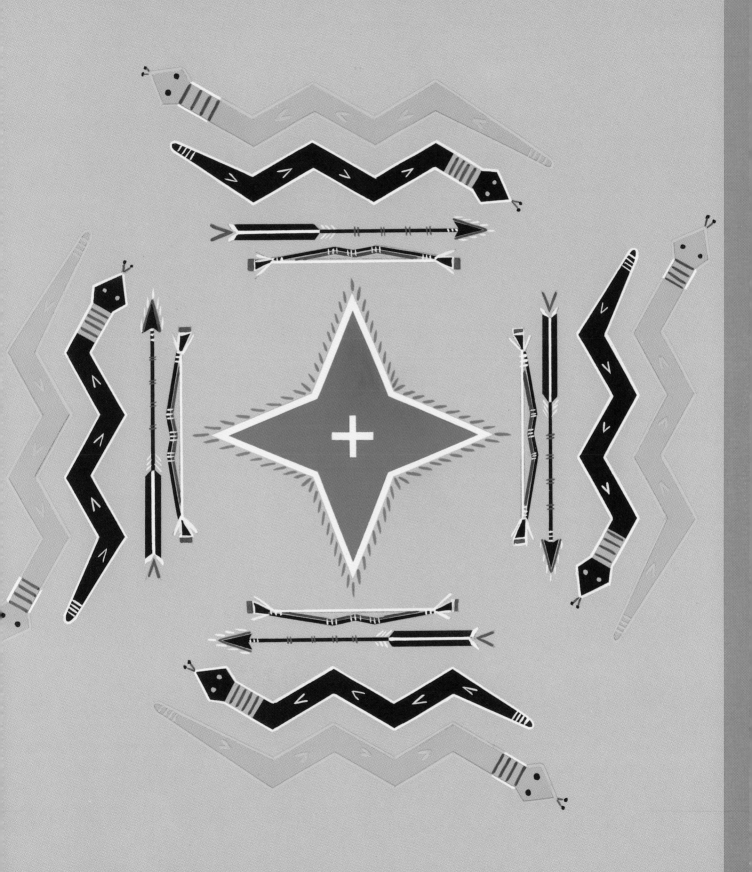

VII

Sǫ'tsohjí Chant—Little Star Form

The yellow star in the center, with star-rays spreading from it, represents light and power. Female cloud people stand on each point. From their elbows and wrists hang rain bundles, made of shá'bitł'óól or rain ribbon. Their faces are covered by brown wind masks. The crosses on their bodies are stars. Near the right hand of each is an arrow point and near the left, a bow.

Medicine Man: Hasteen Klah (Hastiin Tł'aai) who learned it from Tséts'ósí. Collected and painted by Mrs. F. J. Newcomb. Date: 1931-32.

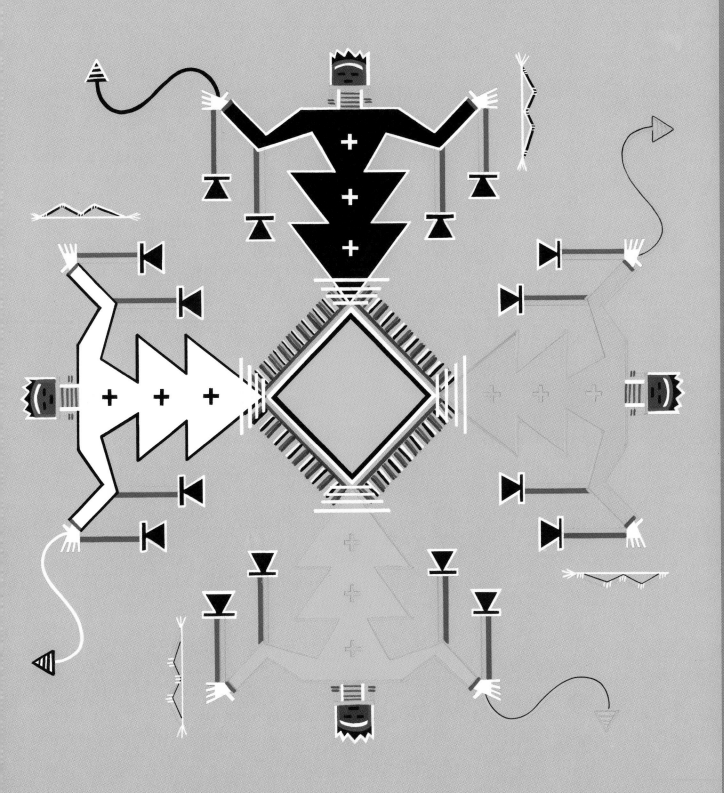

VIII

Great Star Chant—Evil-Chasing Ceremony
The Little Star (2)

Blue-pronged star with armed rain people with brown wind masks standing on it; cords ending in cloud
symbols hang from their arms and their bows and rain arrows are on each side of them.
Medicine Man: Hasteen Klah (Hastiin Tl'aai) who learned it from Tséts'ósí. Collected and painted by
F. J. Newcomb. Place: Near Newcomb. Date: 1931-32.

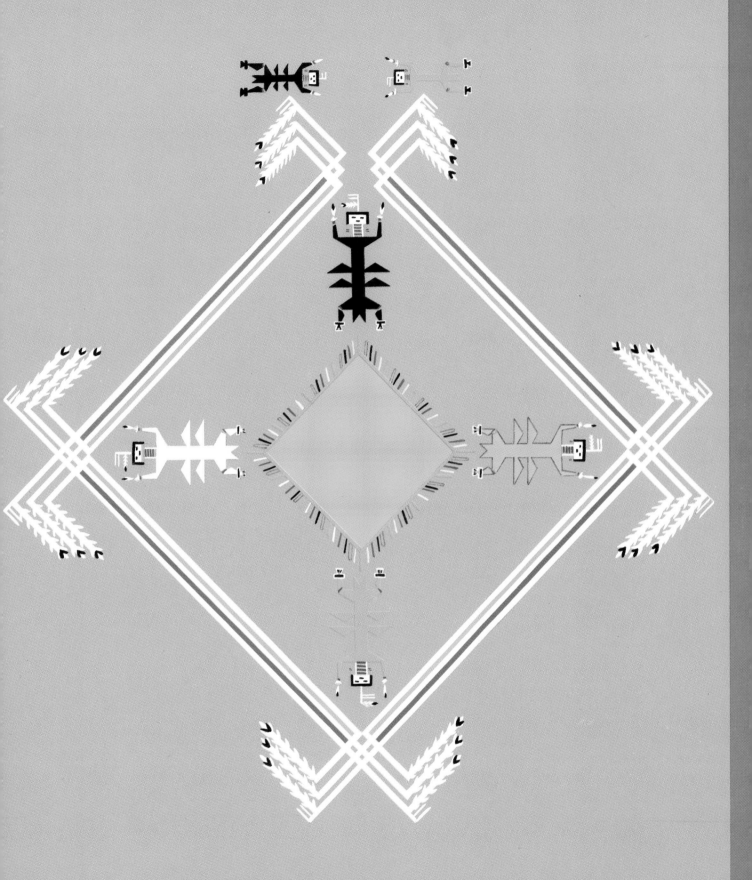

XIII

Great Star Chant—Blessing Form of Ceremony
Second Sandpainting with Feathered Rainbows

This is the second star painting from the Great Star ceremony as given by Ayóó'áníłnézí near Two Grey Hills. He uses a group of five stars with two of the star warriors, with bows and arrows between them to signify extra power. The warriors are carrying lightning arrows and gourd rattles to control wind and rain. The Dǫ'tsoh, or messenger fly, guards each opening to carry messages to and from the ceremony and the star spirits.
Medicine Man: Ayóó'áníłnézí. Collected and painted by F. J. Newcomb. Place: Sawmill near Crystal. Date: 1930.

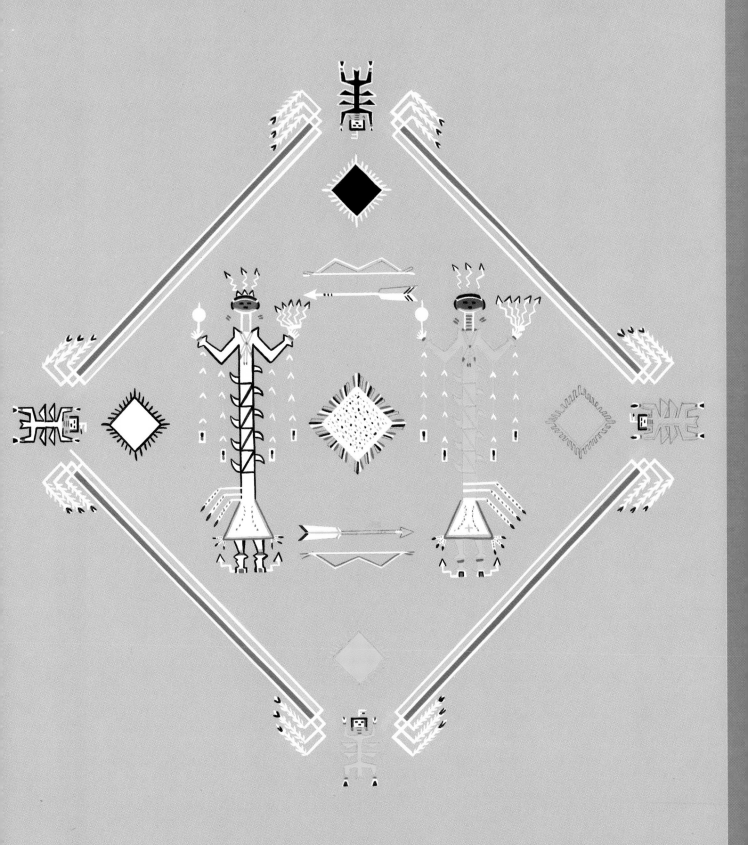

XIV

Great Star Chant—Blessing Form of Ceremony
Feathered Rainbows—Sandpainting of the Fourth Day

The many-colored star of great power with the figure of Naayéé' Neezghání in it, and bows and arrows in four quarters. The four stars of four colors are in the angles of the feathered rainbow.
Medicine Man: Ayóó'aniłnézí. Collected and painted by F. J. Newcomb. Place: Sawmill near Crystal.
Date: 1930.

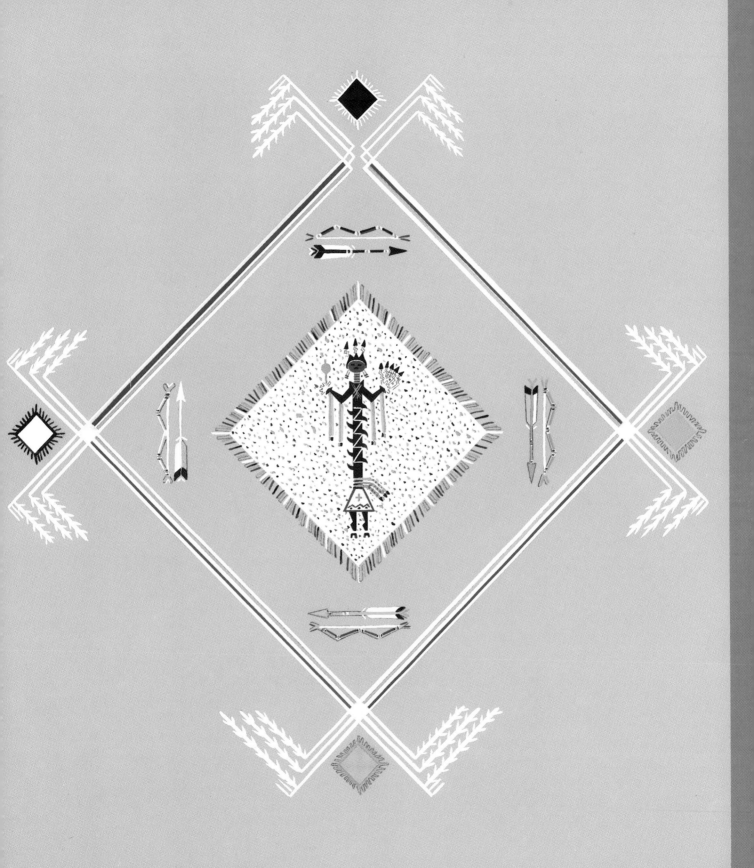

XV

Sandpainting from Ma'iijí Hatáál (or Coyote Chant)

The painting represents the four personified holy times of day. They hold corn, squash, beans, reeds and medicine in their hands, but the eastern dawn figure holds the Sun and Moon. Racer snakes are between the figures of the holy periods of the day.
Medicine Man: Bit'ahnii Bidaghaa'í. Collected by Mary C. Wheelwright. Place: Gallup. Date: 1938.
Painted by Pierre Woodman.

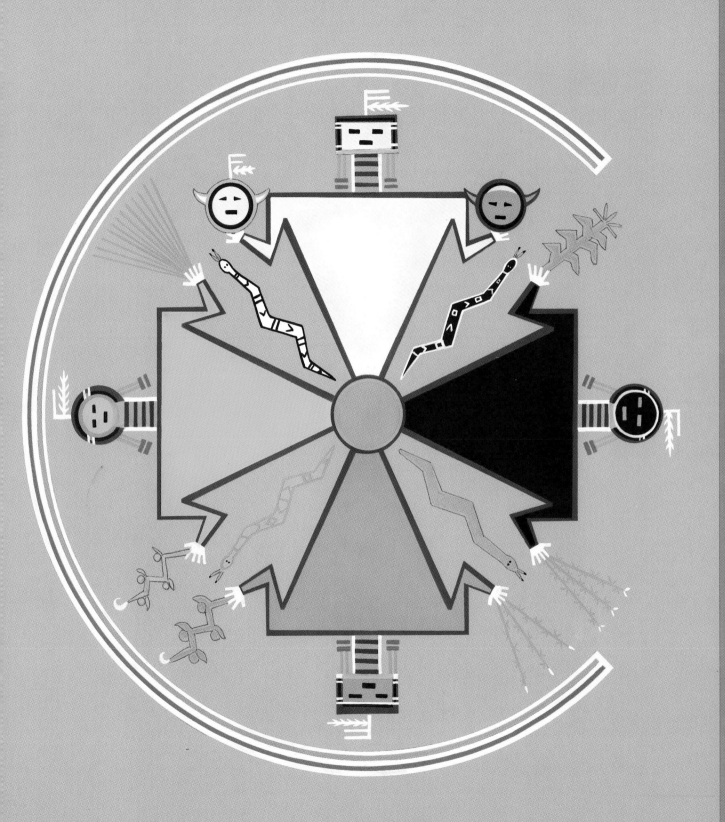

XVI

Ma'iijí or Coyote Chant—First Sandpainting

This painting shows the homes of the different coyotes: of the white dawn, blue day, black night, and yellow evening. Four butterflies are on the paths of pollen leading to the central spring of water. The coyotes call up the rain. This is their function.
Medicine Man: Bit'ahnii Bidághaa'í. Collected by Mary C. Wheelwright. Place: Gallup. Date: 1938.
Painted by Pierre Woodman.

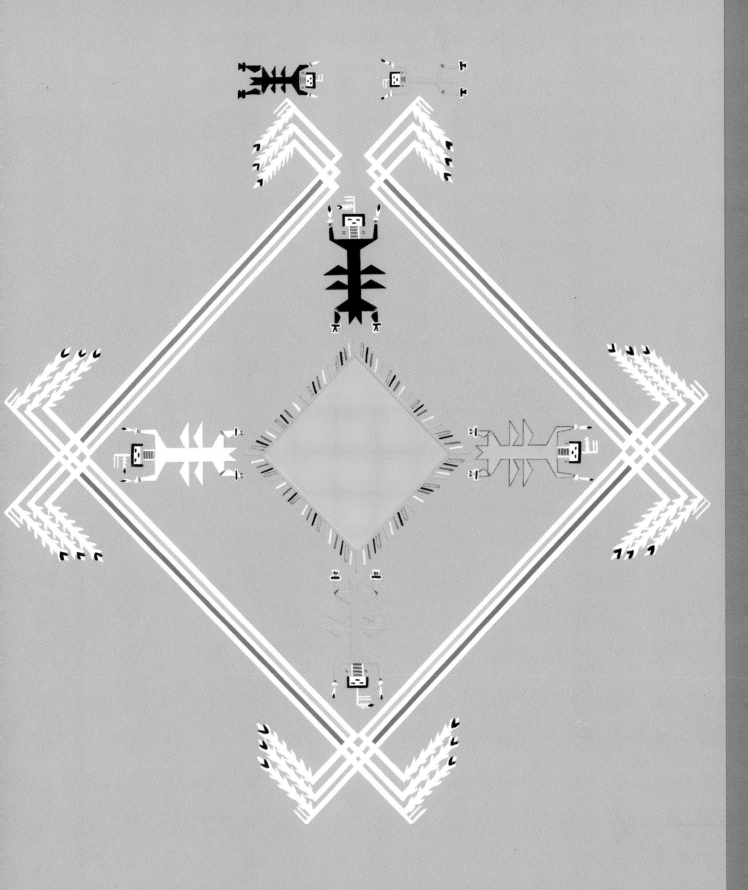

XIII

Great Star Chant—Blessing Form of Ceremony
Second Sandpainting with Feathered Rainbows

This is the second star painting from the Great Star ceremony as given by Ayóó'áníłnézí near Two Grey Hills. He uses a group of five stars with two of the star warriors, with bows and arrows between them to signify extra power. The warriors are carrying lightning arrows and gourd rattles to control wind and rain. The Dǫ'tsoh, or messenger fly, guards each opening to carry messages to and from the ceremony and the star spirits.
Medicine Man: Ayóó'áníłnézí. Collected and painted by F. J. Newcomb. Place: Sawmill near Crystal. Date: 1930.

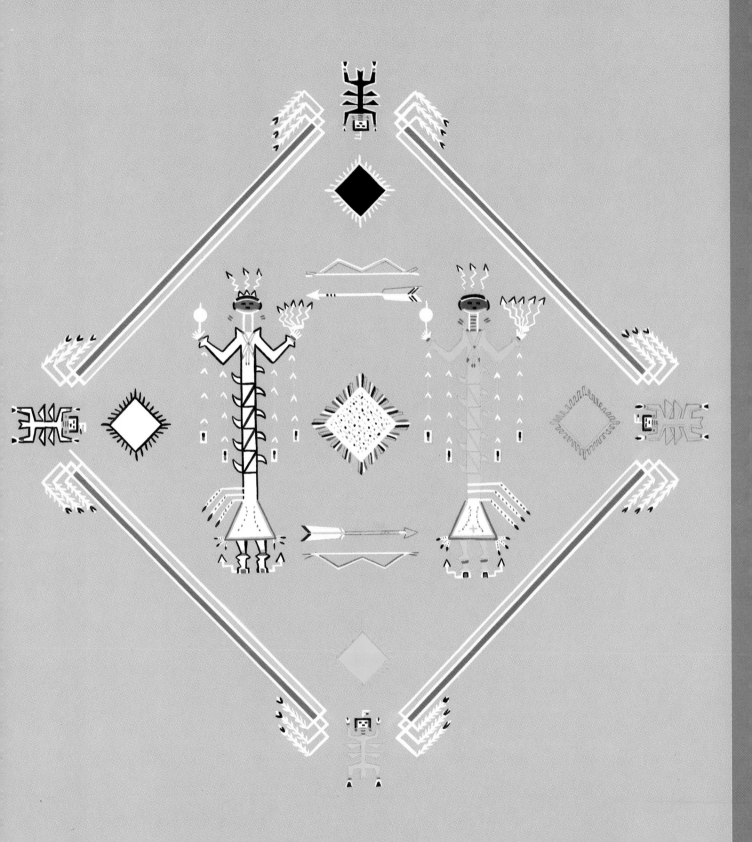

XIV

Great Star Chant—Blessing Form of Ceremony
Feathered Rainbows—Sandpainting of the Fourth Day

The many-colored star of great power with the figure of Naayéé' Neezghání in it, and bows and arrows in four quarters. The four stars of four colors are in the angles of the feathered rainbow.
Medicine Man: Ayóó'aniłnézí. Collected and painted by F. J. Newcomb. Place: Sawmill near Crystal.
Date: 1930.

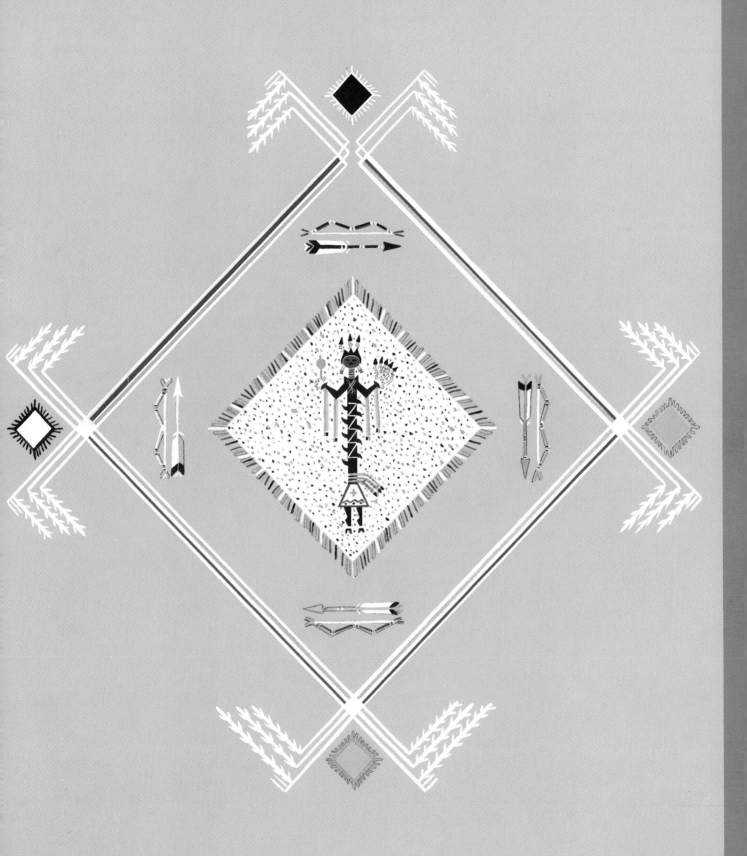

XV

Sandpainting from Ma'iijí Hatáál (or Coyote Chant)

The painting represents the four personified holy times of day. They hold corn, squash, beans, reeds and medicine in their hands, but the eastern dawn figure holds the Sun and Moon. Racer snakes are between the figures of the holy periods of the day.
Medicine Man: Bit'ahnii Bidaghaa'í. Collected by Mary C. Wheelwright. Place: Gallup. Date: 1938.
Painted by Pierre Woodman.

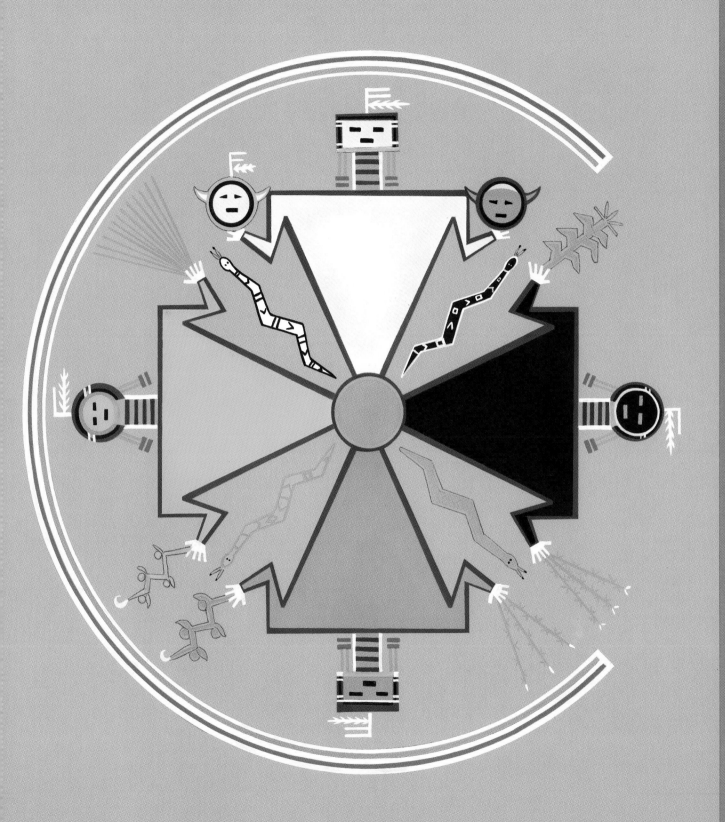

XVI

Ma'iijí or Coyote Chant—First Sandpainting

This painting shows the homes of the different coyotes: of the white dawn, blue day, black night, and yellow evening. Four butterflies are on the paths of pollen leading to the central spring of water. The coyotes call up the rain. This is their function.
Medicine Man: Bit'ahnii Bidághaa'í. Collected by Mary C. Wheelwright. Place: Gallup. Date: 1938.
Painted by Pierre Woodman.

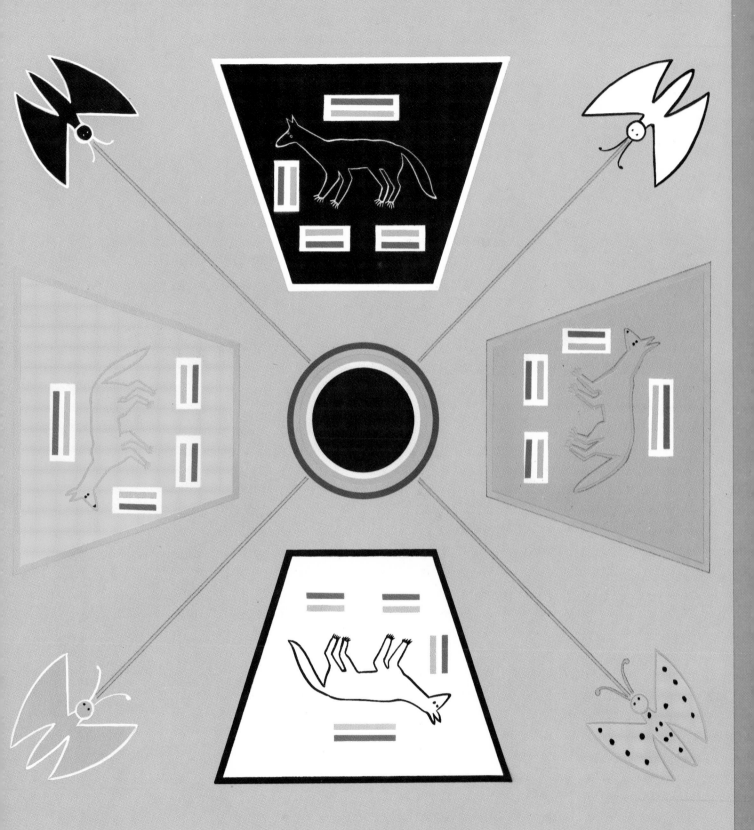

XVII

Coyote Chant—Second Sandpainting

Characters: Sunray and Sunset Coyote girls holding baskets. Under their feet are rainbow to east, sunray to south, sundogs to west, black and white rains to north. Coyotes are walking between Coyote girls. The little animals with feathers (in the girls' hands) are foxes. Eight stalks of corn are growing out of central water.
Collected by Laura Adams Armer. Place: Black Mountain. Date: 1929.
Painted by Mrs. Armer.

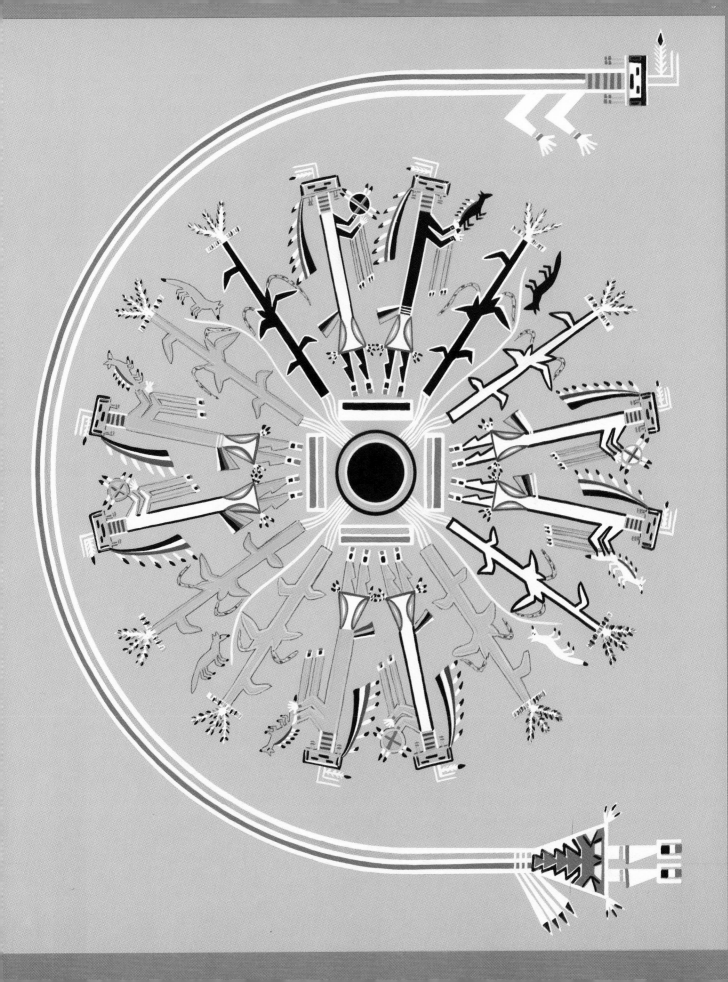

XVIII

Coyote Chant

Coyote girls are shown with baskets and skin rattles in their hands. Four stalks of corn are growing out of
central water. Four foxes with feathered backs are shown.
Collected by Laura Adams Armer. Place: Black Mountain, Arizona. Date: 1929.
Painted by F. J. Newcomb.

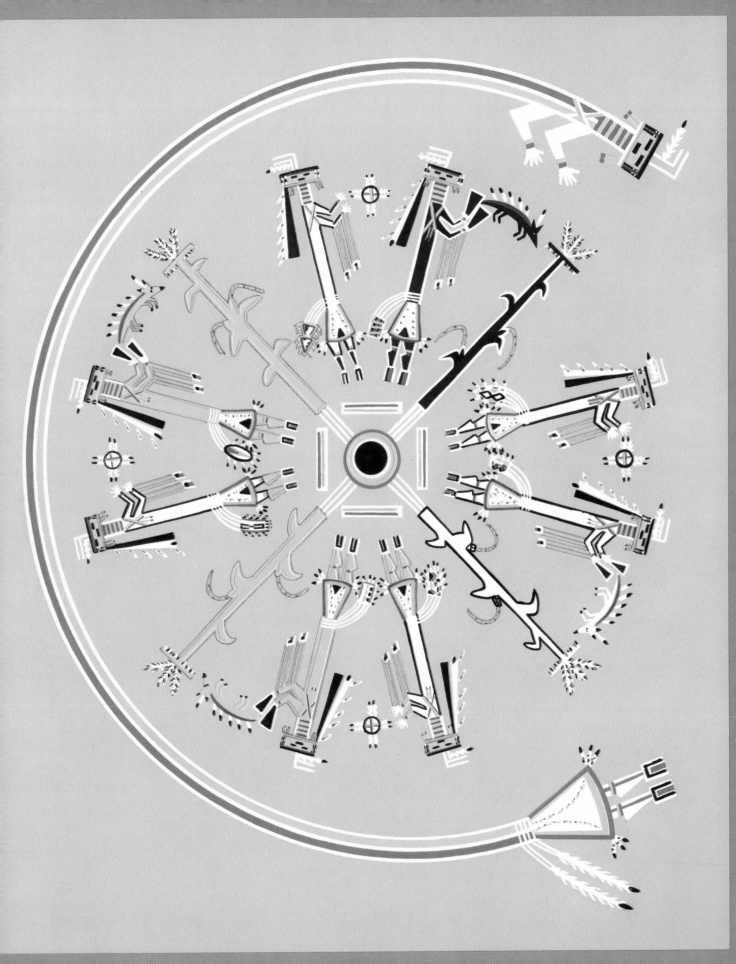

Sǫ'tsohjí Hóchǫ́'íjí
Evil-Chasing Chant
Illustrations

The illustrations on the facing page show the arrangement of mounds (outside the hooghan) which the patient must step over in the ceremonial procedures of the chant. The tsibąąs are also illustrated.

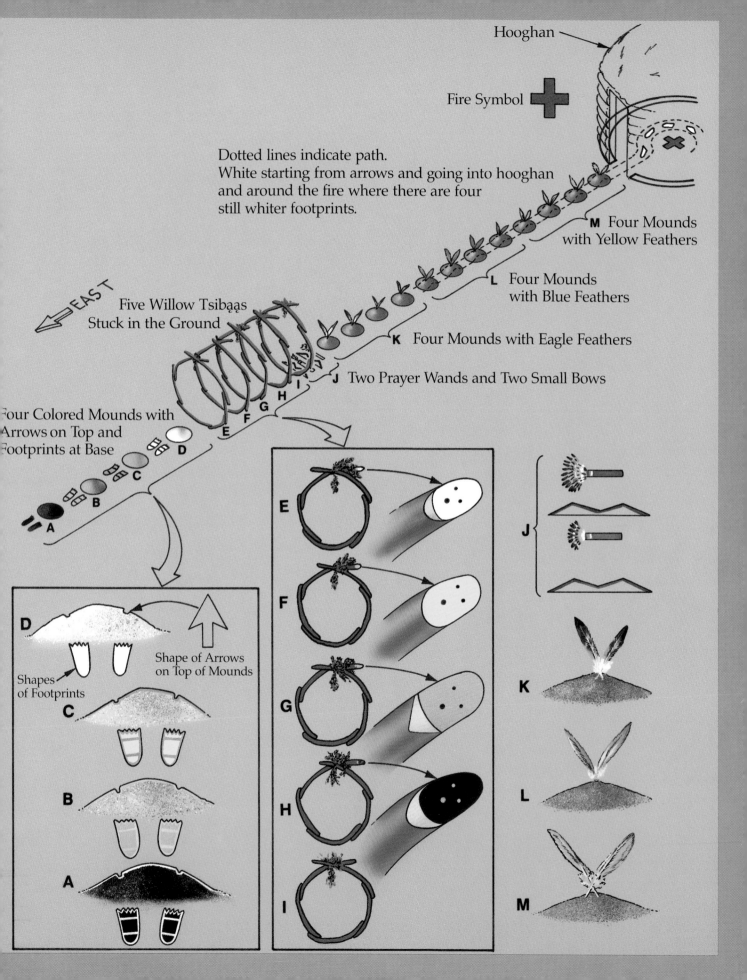

Hooghan

Fire Symbol

Dotted lines indicate path.
White starting from arrows and going into hooghan
and around the fire where there are four
still whiter footprints.

M Four Mounds
with Yellow Feathers

L Four Mounds
with Blue Feathers

EAST

Five Willow Tsibąąs
Stuck in the Ground

K Four Mounds with Eagle Feathers

J Two Prayer Wands and Two Small Bows

Four Colored Mounds with
Arrows on Top and
Footprints at Base

D

C

B

A

E

F

G

H

I

J

K

L

M

D

Shapes
of Footprints

Shape of Arrows
on Top of Mounds

C

B

A

Other ceremonial paraphernalia of the Sǫ'tsohjí Hóchǫ'ijí include reed offerings (k'eet'áán), feathers, and torches of cedar bark (honooyééł).

K'eet'áán,
taken by the hero of the myth
to the sky as a gift to the stars.

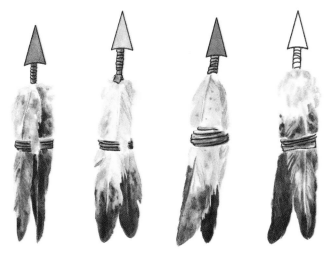

Two eagle feathers bound with two bands of four strands of yucca, 1½ feet high.

Torches of cedar bark, about 1½ feet long,
bound with four groups of four strands of yucca.
Carried by two men.

Body Painting
Illustration

This painting of the body occurred at the end of the holy form of Big Star given by Ayóó'anítnézí, whose sandpaintings are surrounded by fringed rainbows.

For a Male Patient

*(A female patient has the blue star figure on the front
and the black star figure on the back.)*

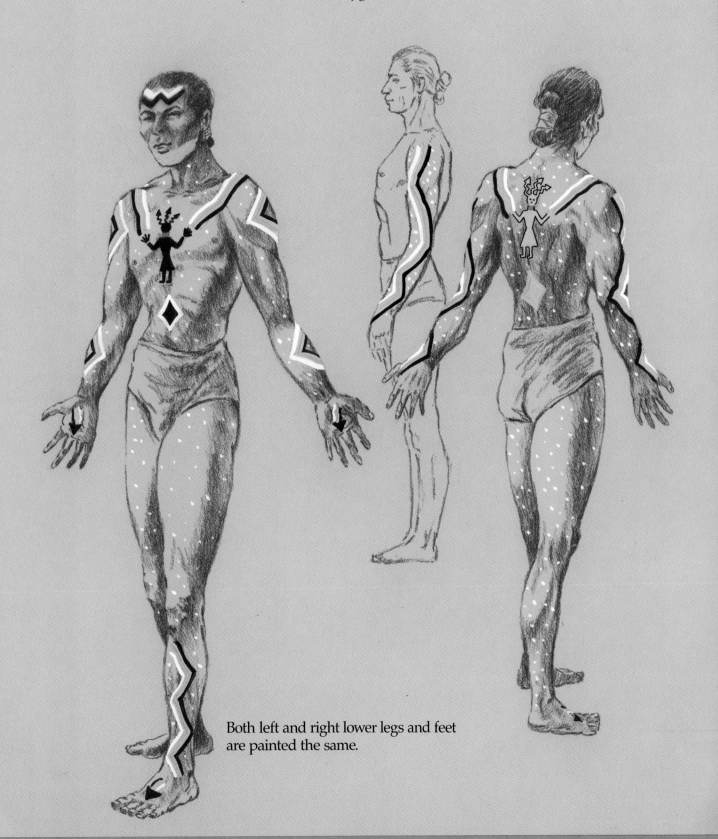

Both left and right lower legs and feet
are painted the same.

Ma'iijí Ceremony
Illustrations

The facing illustrations depict k'eet'áán offerings on the second and third days of the ceremony.

SECOND DAY OF CEREMONY — FIRST K'EET'ÁÁN

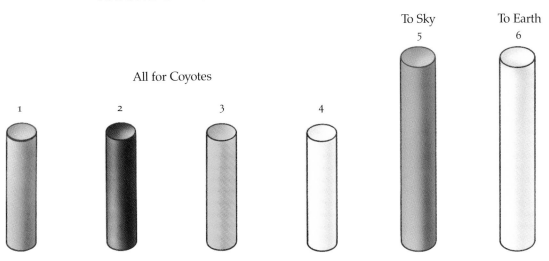

All for Coyotes

To Sky
5

To Earth
6

1   2   3   4

THIRD DAY OF CEREMONY — SECOND K'EET'ÁÁN

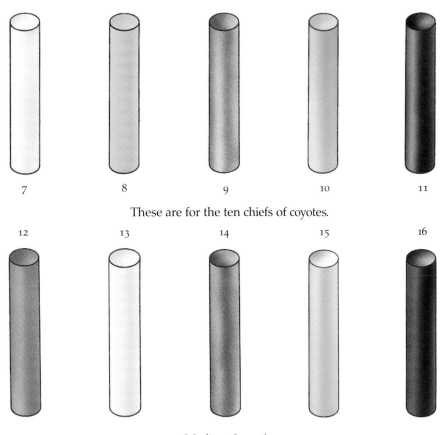

7   8   9   10   11

These are for the ten chiefs of coyotes.

12   13   14   15   16

Medium Length

GLOSSARY

Navajo—English

A

ách'ą́ą́h sodizin	prayer for protection as a shield
ach'íí'náhiniists'e'é	intestines
adooldiz	a dance
ad'ziisį́į́h	see ats'íís
Aghaa'łą́	"Place of Wool," north of Black Mountain, Arizona
ak'ah	fat (see tł'ahnaaschiin)
Akazyiyánii	gland eater
akéé'dahoodzoh	a ceremony using arrows (drawing out by arrows from the body)
ałtahdeedliid	plant burned to make the paint to blacken the body
Anaa'jí	war chant
Aniłt'ánii At'ééd	Corn Beetle Girl ("The Ripener")
ant'eesh	blackening (of the body)
Asdzáán Hataałii	the woman singer who acted as assistant to the medicine man
Asdzáán Nádleehé	Changing Woman
Ashįįh Haagai	"Salt Lake," south of Zuni, named for Salt Woman in the First world and for the Salt Clan
ats'íís	rite of pressing medicine man's limbs and body to those of the patient
Ats'o'osii	feather myth
Awéé'náá'ołí	"Baby-floating-place"
ayahdadi'nił	incense of honey from wasp
ayásh	generic term for small colored birds
ayásh bąąh nanoogáád	a dried substance taken from bat, wren, Dǫ'tsoh, corn beetle, and the ayásh

171

ayeel	medicine in pellet form containing every kind of holy substance connected with a given ceremony; a protection against any sickness; aperient made of wasp
Ayóó'áníłnézí	Tall Man
azdoosįįh	rite of painting the body
azeenitł'iní	hardening medicine

B
Báálók' aa	"Arrow," north of White Cone, Arizona
Be'ek'id Náhásbąsi	"Turning Lake," round lake where the Ancient Ones lived
bijį́	last and most important day of ceremony
Biyahdiigai	"White streak going up"
biyeel	medicine offering (see k'eet'áán)

C
ch'agiiłtsooí	yellow-headed blackbird
ch'eehóyátééh	rite which brings back a person out of sickness and evil
chį́įshtah	a plant
Chį́įshtah Nask'id	"Chį́įshtah Ridge"
ch' il bináá' łees' áán	a food made of seeds
ch' ildiilyésii	gramma grass; one of the four sacred herbs
Ch'ínílí	Chinle, Arizona
Ch'óhazt'i'	"Fir-trees-growing-in-row-at-mouth-of-canyon", north of Ch'ínílį, Arizona
chooshghalii	tanager
Ch'óyáázh Ashkii	"Son of Fir," east of La Plata Mountains

D
Dáádiníléi	Guardians of the entrance
Denihootso	"End of pasture," east of Tuba City, Arizona
Dibé Nitsaa	"Place of the big mountain sheep," La Plata Mountains, Colorado; one of the four holy mountains
didlídii	food plant found on Navajo Mountain
didze'	food plant found on Navajo Mountain
Diné	The People (the Navajos' name for themselves)
Diné Tł'óól	Medicine man (an individual name); see Hastiin Bahozhoni
Diyin Dine'é	Holy People

Diyin K'ehgo Hatáál	holy form of Sacred Chant
dleeshłigaii	white earth
Dook'o'oosłííd	"Sparkling Mountain," San Francisco Peaks, Arizona; one of the four holy mountains
Doonikéí	a Pueblo clan, the Eagle clan
Dǫ'tsoh	Big Fly, Messenger Fly (white-headed fly)
Dził Diłhiłii	"Darkness Mountain"
Dzil Díílt'éhé	"Fourth Mountain," east of Navajo Reservation
Dził Łabáí	"Grey Mountain," north of San Francisco Peaks
Dził Łahdilt'éhé	"Mountain by itself"
Dziłna'oodiłii	"Mountain with something revolving around it," Huerfano Peak
Dził Nidilt'éhé	a mountain
Dził Tált'éhé	"Mountain made of everything"

G
gad ádin	decoction of herbs

H
hááhóyátééh	prayer of liberation
Haashch'ee Bi'aadii	Female God
haashch'éédáá'	coyote bush (see ma'iidą́ą́')
Haashch'éełti'í	Talking God
Haashch'ééshjiní	Fire God
Haashch'é'éwaan	Hooghan God (or Home God)
Hadeeshtł'iizh	south of Manuelito
Hajíínéí	"coming up," where the people came up to this world from below, a lake near Silverton, Colorado
Hastiin Bahozhoni	Medicine man (an individual name): see Diné Tł'óól
hastói	elder men
Hazlíí'	"Made Now" (the Bead People)
hinááh bits'os	feather from a live bird
Hózhǫ́ǫ́jí Hatáál	Blessing Chant

I
I'diilkíísh	a ceremony

J

jidiitłah	rite of resuscitating from a fit
Jóhonaa'éí Iikááh	a sandpainting on buckskin

K

k'eet'áán	an offering; a hollow reed about the size of a cigarette, filled with tobacco, bits of shell, and other precious materials
kétłoh	infusion of herbs
Kin dootł'izh	Blue House
kiva	underground ceremonial chamber
klichee	food plant found on Navajo Mountain
k'oschíín	cloud symbol

L

Ł'ééchąą'i	name of black image of dog in Coyote Myth
lók'aatsoh	big reed
Lók'ajígai	"White field of reeds," north of Ch'íníli, Arizona

M

Ma'ii	Coyote
ma'iidą́ą́'	coyote bush (see haasch'éédáá')
Ma'íí idiizts'ą́ą́'	"The coyote heard it." (What the children roasting corn in the underworld said when the corn popped)

N

Naadą́'ádziil	"Corn Mountain," near Tuba City
Naadahas'éí	mountain south of Zuni, New Mexico
Naadahas'éí Bílátah	"Naadahas'éí Peak," south of the meteor crater near Flagstaff
náá'iiniih	delivering offerings to those above
Naastíín'tsoh	a peak near Black Mountain
Naats'ádziil	Ruler "Mountain," south of Zuni, New Mexico
nááts'íílid	rainbow
Naatsis'áán	Navajo Mountain
Naayéé' Neezghání	Slayer of Enemies
Nahasdzáán	Mother Earth
Nahodiisgiizh	"Where smoke comes out between the rocks," near Blue Mountain
Náhookǫs	Dipper constellation

nahtezh	food plant found on Navajo Mountain
Nakoholdehe	ceremonial name given to the Hunter in the Coyote Myth
Na'ní'áhí	Water Bridge
Nanise'dziil	"Everything-that-grows-on-earth-Mountain"
násodóíłtsoí	mountain lion
Ni'bitádídíín Yeeniiyánii Ashkii	Nourished-by-the-growth-of-the-Earth Boy, or simply Earth Boy
nidii'á	ceremonial plaque
Ni'haldzis	"hollow in rock," near Buell Park
Ni'hodiits'a	"Road of the Left Handed Wind"
Nihookáá' Dine'é	Earth Person
Nihookóó'haniihii	He-who-knows-everything
Niłch'i	Wind
Niłch'i Biyázhí	Spirit Wind, Messenger Wind
Niłch'i Diłhił Biye'	Son of the Black Wind (name of Older Brother)
Niłch'ihołdiiskai	Walking-with-the-Wind
Niłch'ijí Hatáál	Wind Chant
Niłch'ijí Hataałii Biye'	Son of Singer
Niłch'itsoh	December (great wind)
Niłtsą́dziil	"Rain Mountain," in the Chuskai range
nitł'iz	offering of jewels
Nitł'izdziil	"Jewel Mountain"
Níyoltsoh	Cyclone

S	
Saba-kéet	medicine to use after the ceremony of beating the basket
Sisnaajiní	Holy Mountain of the North, north of Taos
Sǫ'tsoh	Great Star
Sǫ'tsoh Deeshzhah	Many-Pointed Star
Sǫ'tsoh Diłhił	Black Star
Sǫ'tsoh Diłhił Biye'	Son of Black Star (the Great Star) (name of Younger Brother)
Sǫ'tsohjí Hatáál	Great Star Chant

T	
Taahdootł'izhi	"Blue-land-goes-into-river"
Taahyilk'id	"Ridge-which-goes-into-the-water," ten miles north of Ch'ínílį

Táchii'nii	Red Soil clan
Tádídíín Ashkii	Pollen Boy
Tádídííndziil	"Pollen Mountain"
Tádídíín Yeeneeyánii	Reared in the Pollen or Blessed with Pollen; name of Older Brother, also name of Younger Brother
Tééhoołtsódii	Water Monster
T'iis Názbạs	Teec Nos Pos, Arizona
tł'ahnaaschíín	ceremonial fat
Tł'iishtsoh	Great Snake
Tł'iishtsoh Asdzáán	Great Snake Woman
Tł'iishtsoh Hastiin	Great Snake Man
tł'oh dahnaayizii	the-plant-that-rolls (tumbleweed)
tł'ohlichi'ii	food plant found on Navajo Mountain
tł'oh nástasii	one of the four sacred herbs
tł'ohtsoh	food plant found on Navajo Mountain
tł'oht'sósí	food plant found on Navajo Mountain
Tó'bájíshchíní	Born of Water, twin brother of Naayéé Neezghání
Tódíníishzhee'	"Streams going out," at north end of Black Mountain
Tónáálị	"Place where water falls," on top of Steamboat plateau
Tónahelįįh	"Crossing water place," crossing of the rivers
Tónaneesdizí	"Where-the-water-goes-round-and-round," near Leupp, Arizona
Tóneinilí	Water God (Water Bearer or Water Sprinkler God)
Tóniteel	the Great Sea
Tónits'ósíkooh	"Narrow-water-canyon,"
tóyikááł	one of the four sacred herbs
tsá' ásdzi'	"Rocks in a row"
tsá'ásdzi'bidee'	horned yucca
tsá'ásdzi'nit'eelí	a land of yucca
tsá'ásdzi' ts'óóz	a kind of yucca
Tsá'ásdzi'tsoozi	the slim yucca
Tsin Hodelkoch	He-whose-stomach-trembles (with hunger), ceremonial name of Yellow Corn Man
Tsah Oshkinzh	Whatever-he-throws-down-spreads-out-flat (vomit); ceremonial name of White Corn Man
Tsé' ááto	"Cave-where-there-is-water," up in Ute country
tsé'azhiih	one of the four sacred herbs
tsé biná' ez' eli	"Rock with surrounding soil washed away," at entrance of Canyon de Chelly, Arizona

Tsé'édééh	place name
Tséhołhót'aáiya	place name
tséiik'ą	powdered rock, for sandpainting
Tséłchíí'Dah'azkání	"Red Rock Hat Brim," a tall rock in Red Rock Valley
Tsénánootł'iizh	"Streak of blue coming down"
Tsén'ást'i'	Sanostee
Tsénáshchii'	"Round Circle Red Rock"
Tséniichii'	"Red Rock Ending," near Gallup, New Mexico
Tséniteel	"Flat Rock," a place known for game animals near Ganado, Arizona
Tsen-koh-oltsin	place name
Tsénoolch'oshii	Rock Wren
Tsét'ąhii	"Thin Rocks"
Tséyaat'i'í	"Pointed Rock," 19 miles east of Náháshch'idí
Tséyi'	Canyon de Chelly
tsibąąs	ceremonial hoop
tsídiiłtsoí	yellowbird
tsiiłchin	food plant found on Navajo Mountain
tsiilkaalii	wood kicking (a game in which they race, kicking a stick along with them)
Tsi' naajinii	Black Streak Clan
Tsin bíil' á	"Trees-growing-on-the-side-of-mountain"
Tsoodził	"Big Mountain," Mt. Taylor, New Mexico, the turquoise mountain of the south; one of the four sacred mountains

W

wóláchíí'	red ant
wooltáád	rite of untying slipknots

Y

Yaasilá	place where the sky and earth meet
yátaał níłch'i	incense made of wax of bee
yé' ibicheii	god
yé'ii	Grandfather God
yé'ii bitsá'ásdzi'	a kind of yucca
Yoo'ii Dine'é	Bead People
Yoo'ídziil	"Bead Mountain"

Z

zaa'nił	powdered herbs, an internal medicine

English — Navajo

*Indicates Navajo word not used in text.

A

abalone	*diichiłí
All-colored (Rainbow) Wind	*Níyolditsǫsí
all sorts of pretty birds; group term	ayash
Ancient Ones	*Anaasází
aperient made of wasp	ayeel

B

basket of jet	bááshjinii ts'aa'
bat	Jaa'abaní
Bead Chant	Yoo'iijí Hatáál
Bead People	Yoo'ii Dine'é
beating the basket	zah-beh kut[1]
bee weed	waa'
Big Fly, Messenger Fly (White-headed fly)	Dǫ'tsoh
big reed	lók'aatsoh
black eagle	*atsáshjiin
blackening (of the body)	ant'eesh
black flint armor	*bééshdiłhiłí
Black Star	Sǫ'tsoh Diłhiłí
Black Streak clan	Tsi'naajinii
Black Thunder	*Ii'ni' Diłhiłí

---

[1]This is in the transcription of M. C. Wheelwright, transcribed differently on page 183.

*Black Wind	Níłch'i Diłhiłí
Blessed Hooghan	*Tádídíín Beehooghan
Blessing Chant	Hózhóójí Hatáál
blue after sunset	*nahoodootł'iizh
bluebird	*dólii
blue flint armor	*bééshdootł'ish
Blue House	Kin dootłizh
blue racer snake	*tł'iishk'aa'
Blue Star	*Sǫ' Dootł'izh
Blue Wind	*Níłch'i Dootł'izh
Born of Water; twin brother of Naayéé' Neezghání	Tóbájíshchíní
brush hooghan	*iłnázt'i'
bull-roarer	tsindi'ni
buzzard	*jeeshóó'

C

Changing Woman	Asdzáán Nádleehé
ceremonial fat	tł'ahnaaschíín
ceremonial hoop	tsibąąs
ceremonial name given to the Hunter in the Coyote Myth	Nakoholdehe
ceremonial plaque	nidii'á
ceremony	I'diilkíísh
ceremony given once	*t'ááłáhídi hatáál
ceremony using arrows; drawing out by arrows from the body	akee'dahoodzoh
ceremony to restore patient when fainting	jidiitłah
chicken hawk	*giní
Chinle, Arizona	Ch'ínílí
cloud symbol	k'oschíín
conch shell	*tseth cheen²
corn beetle, ''The Ripener''	*aniłt'ánii
Corn Beetle Girl	Aniłt'ánii At'ééd
Coyote	Ma'ii
coyote bush	haashch'éédą́ą́', m̨a'iidą́ą́'

²This is in the transcription of M. C. Wheelwright.

"Coyote heard it." (What the children
roasting corn in the underworld said when
the corn popped)   Ma'ii idiizts'ą́ą́
Crystal Hooghan of People of the Rocks   *Tségha'dinídínii Beehooghan
Cyclone   Níyoltsoh

D
dark cloud   *k'os dithił
darkness   *chahałheeł
Darkness Hooghan   *Chahałheeł Beehooghan
December (great wind)   Nítch'itsoh
decoction of herbs   gad ádin
delivering offerings to those above   náá'iiniih
Dipper constellation   Náhookǫs
dried substance taken from Bat, Wren,
Dǫ'tsoh, Corn Beetle, and ayásh   ayásh bąąh nanoogáád.

E
Eagle People   Atsá Dine'é
Earth Boy   Ni'bitádídíín Yeeneeyánii Ashkii
Earth Person   Nihookáá' Dine'é
elder men   hastóí
Entranyas cactus   *kah-obizze[3]
Evil-Chasing Chant   *Hóchǫ́ íjí Hatáál
Evil-Chasing Great Star Chant   Sǫ'tsoi Bihocho'iji
evil spirits   ch'į́į́dii

F
fat   ak'ah (see ceremonial fat)
feather from a live bird   hinááh bits'os
Feather Myth   Ats'o'osii
Female God   Haashch'éé Bi'áadii
Female Great Star Chant   *Sǫ'tsohjí Bi'áádii
Female Wind Chant   *Nítch'ijí Bi'áád
fir   *ch'ó

---

[3]This is in the transcription of M. C. Wheelwright.

Fire God	Haashch'ééshjiní
fire poker	*honiishgish
fire stick	*tł'ééł
flint	*béésh
flint of all colors	*bééshdisǫsii
food made of seeds	ch'il bináá' łees'áán
food plants found on Navajo Mountain	didlídii, dit'ódii, didze', łichíí', tł'ohlich'ii, tł'ohsoh, tł'ohts'ósí, nahtezh, tsiiłchin
from right to left	*shádááh

G

generic terms for small colored birds	ayásh
Gila monster	*tiníléí
Gland Eater	Akazyiyánii
god	Yé'ii
gopher (in the earth pocket)	*na'azísii
gourd rattle	*aghááł
gramma grass	ch'ildiilyésii
Grandfather God	Yé'ibicheii
Great Snake	Tł'iishtsoh
Great Snake Man	Tłi'ishtsoh Hastiin
Great Snake Woman	Tłi'ishtsoh Asdzáán
Great Star	Sǫ'tsoh
Great Star Chant	Sǫ'tsohjí Hatáál
grey barred hawk	tsin yahl shai[4]
grey fir	*ch'ódeenínii
grey hawk	*ayásh dootł'izh
grey short pinyon	*che'ołdeenínii
ground corn meal mush	*gadą́ą́'
Guardians of the Entrance	Dáádiníléí

H

Hail	*Nílóh
Hail Chant	Nílóójí Hatáál

---

[4]This is in the transcription of M. C. Wheelwright.

hardening medicine	azeenitł'ini (see powdered herbs)
heat lightning	*hajilgish
He-who-knows-everything	Nihookóó'haniihii
He-whose-stomach-trembles (with hunger); ceremonial name of Yellow Corn Man	Tsin Hodelkoch
Hooghan God (or Home God)	Haashch'ééwaan
Holy Mountains	Dibé Nitsaa, Dook'o'oosłiid, Sisnaajiní, Tsoodził
Holy People	Diyin Dine'é
Holy Water	*tódiyin
home of yellow hawks	*atsiiłtsoi
horned yucca	tsá'ásdzi'bidee'

I

ice shield	*naagé
incense made of wax of bee	*yátaał nitch'i
incense made of honey from wasp	ayahdadi'nił
infusion of herbs	kétłoh
I-plant-the-small-grains (June)	*Ya'iishjááshchilí
intestines	ach'ii'náhiinists'e'é

J

June (I-plant-the-small-grains)	Ya'iishjááshchilí

L

last and most important day of ceremony	bijí
Left Handed Wind	*Níłch'initł'a
lichen, literally "rock moss"	*tsédláád
Lightning	*atsiniltł'ish

M

"Made Now" (the Bead People)	Hazlíí'
Male Shooting Chant	*Na'ał'oi Biką'jí
Male Great Star Chant	*Sǫ'tsohjí Biką'jí

Male Wind Chant	*Nílch'ijí Biką'
Many-Pointed Star	Sǫ'tsoh Deeshzhah
medicine in pellet form containing every kind of holy substance connected with a given ceremony; a protection against any sickness; aperient made of wasp	ayeel
medicine man (an individual name)	Diné Tł'óó (Hastíí Bahozhoni)
medicine offering	biyeel (k'eet'áán)
medicine pouch	jish
medicine to use after the ceremony of beating the basket	saba-keet
Messenger Fly, Big Fly (White-headed fly)	Dǫ'tsoh
Messenger Wind	Nílch'i Biyazhi (Spirit Wind)
Mother Earth	Nahasdzáán
mountain lion	nashdóítsoh
mountain tobacco	dził nát'oh

N

name of black image of dog in Coyote Myth	Łééchąą'í
Nourished-by-the-growth-of-the-Earth Boy or Nourished-by-Earth Boy	Ni'bitádídíín Yeeneeyánii Ashkii (see Earth Boy)

O

an offering	biyeel (k'eet'áán)
an offering; a hollow reed about the size of a cigarette, filled with tobacco, bits of shell, and other precious materials	k'eet'áán
offering of jewels	nitł'iz

P

The People (the Navajos' name for themselves)	Diné
pinyon	*ché'ol
Place Names:	
Aghaa'łą́	"Place of Wool," north of Black Mountain, Arizona
Ashį́į́h Haagai	"Salt Lake," south of Zuni, named for Salt Woman in the First World and for the Salt Clan
Awéénáá'olí	"Baby-Floating-Place"
Báálók'aá'	"Arrow," north of White Cone, Arizona

Be'ek'id Náházbąsi	"Turning Lake," Round Lake where the Ancient Ones lived
Bhezhin-etsosegi[5]	Black Rock at Red Lake
Biyahdegai	"White streak going up," south of Steamboat Canyon
Chį́į́shtah Násk'id	"Chį́į́shtah Ridge"
Ch'ó Haazt'i'	"Fir-trees-growing-in-row-at-mouth-of-canyon," north of Ch'ínílį, Arizona
Ch'ó Yáázh Ashkii	"Son of Fir," east of La Plata Mountains
Dibé Nitsaa	"Place of the Big Mountain Sheep," La Plata Mountains, Colorado
Denihootso	"End of Pasture," east of Tuba City, Arizona
Dook'o'oosłííd	"Sparkling Mountain," San Francisco Peaks, Arizona
Dził Diłhiłii	"Darkness Mountain"
Dził Dílt'éhé	"Fourth Mountain," east of Navajo Reservation
Dził Ditł'oi	"Hairy Mountain"
Dził Łabái	"Grey Mountain," north of San Francisco Peaks
Dził Náneests'ee'é	"Coiled Mountain"
Dził Ná'oodiłii	"Mountain with something revolving around it," Huerfano Peak
Dzil Łahdilt'éhé	"Mountain by itself"
Dził Nidilt'éhé	a mountain
Dził Tált'éhé	"Mountain made of everything"
Hadeeshtł'iizh	south of Manuelito
Hajíínéí	"Coming up," where the people came up to this world from below; a lake near Silverton, Colorado
Hajíínéídził	"Mountain-where-they-came-up," near eastern end of La Plata Mountains
Lok'ajígai	"White field of reeds," north of Ch'ínílį, Arizona
Naadą́'ádziil	"Corn Mountain," near Tuba City
Naadahas'éí	mountain south of Zuni, New Mexico
Naadahas'éí Bílátah	"Naadahas'éí Peak," south of the meteor crater near Flagstaff
Naat'ádziil	"Ruler Mountain," south of Zuni, New Mexico
Naatsis'áán	Navajo Mountain
Nahodiisgiizh	"Where smoke comes out between the rocks," near Blue Mountain
Na'ni'á	Water Bridge
Nanise'dziil	"Everything-that-grows-on-earth Mountain"

---

[5]This is in the transcription of M. C. Wheelwright.

Nastiintsoh	peak near Black Mountain
Nihodiits'a	"Road of the Left-Handed Wind"
Ni'haldzis	"hollow in rock," near Buell Park
Níłtsądziil	"Rain Mountain," in the Chuska range
Nitł'izdziil	"Jewel Mountain"
Sisnaajiní	Holy Mountain of the North, north of Taos
Taahdootł'izh	"Blue-land-goes-into-river"
Taahyilk'id	"Ridge-which-goes-into-the-water," ten miles north of Ch'ínílį, Arizona
Tádídííndziil	"Pollen Mountain"
Tódínííshzhee'	"Streams going out," at north end of Black Mountain
Tónaalį	"Place where water falls," on top of Steamboat Plateau
Tónahelįįh	"Crossing water place," crossing of the rivers
Tónaneesdizí	"Where-the-water-goes-round-and-round," near Leupp, Arizona
Tóniteel	the Great Sea
Tónits'ósíkooh	"Narrow-water-canyon"
Tse'átó	"Cave-where-there-is-water," up in Ute country
Tsé Biná'az'élí	"Rock with surrounding soil washed away," at entrance of Canyon de Chelly, Arizona
Tsé'édééh	"Rock with wings" (Shiprock)
Tséhołhótááya	a place name
Tséít'eezh	"Rocks in a row"
Tséłichíí' Dah'azká	"Red Rock Hat Brim," a tall rock now called Cheedi in Red Rock Valley
Tsénáshchii'	"Round Circle Red Rock"
Tséniichii'	"Red Rock Ending," near Gallup, New Mexico
Tséníłch'i	"Wind Rock"
Tsenanootł'iizh	"Streak of blue coming down"
Tséniteel	"Flat Rock," a place known for game animals near Ganado, Arizona
Tsét'ąhí	"Thin Rocks"
Tsézhin Hałgizhígíí	"Forked Black Rock," west of Ganado
Tséyaat'i'i	"Pointed Rock," 19 miles east of Náháshch'idí
Tséyi'	Canyon de Chelly
Tsi'keh[6]	"Wooded Hill," near Winslow, Arizona

---

[6]This is in the transcription of M. C. Wheelwright.

Tsilth des-hozhoni[7]	"Sacred Mountain," St. Michaels Mountain, Arizona
Tsilth-nah-niszah[8]	"Wide Mountain"
Tsin Bíil'á	"Trees-growing-on-the-side-of-mountain"
Tsoodził	"Big Mountain," Mt. Taylor, New Mexico, the turquoise mountain of the south; one of the four sacred mountains
Yáhóógai	"Mountain of Light"
Yaasilá	place where the sky and earth meet
Yoo'ídziil	"Bead Mountain"
a plant	chííshtah
plant burned to make the paint to blacken the body	ałtadeedlííd
plant that rolls (tumbleweed)	tł'oh dahnaayizii
Pollen Boy	Tádídíín Ashkii
powdered herbs, an internal medicine	zaa'nił
powdered horsetail plant	ah-teen-sikash[9]
powdered rock, for sandpainting	tséiik'á
pounded dried meat	*ahchonh[10]
prayer	*sodizin
prayer for protection as a shield	ách'áá sodizon
prayer forcing out from danger	ch'ééhóyátééh
prayer of liberation	hááhóyátééh
Pueblo clan, the Eagle clan	Dooníkéí

R

rainbow	nááts'íílid
Rainbow's End	nááts'íílid
Rainbow (all-colored) Wind	*Níyołditsǫsí
Ray of Dawn	*Hayoołkááł
ray of light	*shábitł'óól
Reared in the Pollen or Blessed with Pollen; name of Younger Brother	Tádídíín Yeeneeyánii
red ant	wóláchíí'
Red Soil clan	Táchii'nii
reed	lók'aatsoh

---

[7]This is in the transcription of M. C. Wheelwright.
[8]This is in the transcription of M. C. Wheelwright.
[9]This is in the transcription of M. C. Wheelwright.
[10]This is in the transcription of M. C. Wheelwright.

rite of painting the body	azdoosjjh
rite of pressing medicine man's limbs and body to those of the patient	ats'íís, ats'iisjjh
rite of resuscitating from a fit	jidiitłah
rite of untying slipknots	wooltáád
rite which brings back a person out of sickness and evil	Ch'ééhóyátééh
Rock Wren	Tsénoolch'óshii
rose, rosebush	*chǫh
round cactus	*hoshdijoolí

S

sacred bundle	antranh[11]
Sacred Chant	Diyinjí Hatáál
Sacred form of Holy Chant	Diyin K'ehgo Hataal
sacred herbs	tł'oh nástasii, ch'ildiilyésii, tóyíkááł, tsé'azhiih
salty cactus	hosh dik'ǫzhí
sandpainting on buckskin	Jóhonaa'éí Iikááh
Sanostee	Tsén'ast'i'
scrub cedar	*gaddeenínii
sheet lightning	*hatsol-rah[12]
shield of fire	*kon-noh-gehd[13]
sky	*yá
Slayer of Enemies	Naayéé' Neezghání
slim yucca	tsá'ásdzi'ts'óóz
snake arrow, see blue racer snake	
soapweed (yucca root)	*amole[14]
son-in-law	*shaadaaní
Son of Black Star (the Great Star) (name of Younger Brother)	Sǫ'tsoh Diłhił Biye'
Son of the Black Wind (name of Older Brother)	Níłch'i Diłhił Biye'
Son of Singer	Níłch'ijí Hataałii Biye'

---

[11]This is in the transcription of M. C. Wheelwright.
[12]This is in the transcription of M. C. Wheelwright.
[13]This is in the transcription of M. C. Wheelwright.
[14]This is in the transcription of M. C. Wheelwright.

Spirit Wind	Nítch'i Biyázhí
spruce tree rite	*tróhgish[15]
squirrel plant (medicine)	Hazééłda'a

T

Talking God	Haashch'ééłti'í
tall cactus	*hosh niteelií
Tall Man	Ayóó'áníłnézí
Teec Nos Pos	T'iis Názbąs
tanager	chooshghalii
Thunder (or Lightning)	*Ii'ni'
tiger dance	adooldiz
tumbleweed (the-plant-that-rolls)	tł'oh dahnaayizii

U

| underground ceremonial chamber | kiva |

W

Walking-with-the-wind	Nítch'ihołdiiskai
War Chant	Anaa'jí
Water Chant	Tohí
Water Bearer or Water Sprinkler God	Tóneinilí
Water God	Tóneinilí
Water Horse	*Tééhłį́į'
Water Monster	Tééhhoołtsódii
Water People	Tohí Dine'é
Whatever-he-throws-down-spreads-out-flat (vomit) (ceremonial name of White Corn Man)	Tsah Oshkinzh
Whirling Water	*Tódildǫǫh
White Eagle	*Atsálgai
White-headed Eagle	*Táá'jiłgai
White earth	dleeshłigaií
White Ray of Dawn Hooghan	*Hayoołkááł Beehooghan

---

[15]This is in the transcription of M. C. Wheelwright.

White Shell	Had-at-eh[16]
White Star	Sǫ'tsoh Łigaií
White Thunder	*Ii'ni' Jiłgaií
White Wind	*Níłch'i Łigaií
Wind	Níłch'i
Wind Chant	Níłch'ijí Hatáál
woman singer who acted as assistant to the medicine man	Asdzáán Hataałii
wood kicking (a game in which they race, kicking a stick along with them)	tsiilkaalii

Y

yellowbird	tsídiiłtsoí
yellow-headed blackbird	*chugitso
yellow pine	nídíshchíí'
Yellow Star	Sǫ'tsoh Łitsóí
Yellow Sunset	*Nihootsoi
Yellow Sunset Hoghan	*Nihootsoi Beehooghan
Yellow Wind	*Níłch'i Łítsoi
yucca	tsá'ásdzi'nit'eelí, tsá'ásdzi'ts'óóz, tsá'ásdzi'bid'ee', tsá'ásdzi', yé'ii bitsá'ásdzi'í
yucca root (soapweed)	*amole[17]

---

[16]This is in the transcription of M. C. Wheelwright.
[17]This is in the transcription of M. C. Wheelwright.

INDEX

INDEX